# FINTECH FUNDAMENTALS

# FINTECH FUNDAMENTALS

*Big Data • Cloud Computing*
*• Digital Economy*

**Len Mei, Ph.D.**

**MERCURY LEARNING AND INFORMATION**
Dulles, Virginia
Boston, Massachusetts
New Delhi

Publisher: David Pallai
MERCURY LEARNING AND INFORMATION
22841 Quicksilver Drive
Dulles, VA 20166
info@merclearning.com
www.merclearning.com
1-800-232-0223

L. Mei. *Fintech Fundamentals.*
ISBN: 978-1-68392-838-6

The publisher recognizes and respects all marks used by companies, manufacturers, and developers as a means to distinguish their products. All brand names and product names mentioned in this book are trademarks or service marks of their respective companies. Any omission or misuse (of any kind) of service marks or trademarks, etc. is not an attempt to infringe on the property of others.

Library of Congress Control Number: 2022934841

222324321   Printed on acid-free paper in the United States of America.

Our titles are available for adoption, license, or bulk purchase by institutions, corporations, etc. For additional information, please contact the Customer Service Dept. at 800-232-0223(toll free).

# CONTENTS

*Preface*      *ix*

**Chapter 1:**    **Introduction to the Digital Economy**      **1**

     1.1    Digital Economy      1

     1.2    Infrastructure for the Digital Economy      7

     1.3    Data Center Evolution      11

     References      13

**Chapter 2:**    **Cloud and Edge Computing**      **15**

     2.1    Cloud Computing      17

     2.2    Edge Computing      19

     2.3    High-Performance Computers      21

     2.4    Quantum Computers and Quantum Communication      24

     References      26

**Chapter 3:**    **5G Telecommunication**      **29**

     3.1    5G Communication Technologies      29

     3.2    Software-Defined Network (SDN)      32

     3.3    Private 5G      34

     3.4    Beyond 5G      35

     References      36

| | | |
|---|---|---|
| **Chapter 4:** | **Blockchain and Other Digital Economy** | |
| | **Infrastructures** | **37** |
| | 4.1   IoT Devices and Sensors | 37 |
| | 4.2   Semiconductors | 40 |
| | 4.3   Evolution of Computers Driven by AI | 44 |
| | 4.4   Blockchain | 47 |
| | References | 49 |
| | | |
| **Chapter 5:** | **Big Data and Artificial Intelligence** | **51** |
| | 5.1   What is Artificial Intelligence? | 51 |
| | 5.2   How is Artificial Intelligence Created? | 53 |
| | 5.3   Machine Learning | 55 |
| | 5.4   Big Data | 57 |
| | 5.5   AI Applications | 58 |
| | 5.6   The AI Market | 62 |
| | 5.7   Government's Role in AI | 63 |
| | 5.8   European Approach to AI | 64 |
| | 5.9   Fusion of AI with Biotechnology | 65 |
| | 5.10  AI and Blockchain | 67 |
| | References | 68 |
| | | |
| **Chapter 6:** | **What's New in the Digital Economy?** | **71** |
| | 6.1   Use of Blockchain to Secure IoT Data | 71 |
| | 6.2   Blockchain and Credit Card | 74 |
| | 6.3   Cross-border Retail Business | 75 |
| | 6.4   Counterparty Platform Dapps | 77 |
| | 6.5   AML & KYC | 79 |
| | 6.6   O2O Business | 80 |
| | 6.7   Third-Party Payment | 82 |
| | 6.8   Mobile Wallet and Payment Transfer | 90 |
| | 6.9   European Security Settlement Platform | 91 |
| | 6.10  Credit Rating System | 93 |
| | References | 99 |

**Chapter 7:**    **Financial Services Industries**                      **103**

     7.1   Fintech                                                    103

     7.2   Blockchain and Fintech                                     106

     7.3   Technology-Driven Fintech                                  108

     7.4   Global Fintech Landscape                                   113

     7.5   Major Global Fintech Companies                             127

     7.6   TechFin                                                    131

     7.7   Blockchain Technology for Banks                            133

     7.8   Crowdsale and Crowd Prediction                             135

     7.9   Building MDL for Financial Services                        137

     7.10  Digital Currency                                           139

     References                                                       141

**Chapter 8:**    **Trading and Lending**                                 **145**

     8.1   Security Trading                                           145

     8.2   Commodity Trading                                          147

     8.3   Energy Trading                                             148

     8.4   Alternative Trading System                                 150

     8.5   Peer-to-Peer Lending                                       152

     8.6   Online Lending                                             155

     8.7   Microlending and SME Lending                               156

     References                                                       158

**Chapter 9:**    **Renewed Industries**                                  **161**

     9.1   Wealth Management                                          161

     9.2   Insurance                                                  166

     9.3   Supply Chain Management                                    169

     9.4   Healthcare                                                 171

     9.5   Food Industry                                              173

     9.6   Defense Industry                                           174

     9.7   Cybersecurity                                              176

     9.8   Autonomous Vehicles                                        178

     References                                                       180

**Chapter 10:**  **Industrie 4.0**                                           **183**
  10.1  The Fourth Industrial Revolution                        184
  10.2  Equipment Automation                                    185
  10.3  Factory Automation                                      186
  10.4  Data Automation                                         187
  10.5  From Product Design to Market                           189
  References                                                    189

**Chapter 11:**  **Smart City**                                               **191**
  11.1  What is a Smart City?                                   191
  11.2  Smart City Projects in the World                        194
  11.3  Smart City Project – Transportation                     196
  11.4  Smart City Project – Utility Management                 197
  11.5  Smart City Project – Crime Prevention                   198
  11.6  Smart City Project – Healthcare and Disease
        Prevention                                              199
  References                                                    200

**Chapter 12:**  **Governance, Legal Applications, and Regulation**           **201**
  12.1  Governance and Voting                                   201
  12.2  Regulatory Applications and Issues                      204
  12.3  Overcoming Privacy Issues in Data Collection            206
  12.4  Land Title Registration and Real Estate                 207
  12.5  Law and Justice                                         209
  12.6  Protection of Intellectual Property                     211
  References                                                    212

**Chapter 13:**  **Conclusion**                                               **215**
  13.1  Near-Future Positive Impact                             215
  13.2  Future Job Market                                       217
  13.3  Wealth Redistribution                                   218
  13.4  Technology-Empowered Extremism                          221
  13.5  Longer-term Impact                                      222
  References                                                    223

*Index*                                                         225

# PREFACE

The world is propelling into the era of a digital economy. The signs are everywhere: the digital economy is growing at much faster pace than the overall economy. In the U.S. alone, the digital economy is growing at a rate of 10% a year, while the overall economy is at just two percent annually.

The digital economy is based on data. Data is the crude oil of the digital economy. The volume of data generated is growing exponentially. The digital economy is built upon the foundation of technologies developed in the last six decades – the technology of ICT (Information and Communication Technology). The advance of ICT allows the industry to move into 5G communication, cloud and edge computing, Big Data and artificial intelligence, blockchain technology, Industry 4.0, financial technology (Fintech), digital currency, and many others. These new technologies are altering the landscape of the financial, business, and trade systems today.

Fintech promises to revolutionize the financial industry just as Industry 4.0 revolutionized manufacturing. These new technologies can add trillions of dollars to the global economy. The implications are staggering. On November 9, 2015, the U.S. Department of Commerce unveiled a Digital Economy Agenda to help businesses and consumers realize the potential of the digital economy.[1] Since that time, similar measures have been adopted in many other countries.[2]

These are some aspects of the digital economy. In this book, we will exam the underlying digital technologies required to build the digital economy. We will also discuss basic concepts and elements of the technologies that make a digital economy possible and how they work. We will look at

---

[1] https://www.commerce.gov/index.php/tags/digital-economy
[2] https://hbr.org/2017/07/60-countries-digital-competitiveness-indexed

some of the major applications. We will look into the two most important aspects of the economy: the financial industry (Fintech) and the manufacturing industry (Industry 4.0). This subject is vast and is quickly changing. It is impossible to cover the subject entirely in one book. This book serves as a comprehensive introduction and background to anyone who is interested in the subject in order to do further research on the individual subjects included here. Many references are cited in the interest of research and further exploration. And to conclude the book, we will discuss how the economy and society as a whole may be transformed in the next 20 or 30 years.

Len Mei, Ph.D.
March 2022

# CHAPTER 1

# INTRODUCTION TO THE DIGITAL ECONOMY

In this chapter, we will define digital economy and its impact on the world.

## 1.1  DIGITAL ECONOMY

Since 2010, the world has been propelling into the era of a digital economy. It is evident that the digital sector of the economy in the United States, the world leader in the digital economy, has grown at 10% a year, whereas the rest of the economy grows at two percent a year.[1] In addition, job creation in the digital economy sector is growing at a much faster rate than 10%.[2] The fastest-growing companies are engaged with the digital economy and according to a report published by the Boston Consulting Group, by 2035 there will be 400 million job openings worldwide in these related industries.[3] This number is larger than the current U.S. population. It is estimated that by 2030 the digital economy will increase to $15.7 trillion of the global GDP.

The definition of the digital economy is vague. In the narrow sense, the digital economy includes information and telecommunication services, hardware manufacturing, and the software industry. However, in a broader sense, the digital economy also includes e-commerce, sharing economy, Industry 4.0, and digital services powered by artificial intelligence (AI). The above-mentioned 10% of the U.S. digital economy includes hardware, software, e-commerce, digital media, telecommunication, and supporting services.

The United States is not unique in this aspect; countries around the world are growing the digital economy faster than the general economy. According to one study, the digital economy in Brazil also grows at an annual rate of more than 10% a year.[4]

Brandz,[5] a marketing firm, ranked the ten most recognized brand names in the world: Google, Apple, Amazon, Microsoft, Tencent, Facebook, VISA, McDonald's, Alibaba, and AT&T. Except for McDonald's, which is in the food industry, all the other companies are involved in the digital economy. Many other successful companies of the last two decades are also included, such as Salesforce, Adobe, Splunk, Twilio, etc.

It took only a span of five years for Uber to achieve the same market capitalization which General Motors achieved in 107 years. Apple became the first trillion-dollar company in history, followed by Amazon and Google. There are many other examples: on a single day (November 11, 2019) in China, Alibaba made $38 billion, and the value of Zoom Communication increased from $19 billion to $141 billion in 2020; the digital economy has enabled such incredible growth.

The transition to the digital economy is often considered as the 4th Industrial Revolution, following the last three industrial revolutions. The First Industrial Revolution occurred in 1760 when the United Kingdom invented the steam engine, and other steam-powered machines, such as steamboats, locomotives, and textile machines. This made the United Kingdom the first industrialized country in the world, and subsequently, turned it into a global power.

The Second Industrial Revolution occurred in 1879, 119 years after the First Industrial Revolution. It happened when the electricity generator was invented, together with many devices using electricity, such as electric lamps and electricity-powered machines. Electricity is a form of energy that can be transported much easier than steam. Therefore, its use was spreading more quickly than a vapor form of energy. It spurred the Second Industrial Revolution. Soon, the United States, the country which first set up large-scale power plants, was industrialized and powered by electricity; subsequently, it became a world power.

The electric lamp was a great invention because it extends the useful hours of a day. Now, suddenly, people could work day and night, without any difference, so productivity increased. Many other electricity-powered machines also proliferated quickly, because of this new availability of power.

Sixty-eight years later, at the Bell Laboratories, also in the United States, the transistor was invented. Before the invention of the transistor, computers were made of vacuum tubes. Transistors are much smaller, work much faster, and consume far less energy than vacuum tubes. Since then, computers made by transistors took a quantum leap in performance and computing power. Transistor technology soon got a big push when integrated circuits were invented by scientists at Texas Instruments in 1957. Techniques of making integrated circuits allow one to build more than one transistor on a single chip of silicon. By making transistors smaller, one can fit more and more transistors onto a single chip.

In 1971, a start-up company, called Intel, launched an integrated circuit product, 4004, which integrated 2,300 transistors in a single chip of silicon. It was a milestone achievement. It was merely 14 years after the invention of the integrated circuit. This chip was more powerful in computing than the large-scale computers made out of vacuum tubes a decade earlier.

The founder of Intel, Gordon Moore, predicted that by making transistors smaller and smaller, one could double the number of transistors on a single silicon chip every two years. Intel 4004 was made with 10 μm technology, that is, the size of the transistor on the 4004 chip is about 10 μm large (1 μm is one-millionth of a meter, i.e., it is the size of small bacteria). Gordon Moore's prediction is famously known as *Moore's Law*. Today, almost 50 years later, this prediction still holds true.

Since then, a new industry was born, the industry of integrated circuits, also known as the semiconductor industry, because the chips are made from semiconductors. Consequently, the industry has been dedicated to making transistors smaller and smaller by improving the techniques of printing circuitry, etching, diffusion, oxidation, deposition, and many other techniques of making transistors. Such progress in the semiconductor industry has made all of the electronics that we are using today.

Eighteen years later, in 1989, Intel again broke the record. It created another milestone product, the Intel 80486, containing 1.18 million transistors using 1 microtechnology. Forty years later, in 2010, Intel's Xeon 7400 contained 1.9 billion transistors, using 45 nm technologies (1 nm is 1 billionth of a meter). Today, in 2020, the most advanced chip, such as NVIDIA's GA100, contains 54 billion transistors on a single silicon chip using 7 nm technologies. Soon, we will see chips containing 100 billion transistors or more.

One needs to have some imagination to understand what a chip of 50 billion transistors can do. Today, the cell phone has chips of several billion transistors, and our phones are more than just phones. They are computers more powerful than the large-scale computers of decades ago. However, we need more and more transistors to meet demands of consumers.

Transistors process information in the digital form, 0 and 1. All of the technologies handling data are in digital form. Therefore, we call the economy powered by these technologies the *digital economy*.

Let's compare today with 100 years ago. In 1910, mankind started to construct large-scale power plants to generate electricity, and deliver the electricity through transmission lines to factories and homes. Today, we have large-scale data centers, receiving from and sending data to offices, factories, homes, and individuals. Therefore, we say that the digital economy is powered by data, and data are the most valuable commodity in the digital economy. The huge volume of data as this commodity has acquired a name *"Big Data."* Big Data is the petroleum of the digital economy.

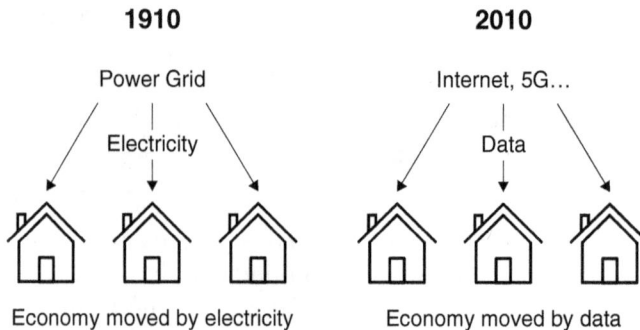

**FIGURE 1.1** Comparison of economies in 1910 and 2010.

The transformation of the digital economy is dramatic. Let us look at one example in our daily life. Not long ago, if you wanted to make an announcement public, you could publish an ad in a newspaper, which has a circulation of 10,000 or more. Unless people search for your ad, it is unlikely it will attract much attention, unless your ad is exceptionally large. Today, to place an ad, you would publish it online. Whoever goes to the page for other information will see your ad. The Internet may circulate millions of copies across the globe. It can be targeted and localized.

Companies like Google receive most of their revenues from advertisements. When you search "vacation to Hawaii," Google knows that you are interested in taking a vacation to Hawaii. It sells your IP address to travel agencies, hotels, airlines, who immediately send an ad to you to promote their businesses. That is why Google's revenue is growing 20% a year since its founding nearly 25 years ago. Today, Google is one of the largest companies in the digital economy; the same is true for Meta (including Facebook) and Amazon.

The digital economy is more than just the Internet. Digital currency is also a disruptive revolution. One of the most well-known digital currencies is *Bitcoin*. Bitcoin, the first cryptocurrency, is probably the most explosive asset in human history. In 12 years, from 2009 to 2021, its market capitalization has grown from zero to almost $1 trillion. Since Bitcoin appeared, there are many other cryptocurrencies springing to life. At the current count, there are over 6,000 different cryptocurrencies. The top 5 cryptocurrencies have a combined market capitalization of over $1.5 trillion.

Digital currency is possible because of its underlying technology – *blockchain*. Blockchain can transform the Internet of information as we know it today, into the Internet of value. It is "money over IP" as coined by Cathie Woods, the founder of Ark Invest. Money can be transferred online, just like data, without the worry that it can be stolen or duplicated. Suddenly, the Internet finds itself capable of performing many financial functions with the security and speed unmatched by the traditional financial systems.

The birth of blockchain technology is due to the maturity of Internet technology itself, the advances in computer science, the spread of cheap computing power, the high speed, high bandwidth communication, and many other factors such as e-commerce and trade globalization.

Blockchain-based smart contracts and distributed apps open up a wide frontier for transaction applications, in addition to the immutable digital identity, which provides a chain of custody and proof of asset ownership.

Another important innovation in the digital economy is AI. Artificial intelligence, machine learning, and Big Data are different aspects of the same thing. Artificial intelligence promises to augment human intelligence and to help humans to accelerate innovations. Applications of AI in healthcare, governance, legal systems, smart cities, factory automation, etc., can greatly improve efficiency.

Recent growth in AI is promoted by the computing power, increase in data volume, as well as investments. Large companies in the digital economy, such as Amazon, Google, IBM, Alibaba, are all offering AI algorithms in their cloud computing services so their customers can build AI-based applications.

As machines become more intelligent, they can perform more human-like tasks, such as strategic games, self-driving cars, medical diagnoses, facial recognition, and many more.

Today's AI capability already includes reasoning, planning, learning, natural language processing, and the ability to move and manipulate objects, and its capability is increasing each day.

Artificial intelligence machines consist of three elements: hardware, software, and Big Data. Hardware is the computer system that mimics a human neuron network. Software is the machine learning algorithm, also known as deep learning, including search, mathematical optimization, methods based on statistics and probability, etc. Big Data is fed into the AI machine to train it. For example, the AI machine that can perform a medical diagnosis learns its technique by studying tens of thousands of X-ray images and their associated diagnoses. In *facial recognition*, AI learns to recognize people by examining millions of faces. Once they are recorded, AI can perform the related tasks better and faster than humans. After all, an experienced doctor can only learn from tens of thousands of his patient's diagnoses, and an AI machine can learn from millions of diagnoses from a worldwide database. A machine can also detect smaller patterns which are imperceptible by human eyes. In autonomous cars, the machine can react in fractions of a millionth second instead of in seconds by a human. The technology of CV-2X[6] (cell, vehicle to everything) constantly connects cars to other devices. AI is also used in the financial industry to detect and flag activity in banking and finance such as unusual debit card usage and large account deposits.

Likewise, the application of digital technologies in the manufacturing industry has revolutionized the industry. Germany calls it *"industrie 4.0"* and we refer to it as Industry 4.0. In a factory of Industry 4.0, manufacturing is entirely automated by robots. These robots have extraordinary sensors: they can see and hear. In addition to sensors, they can also perform certain cognitive services, that is, the services which require pre-acquired knowledge. They can work 24 hours a day and in environments which are dangerous to humans.

At the factory level, the data collected from the entire factory and supply chain will allow the manufacturing execution system to make decisions about production and flow of materials to make the most efficient use of its resources, such as equipment. It can replace much of the managerial work. When the factory is linked to its upstream and downstream supply chain, or even markets, certain tasks can be guided by the requirements of the supply chain. For example, the use of data will allow participants of the delivery, such as shipping and courier companies, to globally track their freight in real time. End customers can even specify how they want their products made. The factory is said to be "personalized." In a personalized manufacturing environment, factories can cater quickly and creatively to meet customer demands. They are flexible and specialized to produce personalized products without hiring and training additional skilled laborers.

When there is no labor required in the factory, there is no need to turn on the lights. Therefore, these types of factories are also known as "lights-out" factories. They can turn out products 24 hours a day without workers.

These are some aspects of the digital economy. In this book, we will examine the underlying digital technologies required to build the digital economy. We will look at some of the major applications. And in the end, we will speculate on how the economy and society will be transformed in 20 or 30 years.

## 1.2   INFRASTRUCTURE FOR THE DIGITAL ECONOMY

As the name implies, the digital economy is the economy driven by digital data. The digital economy involves three aspects of data: the *generation-collection*, *transmission*, and *processing* of data.

The modern economy requires infrastructures like power plants, highways, railways, and public utilities; the digital economy requires different kinds of infrastructures, such as 5G, data centers, etc. These infrastructures all involve high technologies, including semiconductors. The countries which have the capability to quickly build these infrastructures will be able to rapidly develop a digital economy. Since the digital economy ensures the growth of the future economy, building the digital economy infrastructure becomes the number one priority for many countries.

All aspects of data handling require an infrastructure. These infrastructures are the foundation of the digital economy. To grow the digital economy, a country has to grow the digital infrastructure in proportion, both in capacity and capability. The digital infrastructure is to the digital economy as power plants, highways, railroads, airports, and utilities are to the traditional economy.

In the past, the data generation and collection process involved human effort. But increasingly, such a process is automated to a point that human involvement and supervision are not necessary. Data transmission speed is also increasing dramatically with the advancement of 5G telecommunication technology. 5G allows data to be transferred to a large-scale data center, or a cloud computing center, to be processed.

Cloud computing centers have data analysis capabilities, such as AI, blockchain, and many others. As computer power advances, local computer centers also acquire some of the computing capabilities of the large-scale cloud computing centers. These local computing centers are closer to the source of the data. Such a localized computing center is known as *edge computing*, in differentiation from centralized cloud computing.

A large-scale digital infrastructure involves many technologies. We can roughly divide these technologies into three layers:

- application,
- infrastructure, and
- fundamental layers.

The *application layer* is the interface with human beings or users. It allows us to perform the functions we want to achieve in manipulating data. It is very much like the apps we use in our cell phones. The *infrastructure layer* is the physical layer or the hardware that allows us to collect, transmit data, and produce the results we want. The *fundamental technology layer* constructs the infrastructure hardware. For example, the high-performance computer is the building block of data centers. Sensors and the Internet of Things (IoT) are the components used to collect data.

The digital infrastructure is huge. It is composed of millions of components. Any system capable of manipulating digital data has a computer at its core. Each component is composed of both hardware and software. The software includes operating systems and applications. The whole digital infrastructure consists of billions of interconnected computers, cables, transmission towers, IoTs, sensors, antennas, etc., performing different functions coherently based on predefined protocols. These components of the gigantic digital infrastructure belong to millions of independent owners – companies, government organizations, and individuals. And yet, amazingly, they all work seamlessly to perform desired functions.

All the hardware components are made of semiconductor chips. Today, the most advanced chip is manufactured using 5 nm technology. A chip, the size of a nail, contains 60 billion transistors. It is indeed very powerful.

The applications are the technologies that interface with us. For example, in the cell phone, we have many apps, which are built to interface with us. Using these apps, we can send messages, read news, watch videos, listen to music, consult bank accounts, do shopping, and much more. Likewise, the application level of the digital economy allows us to perform certain tasks. A few examples are fintech, artificial intelligence, Industry 4.0, and smart city.

Beneath the applications, there is the layer of infrastructure. For example, the apps in a cell phone are the "application" and the cell phone itself is the "infrastructure." Infrastructure technologies are the platforms that allow us to build applications. Some of the important ones are blockchain, smart factory, Big Data, IoT, etc. For example, you need to use blockchain to make digital currency. You need the Internet of Things (IoT) to make intelligent robots and devices. And you need a smart factory to build Industry 4.0, etc.

In turn, these infrastructure technologies are made from more fundamental technologies, such as HPC (High-Performance Computers), 5G, the Internet, cloud computing, and semiconductors. For example, a data center consists of millions of interconnected computers. Further down the chain, everything is made of semiconductor chips, which collect, transmit, and process digital data.

Most of the applications reside in the cloud. A *cloud* is a data center which offers application software and data storage. This application software can include built-in AI, or blockchain concepts. Today, many companies are offering cloud services: Amazon, Google, Meta, Microsoft, Alibaba, etc.

Companies use a cloud platform when their customer-related services are dedicated applications as opposed to a website. A cloud platform can build and run an application that can leverage the power of hyper-scale data centers: in order to reach users worldwide, to use sophisticated analytics and AI functions, to utilize massive data storage, or to take advantage of cost efficiencies. For example, if you operate a small e-commerce business, you can use a website. But when it increases in size and volume, you may want to have a dedicated application. By using a cloud service, you don't have to buy/lease your own servers, develop your own software applications, and have access to the latest hardware and software.

For example, Vodafone uses Google Cloud services to develop a cloud-based data platform[7] to find new opportunities and improve relationships with customers. It helps Vodafone to create and deploy new digital services in many countries, as well as to gain new insights from customer data to improve relationships and boost customer retention.

Likewise, IBM developed an AI-powered digital assistant chatbot app called TOBi.[8] When consumers ask TOBi questions, it instantly accesses relevant data and answers the questions. It also pulls up customer records for further help.

Amazon, the world's largest cloud service provider, offers its analytics and forecasting services, called Amazon Web Service (AWS). AWS expands in multiple directions. Amazon Web Services (AWS) had an estimated 2018 annual revenue of $25.65 billion. AWS excels in AI, augmented reality, and analytics.

Alibaba is the largest cloud-computing company in China and operates data centers in 23 regions and 63 zones globally, with revenue of $72 billion in 2020. Recently, it is moving into the health, global fashion, and the electric car markets.

*Big Data* is a term used to describe the technology used to handle large volumes of data. Big Data has three characteristics: mega volumes, speed, and it is unstructured. This makes Big Data different from the traditional database. Because of the cost reduction of collection, transmission, storage, and processing of data, an increased volume of Big Data is now cheaper and more accessible than traditional database technologies.

Big Data requires a huge capacity of data handling along with the data path – collection, transmission, storage, and processing. The capacity of data handling must grow in sync with the volume of data. This puts a huge demand on the digital economy infrastructure.

Until recently, most data was generated by humans. With the advent of the Internet of Things (IoT), more objects and devices are connected to the Internet, gathering data on customer usage patterns and product performance. All of these issues prompt the quantity of data to grow exponentially. More data generation puts the demand on data transmission. The transmission technology has moved from 3G to 4G, and now 5G in the last decade.

Finally, data need to be processed: validated, sorted, classified, aggregated, analyzed, and reported. In addition to constructing a Big Data center to increase capacity, the capability of data handling also needs to be improved. To alleviate the congestion, software libraries such as Hadoop and Spark have been developed to allow for the distributed processing of large data sets across clusters of computers, using simple programming models. They allow the clustering of multiple computers to analyze massive datasets in parallel. Each of these multiple computers offers local computation and storage. The library can detect and handle failures at the application layer, thus delivering a highly available and reliable service on top of a cluster of computers.

## 1.3   DATA CENTER EVOLUTION

In the digital economy, all economic activities are evolving around data. Therefore, data centers play a key role in the digital economy. This is similar to how the power plants played a key role in the Second Industrial Revolution.

Fundamental technologies are the foundation of building the infrastructure of the digital economy. All applications and infrastructure layers are constructed on the fundamental technologies. They include HPC (High-Performance Computers), 5G telecommunication, the Internet, cloud computing, and most important of all – semiconductor technology.

Cloud computing resides in the data centers. Data centers evolved from large computing centers in the early 1970s. When inexpensive networking equipment was available in the 1980s, it became possible to put many servers in a specific room inside the company to serve the entire company. When the Internet became prevalent, data centers started to appear to serve the public instead of private data centers belonging to a single company.

The original data center, in the 1980s, was used mostly for data storage purposes. They were called *"Infrastructure as a Service,"* in short, "IaaS." In the 1990s, data center companies started to offer operating systems to their customers. With a *dumb terminal*, one can log into a data center computer and use it as a remote computer. This type of service is called *"Platform as a Service,"* or "PaaS." Beginning in 2000, data centers offered not only operating systems but also application software on data centers. This type of data center is called *"Software as a Service,"* or "SaaS." For example, Microsoft 365 is an office application offered by Microsoft data center.

Since 2010, data center companies have offered much more sophisticated application software, including blockchain, AI, etc. The data center has acquired many different names, such as "Blockchain as a Service," "AI as a Service," etc. Suddenly, customers without the know-how of blockchain or AI can ask the service providers to develop their own blockchain-based or AI-based applications. All they need to know is how they want their applications to be used.

With such a capability, the market for cloud computing grows explosively. The global cloud computing market grew to $266 billion in 2019 and is forecasted to grow by 15% a year until 2027. The United States currently has almost half of the global market.

The deployment of these services can save operating costs of companies by leveraging the established hardware and software. In addition, the added capabilities will help boost their business performance. Therefore, companies are proactively outsourcing cloud computing instead of building their own IT infrastructures. For example, Stelco Holdings, a Canadian steel company, uses the AI-enabled cloud platform Canvas Analytics[9] to digest its operational data to obtain real-time analytics solutions. Similarly, in the healthcare industry, Nuance Communications Inc., acquired by Microsoft in 2021, offers a cloud-based AI platform to healthcare providers.

Such cloud-based systems are a boom for small and medium enterprises (SMEs). Suddenly, SMEs find that the highly sophisticated and expensive tools which were previously inaccessible to them, are at their fingertips for reasonable costs. This increases their competitive advantages to the same levels as larger competitors. According to some estimates, up to 60% of companies are currently using cloud services rather than their in-house computer systems.

With the huge amounts of data being transferred, data security becomes a concern. There are two ways to protect data: (1) to prevent hacking of existing data and (2) to create the data so it is free from hackers. That is where blockchain technology becomes valuable. The encrypted and distributed nature of the blockchain database provides high security to sensitive data. Blockchain methods provide a solution for such security issues.

# REFERENCES

1. *https://www.bea.gov/data/special-topics/digital-economy.*

2. *https://www.researchgate.net/figure/2010-2015-Percent-Change-in-Digital-Economy-Jobs-and-Establishments_fig4_323701244.*

3. *https://image-src.bcg.com/Images/BCG_Year-2035_400-Million-Job-Opportunities-Digital%20Age_ENG_Mar2017_tcm52-153963.pdf.*

4. *http://www.csstoday.com/Item/6662.aspx.*

5. *https://www.kantar.com/campaigns/brandz-downloads/brandz-top-100-most-valuable-global-brands-2020.*

6. *https://www.zdnet.com/article/what-is-c-v2x-and-how-it-changes-the-driving-smart-cities/*

7. *https://cloud.google.com/press-releases/2019/1120/vodafone-chooses-google-cloud-as-strategic-cloud-platform/.*

8. *https://newsroom.ibm.com/Boosting-Digital-Contact-in-a-Contactless-World-with-AI-and-Hybrid-Cloud.*

9. *https://www.plant.ca/general/stelco-supports-its-intelligent-operations-with-ai-deal-181902/.*

# 2

# CLOUD AND EDGE COMPUTING

The modern digital system consists of hardware and software. The hardware consists of a data processing unit, a data storage unit, and an interface. The software consists of an operating system and application software. The operating system is the interface layer which performs the translation between machine language that the computer understands and the programming languages that humans understand. The application software performs a specific task that the user commands the computer to do.

Any large-scale computing system is composed of many smaller systems that communicate with each other. The basic computing system can be compared to a brick, and the large computing system is like a building.

The infrastructure of a digital economy is comprised of data collection, data transmission, and data processing. Data are collected from a human or from an object, using sensors and IoT.

When you send a message or compose an email, you generate data. Sometimes, you generate data unconsciously: for example, when you make a credit card transaction, take a ride on Uber, or purchase online, you are also generating data.

Currently, however, data are increasingly being gathered from objects. When we attach a sensor such as a camera to the object, it acquires vision. It can take pictures. An object is connected to the Internet through IoT. It can then send the data, such as a video or a picture, over the Internet to a destination. For example, a surveillance camera sends video online.

The second component of digital infrastructure is data transmission. The data are transmitted through the telecommunication network. In 2020, the telecommunication network is entering 5G or the 5th generation. Compared to 4G, 5G has a bandwidth that is 1000× as large. It can connect 100× more devices simultaneously. Its download speed is 100× faster than that of 4G, and the response time is 5× faster. The 5G telecommunication network will allow more data to be transmitted and therefore processed.

Creating AI requires data, and more data can provide AI with more intelligence. Therefore, 5G serves not only human-operated but also AI-controlled machines.

We have mentioned that data from objects are collected by sensors and transmitted to the internet by IoT. IoT installation is witnessing exponential growth globally. Currently, in 2021, there are 36 billion IoT systems installed. It is forecast that by 2025, the number will double.

Many companies are already using IoT to monitor their equipment. For example, Caterpillar, the world's largest manufacturer of agriculture machinery, installs IoT on its tractors.[1] No matter how far out the tractors are in the field, Caterpillar can monitor their performance in real time. It knows the exact location, the working condition, and when and how a tractor breaks down, eliminating the need for fault diagnosis.[2] In this way, Caterpillar can provide assistance much faster.

Samsung's smart refrigerator has sensors and IoT.[3] It can tell you exactly what food you have in the refrigerator, without you having to open it. You can check it using Samsung's app, in your phone. When you are at the supermarket wondering whether or not you have eggs at home, just open the app.

Doctors can monitor a patient's vital signs, such as blood pressure or erratic heart beats, remotely and in real time, which helps to prevent serious mishaps.

In the supply chain, IoT can track valuable assets along their supply route. Any deviation can be detected and corrected more quickly. Warehouse inventory can be tracked using IoT.

In the utility industry, with the help of IoT technology in the electrical grid, engineers can collect necessary data to monitor the performance and power consumption. This information can help in channelizing the flow of electricity to the homes. So, the pressure to create more electric power during peak consumption hours can be distributed. With IoT-driven electric smart meters, the utility company can guide households about their pattern of power consumption and ways in which they can reduce their dependence on electricity.

IoT used in the industry is called IIoT. It can gather data from machines and materials around the factory to track any deviation in performance parameters, and promptly eliminate the glitches so that the production process is not hampered.

Sensors are important components in the digital infrastructure. A sensor is an interface between the digital world and the real world. There are many types of sensors: the camera is a vision sensor; the microphone is a sound sensor. There are sensors for pressure, temperature, chemical concentration, speed, magnetic field, electrical field, gyroscope, moisture, biological parameters, and many others. Sensors collect ambient data and send these data through IoT to remote data centers through the Internet.

There are also robots, which can act on objects as instructed. Robots are mechanical arms. In many automated factories, robots replace human labor. The global market for robots is growing exponentially. In 2020, it was worth about $45 billion. It is expected to grow to $67 billion by 2025.[4]

## 2.1 CLOUD COMPUTING

Cloud computing is the central component of digital infrastructure. It evolves from the data center. It refers to computing services over the Internet ("the cloud") to offer faster innovation, flexible resources, and economies of scale. Cloud computing infrastructure, composed of both hardware and software, includes HPC servers, data storage, databases, networking, software, analytics, and other new technologies such as AI and blockchain.

Cloud computing allows many customers to share the same computing resources so that the cost of IT is reduced, and the development and deployment of applications are much faster. There is no need to procure expensive computer systems to install the operating system and application software, which also reduces all the associated maintenance costs.

In addition, the cloud environment has better cyber-security. Cloud service can also be scaled easily as needed. Cloud service providers are increasingly offering new technologies such as AI, blockchain, and many others so that even a company that does not have expertise in the area can develop applications together with the cloud service provider. It also has the added advantage of the automatic update—you are always using the latest version.

From the point of view of cloud resource ownership, there are three types of cloud—public cloud, private cloud, and hybrid cloud.

Public cloud makes computing and data storage resources available to many users over the public Internet. The public cloud provider owns and manages the data centers, hardware, and infrastructure. It is a multi-tenet environment—the data center infrastructure is shared by all cloud customers, sometimes numbering in millions.

Examples of public clouds are Amazon Web Services (AWS), Google Cloud, IBM Cloud, Microsoft Azure, and Oracle Cloud. The global public cloud market is growing rapidly. Marketing firm Gartner[5] estimates that the worldwide public cloud market will exceed $330 billion by 2022.

Due to its more open platform, public cloud is vulnerable to privacy invasion and data hacking. The alternative is to use a private cloud service. *Private cloud* is dedicated for a single customer only. Its infrastructure is on-premises. Private cloud retains many of the benefits of cloud computing—including elasticity, scalability, and ease of service delivery—with the access control, security, and resource customization of on-premises infrastructure.

Because of the data security concerns, regulatory compliance requires certain types of sensitive information to be stored on-premises, such as confidential documents, intellectual property, or any other sensitive data. Private cloud can meet such requirements better than public cloud. Customers with such sensitive data usually choose private cloud. If public cloud is like an apartment building, private cloud is like a single-family house.

The *hybrid cloud* is the combination of public cloud and private cloud. The user of a hybrid cloud has an on-premises private cloud; yet it can redirect the excess demand to a public cloud.

A hybrid cloud integrates a company's private cloud and public clouds into a single, flexible infrastructure. The company must decide what data can be stored in its private cloud and what can be stored in its public cloud. By mixing the public and private cloud resources, the company can choose which cloud to use for each workload and/or to move workloads freely between the two clouds according to changing circumstances. This enables the company to meet its IT objectives more effectively and cost-efficiently.

## 2.2    EDGE COMPUTING

In recent years, edge computing has attracted substantial attention because its proximity to the source of data can reduce the overheads of data transmission. This allows faster response time and better bandwidth availability. It is complementary to cloud computing. In many situations, edge computing is even preferred when there is a need for low latency and quick actuation, as in self-driving cars or privacy concerns over the transfer of sensitive data or massive amounts of data to the remote cloud. A reduction in the transmission of data to external locations also means fewer open connections and fewer opportunities for cyber attacks.

The edge computing infrastructure is expanding even faster than cloud computing facilities. By 2025, more data will be generated and processed at edge computing facilities than by using cloud computing.

Edge computing is like a localized cloud. It requires the same kind of support as cloud computing. In some aspects, the requirements of edge computing are even more demanding than those of cloud computing. This is because edge computing must support hundreds or even thousands of edge devices, and its workflows must be more flexible. At the same time, it is more vulnerable than cloud computing because of its greater exposure to the outside environment.

A new method of constructing edge computing infrastructure is emerging: *composable infrastructure*. Infrastructure composing is a technique to abstract hardware resources from a physical location, and use software to apply those resources where needed. The 5G Virtual Network is an example.

A composable infrastructure allows the speedy operational deployment, enabling the business to quickly deliver new products and services to the market. It also eliminates the need for workload-specific environments and configures the resources as desired to meet the unique needs of an application. It improves performance and flexibility, reduces under-utilization, and creates a more agile, cost-effective data center.

With composable infrastructure, edge computing can be deployed as quickly as cloud computing, even though its environment is much more complicated because it connects to a huge number of external devices. Without changing physical workloads, composable infrastructure can support the virtual workload of different environments. This is done through software-defined intelligence with logical pooling of resources.

Even supercomputers are moving to the edge to meet the ever-increasing demand for computing power at the edge. Because of the nature of edge computing, these supercomputers for the edge are specially designed. Specifically, they are a cluster of computers working as a supercomputer. Together with supercomputers, edge computing is also developing its AI capability. Increasingly, robots with machine vision are no longer programmed with deterministic commands, but with an AI algorithm instead. This greatly increases the flexibility of robots. They are more human-like and can perform intelligent tasks, like quality control or even real-time process optimization. Such a capability exists when robots are driven by AI in edge computing.

Special tools are needed to develop edge computing solutions. Google's cloud service provides tools with an integrated software and hardware stack for implementing machine learning, both in its cloud computing and its edge computing. This provides Google's cloud/edge solution advantage of leveraging data directly at the edge.

Google's cloud/edge tools include the Edge TPU (Tensor Processing Unit) chip, Cloud IoT Edge software, and a development kit. In essence, Google provides a one-stop shopping solution to customers who want to develop both cloud and edge computing capabilities.

The combined system of the Edge TPU chip and the Cloud IoT Edge software runs TensorFlow Lite machine learning at the edge. The software has two functions: the Edge IoT Core gateway functions and a machine learning function. Edge ML, a TensorFlow Lite-based model, provides machine learning functions on edge devices. The development kit includes a system-on-module (SOM) that combines the Edge TPU, an NXP CPU, Wi-Fi, and Microchip's secure element.

Edge computing also has its downside. Connecting to a large number of edge devices can expose data to security risks. Typically, edge devices are less secure than a centralized data center. The extensive data transmission between edge devices and edge computing centers over the Internet means that data will be more exposed than in a controlled centralized cloud environment. This means that edge infrastructures will need stronger security measure to facilitate secure data sharing, to collaborate efficiently between the edge device and the data center; and to consolidate security auditing.

Many edge infrastructures today have limited processing capability and storage space. Some are designed for harsh environments and rough operational conditions.

Edge computing pushes the frontier of computing applications, data, and services away from centralized nodes to the logical edge of a network. It leverages resources that may not be continuously connected to a network.

## 2.3    HIGH-PERFORMANCE COMPUTERS

The services offered by cloud and edge computing are growing fast. Both edge and cloud computing centers are run using High-Performance Computers (HPC). HPC is the generic name of the powerful and advanced computers capable of processing data and performing complex calculations at high speeds ~ at the order of quadrillions of calculations per second, or a million times faster than the PC. The frontier of HPC is propelled by the supercomputer, the AI computer, and the quantum computer.

A cloud computing center is a cluster of thousands of HPCs and data storage units connected together by an internal network. It is also connected to the Internet to receive and send data. A cloud computing center requires a special operating system that ties them together to work seamlessly and in parallel, so that they work as one computer. There are also many software applications that are built for specific applications.

The supercomputer can be considered as the top-of-line HPC. Today, the performance of a supercomputer achieves well over Peta FLOPS ($10^{15}$ Floating Point Operations per Second).

In 2021, the world's fastest supercomputer was the Japanese Fugaku. It has 7,630,848 cores with a performance of 442 petaFLOPS. However, using the new HPL-AI benchmark, instead of the traditional HPL (High-Performance Linpack software package for benchmark), its performance is at 2 exaFLOPS. So, it can claim to be the world's first exascale computer.

The HPL-AI benchmark seeks to place more emphasis on AI workloads. AI-based benchmark's demands are lower on the accuracy, but higher on data classification and recognition fidelity. This reflects a more realistic situation for the upcoming increase in AI workloads for the majority of supercomputers.

The second position is claimed by the Summit, made by IBM and housed at the Oak Ridge National Laboratory (ORNL), having 2.4 million cores, with 150 petaFLOPS performance.[6] Summit is built specifically for AI. Its architecture combines IBM POWER9 CPUs with NVIDIA GPUs. It has 4,600 nodes, with six NVIDIA Volta Tensor Core GPUs per node. All of the world's top 500 supercomputers are petascale computers.

While these petascale systems are quite powerful, the next milestone in computing achievement is the exascale (ExaFLOPS)—a higher level of performance in computing that will have profound impacts on everyday life. At a quintillion ($10^{18}$) calculations each second, exascale supercomputers will more be realistic to simulate the processes involved in precision medicine, regional climate, additive manufacturing, the conversion of plants to biofuels, the relationship between energy and water use, the unseen physics in materials discovery and design, the fundamental forces of the universe, and much more.

Exascale supercomputers will be able to quickly analyze massive volumes of data and more realistically simulate the complex processes and relationships behind many of the fundamental forces of the universe. This will have practical applications in everything from precision medicine to regional climate, water use to materials science, and nuclear physics to national security. Exascale computing has the potential to drive discoveries across the spectrum of scientific fields and to improve both our understanding of the world and how we live in it. Exascale AI will enable scientific breakthroughs with massive scale. Exascale computing is more than just making processors faster, it needs to address disruptive changes in computer architectures and the complexities of tackling exascale modeling, simulation, and analysis.

The US Department of Energy has an Exascale Computing Project (ECP) to accelerate exascale computing research. It is working with the Interoperable Design of Extreme-scale Application Software (IDEAS) team to build an exascale software ecosystem that enables transformative next-generation predictive science and decision support. The IDEAS-ECP project brings together experts throughout the DOE community.

NVIDIA builds the world's fastest AI computer called Perlmutter. It is also at number 5 in the TOP500 supercomputer list in January 2021.[7] It can run at 65 PetaFLOPS. Nvidia is also delivering a 2,240-GPU Polaris Supercomputer for the Argonne Leadership Computing Facility (ALCF) together with HPE. Polaris is a supercomputer to prepare critical workloads for future exascale systems. It will enable scientists to test and optimize software codes for AI applications. It is being prepared for the forthcoming exascale supercomputer, Aurora, a joint collaboration between Argonne, Intel, and HPE.

NVIDIA's GPU-accelerated computing platform provides pioneers like the ALCF breakthrough performance such as Polaris that let researchers push the boundaries of scientific exploration. Harnessing the huge number of NVIDIA A100 GPUs will have an immediate impact on data-intensive and AI workloads, allowing Polaris to tackle some of the world's most complex scientific problems.

NVIDIA is the only company in the world listing two supercomputers in the Top 10 in 2021. For NVIDIA's contribution to the graphics, AI, and supercomputer technologies, its CEO Jensen Huang was named one of Time magazine's top 100 most influential people of 2021.[8]

While the exascale supercomputer is powerful enough, the ability to integrate into cloud computing is a giant step forward to empower cloud computing. As one of the most important and emerging cloud computing applications, AI deep learning requires huge computing power. The ever more powerful HPC accelerates the deep learning of AI. The fields of supercomputing, AI, and cloud computing are converging quickly. Such a combination will boost AI development to a great extent.

China has recently integrated the Tianhe-3 exascale supercomputer into cloud computing. Tianhe-3 uses China's native multi-core Arm-v8-based Phytium 2000+ (FTP) and the Matrix 2000+ (MTP) processor/node architecture.

Europe launched the EuroHPC Joint Undertaking (JU) in 2018. It comprises 33 member states, including all nations in the European Union. It developed several EuroHPC systems by 2021 including several petascale systems; all made it to the Top 500 list in 2021.[9] Pre-exascale systems will be expected in 2022.

Likewise, Japan's National Institute of Advanced Industrial Science and Technology built an AI Bridging Cloud Infrastructure (ABCI)[10] using a supercomputer for AI and deep learning. The computer has a $1.30 \times 10^{17}$ FLOPS performance.

Germany TOP500 has published the world's TOP500 supercomputer ranking since 1993, twice a year. On June 28, 2021, it published the 57th edition of the TOP500 list. Out of the top 10, the United States has claimed 7 positions, China 2, and Japan 1. Out of the top 500, China has 188 systems, the United States 122 systems, Europe 72 systems, Japan 34 systems, and others 59 systems. Even though China has more systems in the top 500, the United States has more aggregated performance (adding total FLOPS), 30.7% of the total, and China has 19.4% of the total.[11]

## 2.4 QUANTUM COMPUTERS AND QUANTUM COMMUNICATION

Another distinct HPC technology is the quantum computer.[12] Quantum computing is a class of computing by itself and is radically different from traditional computing using binary states. Quantum computing can use any state in-between 1 and 0. This state is called a qubit, the basic unit of quantum computing.

A quantum computer can be constructed using a number of technologies: superconducting, photonics, trapped ions, spin/quantum dot, cold/ neutral/ Helium atoms, NV/ Diamond/ NMR, adiabatic, and topological. There is no clear winner at this moment. For example, the Chinese quantum computer Zuchongzhi uses photonics technology to manage and process its qubits, whereas Google's Sycamore is based on electrons and superconductors.

The United States and China are leading quantum computer research as measured by the research publications. Benchmarking the performance of a new quantum computer in qubits is another way to win the race. Many other countries, in particular Europe and Japan, also have aggressive programs in quantum computing. Most of the research and development effort is through government-sponsored programs such as the Quantum Flagship program in the EU, the Q-LEAP program in Japan, the Digital Economy National Program in Russia, and the UK National Quantum Technologies program. The US government is also championing quantum computer R&D, through the National Quantum Initiative Act.

In addition to many programs carried out by private enterprises, there are also industry-sponsored initiatives, such as QED-C (Quantum Economic Development Consortium) in the United States, QuIC (European Quantum Industry Consortium), the Council for New Industry Creation through Quantum Technology in Japan, and QUTAC (Quantum Technology and Applications Consortium) in Germany. India is collaborating with Amazon Web Services (AWS) to create a quantum computing applications lab in the country, to coordinate quantum computing-led research and development. The lab will be open to government bodies as well as researchers, scientists, academicians, and developers working in different industries, such as manufacturing, healthcare, agriculture, and aerospace engineering.

According to some estimates, the size of the global market for quantum computing was roughly $300 million dollars in 2020 and is expected to grow at an annual rate of 27%.[13] The real breakthrough will come when quantum computing is successfully integrated into cloud computing.

Quantum computers leverage quantum physics phenomena, such as superposition and entanglement. The quantum computer operates in the quantum space versus the classical binary digital space, and could potentially solve problems far beyond the capabilities of classical supercomputers. Quantum computing is more than just another advanced computing system. Quantum computing offers significant performance advantages for certain applications in solving problems that no classical computer can handle in a feasible amount of time. It complements the existing computing architecture, rather than replacing it.

The quantum computer is particularly well suited to machine learning because of its linear nature, in that it can be expressed anywhere between 0 and 1. It can also be suitable for biological computation. It can drastically reduce the time to sequence a human genome.

The development of the quantum computer involves more than just constructing the computer or the hardware. Entirely new software, including the operating system, application software, and algorithm needs to be developed. Since the quantum computer is so specialized, rather than the standalone quantum computers available for the public, it is most likely that quantum computers will be integrated into the cloud to perform special tasks that traditional computers cannot accomplish within a reasonable timeframe. When this is achieved, it is expected that the market for quantum computing will take off. As quantum computing offers increasing utility, it will likely be implemented within advanced computing infrastructures in the next decade or so.

Google's 54-qubit Sycamore quantum computer was reported to have out-performed Summit, the world's fastest supercomputer in 2020 by 3,000,000 times. In 2020, IBM's most powerful quantum computer had 65 qubits. However, it promised to show a 1000-qubit computer by 2023. Google has a plan to build a million-qubit quantum computer within 10 years.[14] In July 2021, China reported a milestone in quantum computing. Researchers in China unveiled a 66-qubit quantum computer called Zuchongzhi,[15] almost on par with the IBM quantum computer.

A related area of technology development is quantum communication.[16] Quantum communication uses Quantum Key Distribution (QKD) to send encrypted data as classical bits over networks. The keys to decrypt the data are encoded and transmitted in a quantum state using qubits.

The encryption key is in the form of qubits. The qubits can be sent through a fiberoptic cable. By comparing the state of the sender's and receiver's qubits—a process known as "key sifting," the sender and receiver can know whether or not they hold the same key. If the key is intercepted by a hacker, the quantum state of the key will collapse. Then the sender and receiver will have different keys. The sender can resend the key until the receiver receives the same key. Since the signal travels at the speed of light, there is practically no perceived delay.

China has installed a quantum communication line between Beijing and Shanghai, a 1,263-mile-long ground link. There are[17] banks and other financial companies already using it to transmit data. In the United States, a company named Quantum Xchange has setup a similar 500-mile fiberoptic cable running along the East Coast.[18]

Such a line does not need to be land-based. The Chinese satellite, Micius, demonstrated such quantum communication in 2017. The Chinese team, along with researchers in Austria, demonstrated the world's first quantum-encrypted virtual teleconference between Beijing and Vienna.

## REFERENCES

1. *https://www.iot-now.com/tag/caterpillar/*

2. *https://fieldserviceasia.wbresearch.com/blog/caterpillar-and-iot-a-partnership-set-to-move-the-earth*

3. *https://www.samsung.com/us/refrigerators/*

4. *https://www.mordorintelligence.com/industry-reports/robotics-market*

5. *https://www.gartner.com/en/newsroom/press-releases/2019-04-02-gartner-forecasts-worldwide-public-cloud-revenue-to-g*

6. *https://ourworldindata.org/grapher/supercomputer-power-flops*

7. *https://www.top500.org/news/fugaku-holds-top-spot-exascale-remains-elusive/*

8. *https://venturebeat.com/2021/09/15/nvidia-ceo-jensen-huang-named-one-of-times-most-influential-people/*

9. After Roadblocks and Renewals, EuroHPC Targets a Bigger, Quantum Future (*hpcwire.com*)

10. *https://bgr.com/tech/worlds-fastest-computer-japan-abci-supercomputer-5460526/*

11. Home—TOP500

12. *https://en.wikipedia.org/wiki/Quantum_computing*

13. Quantum Computer Market Headed to $830M in 2024 (*hpcwire.com*)

14. *https://www.quantamagazine.org/google-and-ibm-clash-over-quantum-supremacy-claim-20191023/*

15. *https://www.msn.com/en-us/news/technology/record-breaking-chinese-supercomputer-marks-new-quantum-supremacy-milestone/ar-AAM7VFM*

16. *https://www.sciencedirect.com/topics/chemistry/quantum-communication*

17. *https://scitechdaily.com/china-builds-the-worlds-first-integrated-quantum-communication-network/*

18. *https://quantumxc.com*

# CHAPTER 3

# 5G TELECOMMUNICATION

In this chapter, we see the advantages of 5G technology in network communications.

## 3.1 5G COMMUNICATION TECHNOLOGIES

5G is 5th generation communication technology. Cell phone technology was first commercialized on a large scale in the early 1980s. Since then, in every decade, the technology has evolved into a new generation—1G in the 1980s, 2G in the 1990s, 3G in the 2000s, 4G in the 2010s—and now we are entering the 5G era.

Compared to 4G, a 5G cell phone can take 1000× more data volume, has a 10× to 100× faster data download rate, and 5× faster latency. It can be connected to 10× to 100× more devices at the same time. 5G technology is also radically different from the previous generation in that its network is software-defined rather than hardware-defined.

5G connects not only to cell phones but also to any object in which the Internet of Things (IoT) is installed. In other words, IoT enables any object to be connected to the Internet. This opens up a huge source of data. In the year 2018, the number of IoT systems installed exceeded the number of cell phones in the world. The volume of data in the world will reach 163 zettabytes (ZB) by 2025, mostly generated by IoT. Because data create AI, we can say that 5G is the enabler of AI. 5G-enabled devices allow us to power edge computing and manage the movement of crucial data between locations. As a result, 5G is making substantial changes to edge devices and data center infrastructures.

5G uses New Radio (NR) frequency ranges: (1) sub-6 GHz frequency bands, and (2) 24–100 GHz frequency bands in the mmWave range. Because these wave ranges are new in cell phone technology, the 5G network is known as the New Radio (NR) network. In this section, we will discuss the structure of the 5G network.

A 5G network is radically different from its 4G counterpart. It is software-defined, in contrast to 4G which is mostly hardware-defined. This enables it to optimize the network performance, and increase the efficiency, flexibility, and capacity of the infrastructure. This is called *virtualization*. Virtual networks are not new in 5G. The most well-known virtual network employed in 4G is the Virtual Private Network, or VPN. Functionally, 5G consists of 4 logical networks: Core Networks, Radio Access Networks (RAN), an Interconnect Network, and a Transport Network. Each logical network performs certain functions.

The core network is the command center of 5G. It resides in a cloud. It has a Service-Based Architecture (SBA), which is built using IT networking principles and cloud native technology. It establishes connectivity and access to its services and handles mobility throughout the network. In this sense, 5G is greatly integrated into the cloud service.

A Radio Access Network (RAN) consists of the Remote Radio Unit (RRU) and Baseband Unit (BBU).[1] The RRU is mounted in the cell tower, near the antenna. It is the final connection between a cell phone and a network. Data traffic arrives from remote locations via underground optical fibers through the BBU to the RRU. The BBU is connected to the RRU via the Common Public Radio Interface (CPRI). Among many other functions, the BBU converts the voice signal that people understand into a digital signal for transmission.

Before 5G, the BBU resided mostly in a Radio Tower.[2] In 5G, due to the shorter transmission distance of new radio frequencies, the number of radio towers has increased. It becomes expensive to build a BBU into every tower. The functions of the BBU are separated into Distributed Units (DUs) and Centralized Units (CUs). A Centralized Unit (CU) is moved to a central location, usually in the cloud. It is shared by many towers and is therefore more cost effective. A Distributed Unit (DU) may or may not be located in the radio tower. This means that some network functions are moving away from Radio Towers.

Before the split, the connection between RRU and BBU was called the front haul, and the connection between the BBU and the Core Network was called the back haul. After the split, the connection between the DU and CU is inserted between the Core Network and the RRU. Therefore, the connection from the DU to the CU is known as the middle haul. The network which provides connectivity between all the disaggregated components of the BBU and the RRU is called the Transport Network. In effect, the Transport Network has three segments: front haul, middle haul, and back haul.

In addition to the reduced cost, splitting the BBU also offers more flexibility in locating functions, and maximizes performance. There are many options for the split, depending on the deployment scenarios.[3] The division of network functions between the CU and DU has trade-offs in the performance features, such as latency and cost. Network engineers must decide among load management, real-time performance optimization, and adaptation to various use cases to maintain the quality of service. While CUs will maintain BBU-like functionalities such as digital processing, DUs are software-based and could contain some functions related to the Remote Radio Head (RRH) contained in the RRU.

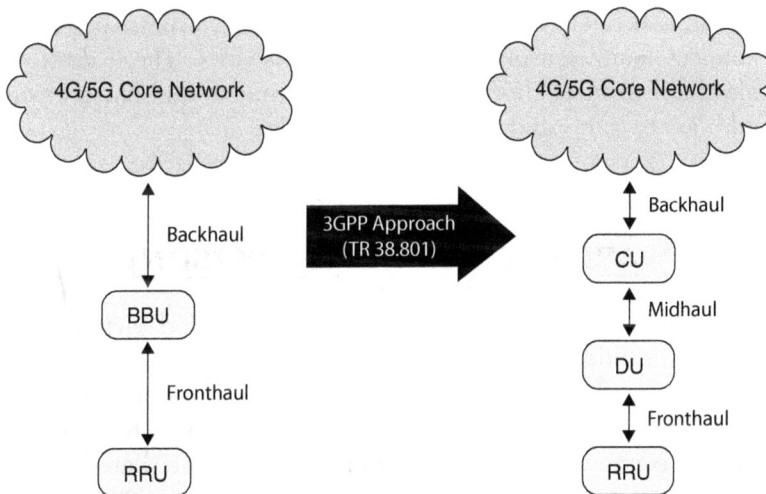

*FIGURE 3.1* RAN architecture.

Further, instead of separating the BBU into CU and DU, why not just remove the entire BBU from the Radio Tower? In this case, the BBU can be shared by many towers. In other words, one master Base Unit serves many ratio towers. Furthermore, such a BBU can exist in a cloud. If the BBU resides in a cloud, the RAN is known as a Cloud-based Radio Access Network (C-RAN).

5G networks need to co-exist with 4G networks for a long time to come because not all phones will be upgraded to 5G. Therefore, some 5G networks must work with 4G signals. This kind of 5G network is called the Non-Standalone (NSA) network. On the contrary, if it does not work with 4G signals, it is called a Standalone (SA) network.

5G is not just a replacement for 4G. It supports many new infrastructures of the digital economy, such as edge computing and mobile computing in autonomous vehicles. 5G connectivity in the new mobile computing of autonomous vehicles requires superfast latency in order to respond to quickly changing traffic situations. This means redesigning many of the core components, including RF antennas, power requirements, new hardware and firmware, new safety and regulatory testing, and cyber-security tools.

There are many important factors to consider in incorporating 5G into edge devices, such as low power usage, the integrity of the radio frequency signal, and safety concerns. 5G needs to have a massive system capacity to connect many sensors and other edge devices. These devices themselves also have to meet the requirements for remote and harsh environments, in addition to safety and regulatory standards.

## 3.2 SOFTWARE-DEFINED NETWORK (SDN)

A 5G network is sliced into many networks called Virtual Networks (VN)[4] by software-defined networks (SDN). This is different from the traditional hardware-defined physical network. Each VN works independently. Network slicing permits the logical separation of a network so that each slice provides unique connectivity—but all slices run on the same shared infrastructure.

5G virtualization provides a new level of flexibility, allowing operators to, for example, devote a network slice to certain kinds of devices. To the user, each VN is like an independent network on its own. Nevertheless, it resides in the same physical infrastructure as the other virtual networks. The VPN (Virtual Private Network) is the most popular virtual network.

To efficiently support certain services, each network slice can access different types of resources, such as infrastructure (e.g., VPNs and cloud services) and *virtualized network functions* (VNFs). With 5G virtualization, operators will be able to create custom networks with unique sets of capabilities.

VNs can be highly dispersed over many locations in the edge cloud servers and core data centers. For them to work seamlessly together, they must be interconnected with the *physical network functions* (PNFs) to provide end-to-end services. The interconnect network connects PNFs and VNFs in a unified and scalable manner. This is achieved by the interconnect network as shown in Figure 3.2.

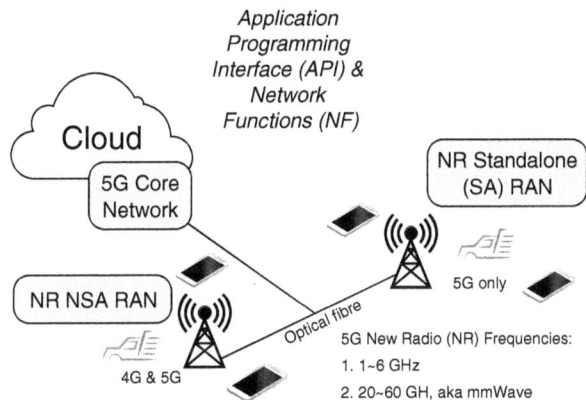

**FIGURE 3.2** A 5G network.

The 5G transport network holds together the disaggregated RAN components, connecting the cell site to the core network. While the RU is at the cell site, the DU and CU may be located remotely, virtualized, and operated as a pool of resources to reduce costs. This flexible RAN disaggregation has specific performance requirements for front-haul, middle-haul, and back-haul implementation, corresponding to the various RAN deployment options as shown in the diagram. Each imposes requirements for latency and distance.

Cell phone infrastructure is expensive. Therefore, many operators share the same infrastructure. This is more prominent in 5G. The infrastructure belongs to a Mobile Network Operator (MNO).[5] The cell phone service providers lease part of the network from an MNO. They are known as the Mobile

Virtual Network Operator (MVNO). Think of the MNO as the landlord and the MVNO as the tenant in an apartment building.

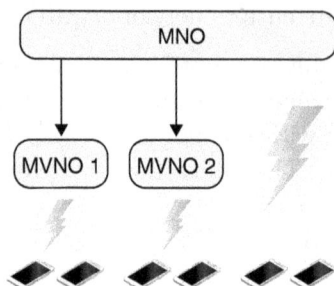

**FIGURE 3.3** MNO and MVNO.

The MNO buys radio spectrum and provides end-to-end service (voice or data) to its subscribers. It sets up the cellular network, including mobile network towers, and also issues SIM cards to mobile phone users. The MNO purchases radio spectrum from regulators. The popular MNOs are Verizon Wireless, T-Mobile, Vodafone, etc.

An MVNO is an operator which offers mobile services to end users. MVNOs do not have a government license to use their own radio frequencies. The MVNO buys spectrum from the MNO. The MVNO is basically a reseller of wireless communication services. The MVNOs buy voice and data packages in bulk from MNOs and sell them to their subscribers/users. The MNO can also offer end-to-end cell phone services directly to customers.

The cellular network elements include transmission links, control functions, and mobility management functions which keep track of the location of mobile handsets. This helps the service providers to provide voice call services as well as data services.

## 3.3 PRIVATE 5G

5G opens up the possibility of private 5G networks because of its Cloud Network Functions (CNFs). CNFs are built using a micro-services methodology. CNFs can be deployed in public, private, or hybrid networks with 5G, delivering ultra-low latency and high bandwidth connections. Improved local processing allows machine learning algorithms to handle massive amounts of data on the edge. Such capability makes it possible to work with both multi-access edge computing (MEC) and core cloud architectures that support AI without ever leaving the private domain. Factories, distribution centers, and other organizations which require more secure data networks can benefit from the deployment of such private 5G infrastructures.

The private 5G network is built by a network slicing technique with the 5G Service-Based Architecture (SBA). Each slice retains independent control and user plane functions. Mobile network operators can partition their public networks, creating a practically unlimited number of private 5G networks to support their customers. Data traffic can be dynamically directed to either the customers' private networks or to a software-defined VPN.

For example, Microsoft's Azure private MEC brings together Microsoft's computing, networking, and application services, all managed from the cloud. Operators and system integrators can use such a service to deliver high performance, low-latency connectivity, and IoT applications on the edge, to achieve digital transformation for their customers.

The major business target for private 5G is industries, which can both benefit from simplified business operations with cloud-based network management, keeping sensitive data on-premises, as well as gain the ability to scale up in location coverage and data traffic when needed. It is simple to install and flexible to connect to existing production IT, and to scale up to meet future challenges. A private 5G network addresses key trends in the enterprise cellular market. It can also track assets and perform real-time automation to improve productivity in warehouses, with digital twins to optimize manufacturing operations. Working with augmented reality can improve the efficiency of quality inspections.

## 3.4  BEYOND 5G

The world will not stop at 5G. Even before 5G has been fully deployed, 6G research is already underway. It is believed that 6G networks will be another quantum leap from 5G in supporting applications far beyond anything we know today, such as virtual and augmented reality (VR/AR), ubiquitous instant communication, and pervasive intelligence. Mobile network operators will adopt flexible decentralized business models for 6G, with spectrum sharing, infrastructure sharing, mobile edge computing, artificial intelligence, and blockchain technology. Blockchain-enabled telecommunications will provide data security to the Internet. In other words, high security, secrecy, and privacy should be the key features of 6G. By then, the entire Internet will be as secure as Bitcoin is today. According to the schedule, the launch of 6G is expected in the year 2035.

In the United States, the FCC has taken the first step of opening up a terahertz wave spectrum (between 95 GHz and 3 THz). Many countries and companies are also funding or starting research on 6G. ATIS, the Alliance of Telecommunication Industry Solutions, launched the Next G Alliance in late 2020 for the development of 6G and beyond. ATIS includes prominent members such as Verizon, T-Mobile, AT&T, Microsoft, Samsung, Meta, Apple, Google, Ericsson, Nokia, Qualcomm, and others. In November 2020, China launched the world's first 6G satellite[6] to test ultra-high speeds using terahertz waves.

## REFERENCES

1. *https://www.verizon.com/about/our-company/5g/5g-radio-access-networks.*

2. *http://3yuangroup.com/news/industry-news/348.html.*

3. *https://www.5g-networks.net/5g-technology/gnodeb-gnb-cu-du-split/.*

4. *https://www.vmware.com/topics/glossary/content/virtual-networking.*

5. *https://en.wikipedia.org/wiki/Mobile_network_operator.*

6. *https://www.bbc.com/news/av/world-asia-china-54852131.*

# 4

# *BLOCKCHAIN AND OTHER DIGITAL ECONOMY INFRASTRUCTURES*

There are many other infrastructures that are important for the digital economy besides HPC and 5G. In this and the next chapters, we are going to discuss some of which are the most significant.

## 4.1  IoT DEVICES AND SENSORS

The Internet of Things (IoT) and sensors are the frontline components of the digital economy. They collect data and transmit to a data center. IoT is a breakthrough technology derived from the Internet. For the first time in history, objects are no longer isolated physical entities. Objects equipped with IoT and sensors can sense their environment, collect data, communicate with other objects and people, and perform tasks as instructed, all through the Internet.

The data that are collected constitute a part of Big Data. Big Data, in turn, trains AI through machine learning. AI can instruct an object to perform a function through IoT. The entire world of lifeless objects is activated by the IoT. IoT promises to bring us into the 4th industrial revolution, following the invention of the steam engine, electricity, and the computer. IoT integrates people and objects to form a gigantic network. Messages and data are sent and received not only between people, but between people and objects, and between objects and objects. IoT is widely adopted in a variety of industries and consumer markets.

Today, the number of IoT devices installed worldwide exceeds the population of the entire world. By 2025, there will be 75 billion IoT-connected devices worldwide, according to a recent forecast.[1]

An object that is classified as IoT, with RFID and sensors, becomes a part of the Wireless Sensor Network (WSN) (Figure 4.1).[2]

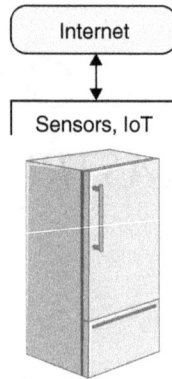

*FIGURE 4.1* An IoT-connected object

It can infer, see, hear, and measure any environmental parameters (temperature, humidity, chemical composition, etc.) through multiple types of attached sensors and actuators. It collects the data as desired and shares the data with the outside world. Through two-way communication, it can receive external instruction to perform functions requested by an external source. In this way, the object is no longer isolated but forms an integral part of a much larger system. The exchange of data between an object with IoT and the remote server allows the object to be monitored and controlled. It makes the management of a remote system possible. This results in increased system efficiency and improved cost monitoring. Through IoT, objects can also be activated to perform certain tasks by human command, a preprogrammed instruction set, or even by artificial intelligence.

IoT promises to be the next revolutionary technology that integrates all the objects into the Internet. With industrial devices and applications, IIoT (or Industrial IoT), each machine or device runs the full range of productivity improvements—from predictive maintenance of the equipment to the customized configuration of products in the production line. It also provides equipment vendors with invaluable performance data from the field, and the capability of remote diagnosis and troubleshooting to improve their equipment.

*Blockchain technology* further unleashes the power of IoT. The combination of IoT and blockchain will allow any type of transaction to occur between two IoT-enabled objects. The industry can create a tamper-proof history of the products, from their component supply chain to their field operation, in complex value networks with many stakeholders. The possibilities include connected cars, connected light bulbs, HVAC in "green building" management systems, the equipment used in hospitals, tracking devices in container ships, and many others.

With the reduced cost of IoT, these devices will become ubiquitous—in consumer product packages, medical devices, hardware scanners, drones—almost anywhere. The blockchain adds security to the IoT data and allows not only information transfer, but also valuable assets to be sent over networks. This makes it possible for two objects to transact with each other without human intervention. For example, in a factory, parts passing the quality inspection check can be automatically routed to the production line. Otherwise, they might be routed to scrap or downgrade bins. A proprietary recipe of a pharmaceutical process producing a new drug developed in the company's R&D laboratory can be sent over to the factory's production IoT platform when released for manufacturing, without the risk of being hacked.

Alternatively, a highly sensitive technical specification of a sophisticated system in development can be shared among different devices between different collaboration partners using an IoT platform. A smart contract can be sent over the blockchain to a contractor's IoT platform in the supply chain to trigger a specific event in the contract. When a container of goods is loaded on a cargo plane connected by IoT, the smart contract immediately triggers a payment without the involvement of a third party, such as a bank.

The combination of blockchain and IoT creates tremendous potential in industrial use. Samsung and IBM are creating decentralized networks of IoT devices using blockchain. IBM's Watson IoT platform enables IoT devices to send data to blockchain ledgers. The platform is called ADEPT (Autonomous Decentralized Peer-to-Peer Telemetry).[3] ADEPT records the transactions carried out by the IoT devices without the need for central control and management. It utilizes hybrid PoW / PoS to secure transactions. The three building blocks of the platform are BitTorrent for file sharing, Ethereum for smart contracts, and TeleHash for peer-to-peer (P2P) messaging. IoT serves to bridge blockchain with the real world.

A fintech company in China, ZhongAn Technology,[4] a subsidiary of ZhongAn Insurance, developed a blockchain-based system that aims to track the entire process of chicken farming, in partnership with Wopu, an IoT company in China. The blockchain application will give each chicken an identity by attaching it to an IoT device and using mobile applications to check each transaction recorded on the blockchain. It can trace and record information of its birth, the farms on which it was raised, and the processing factories and logistic suppliers it reaches on its way to market. ZhongAn is also rolling out the first blockchain application in the country's agricultural industry.

Walmart collaborated with Tsinghua University and IBM Blockchain to form WFSCC (Walmart Food Safety Collaboration Center) in Beijing.[5] The project will use blockchain technology to explore the traceability of the food supply chain and establish its authenticity.

In addition to these examples, many more companies are rushing into this new arena, including Fortune 500 companies and startups: Ambisafe, BitSE, Chronicled, ConsenSys, Distributed Global, Filament, Hashed Health, Ledger, Skuchain, Slock.it, BNY Mellon, Bosch, Cisco, Gemalto, and Foxconn are a few examples. Leading manufacturing and IT companies, blockchain companies, and financial institutions, such as Cisco, Foxconn, Bank of New York Mellon, BitSE, Bosch, Gemalto, Chronicled, and ConsenSys formed a consortium to develop blockchain-based IoT applications. The consortium wants to establish a decentralized and immutable blockchain protocol as a shared platform to build IoT devices, applications, and networks. The consortium is working to initially set the shared protocol. It will then begin to explore structures of IoT networks and design appropriate applications.

In addition to the manufacturing industry, service industries such as healthcare can also use IoT plus blockchain to drastically improve their services, by attaching monitoring and tracking devices to patients. Multiple parties can gain real-time access to information being distributed and recorded onto a public blockchain, such as insulin levels or heart rates. The potential of the IoT and blockchain combination is beyond imagination.

## 4.2 SEMICONDUCTORS

Whether or not semiconductor technology can meet AI's processing demands will depend on the so-called "Moore's Law." Analysts debate whether Moore's Law is no longer valid, after five decades of infallibility in predicting the progress of semiconductor technology. Much of the debate is centered on the issue that the size of transistors is approaching its physical limits—the size of atoms. You cannot build transistors with only a few atoms. The physics of the transistor structure no longer works in terms of increased size.

In reality, there are two ways to describe Moore's Law: by the size of the technology node and by the number of transistors per chip. Until recently, when one plots the size of the most advanced technology node or the maximum number of transistors, in log scale vs. years (from 1970 to 2020), Moore's Law is linear. In fact, the original prediction of Gordon Moore was, by definition, that the maximum number of transistors per chip doubles every two years. By this definition, Moore's Law is still valid, even if the transistors cannot be made smaller than 2 nm. There is nothing to prevent building transistors into the third dimension. The vertical dimension buildup allows the number of transistors on a chip to continue to increase.

Until now, the transistor has been built on the surface of a silicon substrate. However, new technologies allow building devices vertically, different from the silicon substrate. In fact, in 3D NAND flash, the chip already has more than one hundred layers of memory cells. Nanowire technology builds transistors using deposited materials, which can be extended vertically.

In view of the growing market, chip companies are rushing into offering chips designed especially for AI applications, which require handling huge workloads to process machine learning and deep learning. These players include Intel, AMD, NVIDIA, IBM, and many others.

To overcome issues with Moore's Law, next-generation chips are using technologies like advanced packaging to build chips in 3D, alternatives to the planar CMOS and CIM (Compute In-Memory).

Because data are processed by processors and stored in the memory, not only do the processors and the memory need to be fast, but the bandwidth of data transfer between processors and memory must be large so that transfers are not slowed by bottlenecks. In order to achieve this, the memory's read/write cycle needs to be fast and the transfer path must allow large amounts of data to be transferred in parallel. This means the memory/processor architecture must be changed.

The breakthrough in the memory speed will come from fabrication technologies and the new types of semiconductor memories using new materials. New types of memory technology use different data storage mechanisms and memory cell materials to store the information, such as Magnetic Random Access Memory (MRAM), Resistive RAM (ReRAM), Phase-Change RAM (PCRAM), and Ferromagnetic RAM (FeRAM). These new memory types increase memory density, are faster in storing and retrieving data (read and write), have lower power consumption, and are non-volatile (data will not dissipate when power is off); they also allow the construction of high-bandwidth memory (HBM) on the chip. HBM in the CIM architecture allows memory to be located near the processing core, to store and retrieve large arrays of data simultaneously, in order to speed up the processing. These advancements meet a surging demand for memory capacity in training neural networks. These qualities are needed to contend with the sharp rise in AI workloads.

High Bandwidth Memory (HBM) is indispensable in the exascale HPC as the primary, on-node memory. HBM is a DRAM stacking technology that vertically stacks multiple DRAM dies and directly connects them with through-silicon vias (TSVs). Both HBM and DDR use the same DRAM technology, and both support multiple independent channels to access the memory. However, their architectures in the width of the interface differ. The interface width determines how many bits of data can be transferred in parallel between memory and processor in one cycle of the computer clock. Each HBM channel uses a 128-bit, wide I/0 interface, and each connection can operate at a data rate of up to 2Gbps. This extremely wide, parallel interface is the key technique used by HBM to deliver such high bandwidth rates. The total bandwidth of a single HBM2 channel can reach 32GB/s with a stack capable of delivering 256GB/s. The access latency of HBM is comparable to that of conventional DDR DRAM technology. The newer version HBM3 doubles the density of the individual memory dies from 8Gb to 16Gb and will allow for more than eight dies to be stacked together in a single chip, with up to 64GB of memory capacity possible. When employing multiple stacks, the total amount of memory bandwidth available per socket could be several terabytes per second, by the year 2023.

Likewise, in the computer processor area, AMD and Xilinx make heterogeneous types of computing chips to meet the demands of deep learning. AMD's "EPYC" server chip combines multiple and heterogeneous "chiplets," including the CP, GPU, neural processor, and memory chips, into a single package, interconnected by a high-speed memory bus. Field-Programmable Gate Arrays (FPGAs) can handle not only the matrix multiplications of AI but also the parts of traditional software execution, together with the machine learning operations.

Google's Tensor Processing Unit (TPU) chips are designed for machine learning services. However, even Google's huge data centers, having a million racks filled with TPUs, are not nearly enough to meet the demand. Google plans to increase TPU performance by tenfold in the next few years.

A top-of-the line chip for deep learning training, such as NVIDIA's Tesla V100, runs at 112 trillion FLOPS or 112 TeraFLOPS. Even if Moore's Law continues, the increase in chip power is still outpaced by the demand. The only way to go around is to build bigger and bigger cloud computing centers.

NVIDIA, a leader in AI chips, offers GPU using the proprietary NVLink technology—the most popular AI chip to date. IBM's CPU Power9 can crunch the huge amount of data in AI and machine learning, such as image and voice recognition and credit card fraud prevention.

Intel's Nervana Neural Network Processor (NNP), built for deep learning, provides the flexibility to support all deep learning primitives efficiently. It is called the Neural Network Process because the parallelism in its architecture allows neural network-like parameters distributed across multiple chips to accommodate larger models to capture more insight from data.

Advanced Micro Devices launched the newest EPYC server and Vega graphics chips for AI tasks. Google, although not a chip company, has also forayed into designing its own chip, named TPU V2 (the Tensor Processing Unit),[6] to power its cloud computing business.

The basic circuit in the neural network is called the Multiply-Accumulate Circuit, or MAC, which was originally patented by Motorola in 1998.[7] The MACs perform linear algebra computations known as tensor math. In the multiplication operation, the input data form vectors are multiplied by the neural network weights. In the accumulation operation, the products of these multiplications are added together. More MACs on a chip increase parallelization and can improve machine learning.

Both NVIDIA and Intel have tried to adapt their products to take advantage of those atomic linear algebra functions. NVIDIA has added tensor cores to its Tesla GPUs, to optimize the matrix multiplications. Intel has bought companies such as Mobileye, Movidius, and Nervana Systems, in the deep learning chip design space.

Microsoft has an Azure cloud service called Project Brainwave. Amazon is also developing its own custom chip called Inferentia, as is Meta.

In addition to these large companies, there are also many startups specialized in the design of AI chips. Their goal is to design chips with large numbers of MAC units. Graphcore, a UK company, is one of the farthest along among the startups, being the first to ship production chips, called Colossus, to customers. Colossus contains 1,024 Intelligence Processor Cores (IPCs). Each core embeds 296KB of SRAM, making the total amount of memory in the chip 304MB. The chip size is huge, measuring 806 mm$^2$, because of its large on-board memory. The embedded memory with low latency will provide much faster processing power. Graphcore also builds its own programming software, called "Poplar." Poplar not only translates the frameworks but also assigns parallel computations to MAC and vector units on the chip. It breaks up the computing graph of a neural network into "codelets" and distributes each codelet to a different core of Colossus to optimize parallel processing.

Other companies are not to be left behind. Cerebras Systems, also a UK company, has announced its 2nd Generation Wafer Scale Engine processor. The new chip, as large as a single 300-mm wafer, has a die size of approximately 46,225 mm$^2$. The chip is fabricated using TSMC's 7nm technology and consists of 2.6 trillion transistors. In comparison, NVIDIA's A100 measures 826 mm$^2$ and contains 54.2 billion transistors.

The worldwide market size of semiconductors is growing ever faster because the demand of semiconductors is increasing in sync with the increase in the volume of data. The generation, collection, transmission, and processing of data all require semiconductor chips. The semiconductor market was $200 billion in 2000 and grew to $300 billion in 2012. It took 13 years to increase by $100 billion. Yet, to grow from $300 billion to $400 billion took only four years (2013 to 2017). In 2021, it reached $500 billion. Likewise, the semiconductor capital investment in 2020 was $107 billion and grew to $140 billion in 2021. It is safe to say that such trends will continue as long as the volume of data grows.

## 4.3   EVOLUTION OF COMPUTERS DRIVEN BY AI

Today's computing system is based on the concept invented by Alan Turing in 1936. The Turing machine is known as the foundation of modern computing. Today, some eight decades later, such a computer system is finally running into limitations. The reason is that the Turing machine is not ideal to imitate neural network calculations or machine learning.

The use of machine learning, by which AI gains its intelligence, is quickly growing. Machine learning will soon be poised to take over the majority of the world's computing activity. According to OpenAI, the demand for computing by deep learning networks has been increasing by 10x every year since 2012. AI workloads in data centers worldwide could eventually consume as much as 80% of all computing power and 10% of global electricity within the next two decades.

As a result, AI and machine learning are changing the way computers are built and being used. This is pushing the boundaries of what today's computers can do, in terms of both capability and capacity. Current hardware capabilities and software tools encounter serious limitations, but a major breakthrough in computing has been achieved through the use of AI and machine learning methods.

The breakthrough came from both chip design and computer architecture. For example, Graphics Processing Units (GPUs) lead to greater parallelization of computing. The GPU-based system can train vastly larger networks than systems made of Central Processing Units (CPUs). Such a distributed processing method is required to train an AI network in parallel. Modern neural networks such as OpenAI's GPT-2 have over a billion parameters that need to be "trained" simultaneously. Such a job cannot be easily handled by the traditional CPU-based computers.

These advances are considered to be the paradigm shift in making computer chips. They require much more collaboration between hardware designers and software programmers. Machine learning might open new opportunities for analog computing as well, to eliminate the digital layer between the real-numbered neural nets and the underlying analog devices.

Microsoft offers tools, turnkey solutions to allow developers to create AI apps on its Azure platform. Such a tool can be used in virtual machine images, networking, storage, the blockchain, security and identity, databases, and others. Many of these have direct applications in fintech.[8] Many companies are forming partnerships to leverage each other's expertise, for example, Microsoft is working with Huawei, and Facebook has partnered with Qualcomm.

AI is by no means limited to the large machines. Even mobile devices rely on AI. Apple's new iPhone has a neural engine, so does Huawei's Mate 10. Big companies designing mobile chips, such as Qualcomm and ARM, are gearing up to supply AI-capable hardware to power mobile devices. AI hardware promises to offer better performance and better battery life, privacy, and security. AI chips can perform more data-crunching on a device instead of sending everything via the cloud. This means improved privacy. AI is more than just hardware; it is the combination of hardware and apps. Both Android and Apple iOS have APIs that can tap the power of the neural hardware. These APIs leverage the capability of deep learning frameworks such as Google's TensorFlow[9] or Meta's Caffe2.[10]

The R&D spending on AI-oriented microprocessors has ramped up dramatically. Some estimate that AI chip sales reached $35 billion in 2021 from $6 billion in 2016.[11] AI chips power AI just as microprocessors power computing. AI will be omnipresent in the near future.

One of the most common benefits and effects AI has in nearly every industry is an opportunity for automation. In addition to AI reducing the manual expense management problem, it can automatically generate expenditure and expense reports quickly, efficiently, and without errors.

AI understands approval workflows and allows companies to restructure and automate the expense-tracking process. It also helps to prevent reimbursement fraud and guides organizations with their budgeting efforts, thanks to automated reports.

One of the most valuable benefits AI brings to organizations of all kinds is data. The future of fintech is largely reliant on gathering data and staying ahead of the competition, and AI can make that happen. With AI, one can process a huge volume of data, which will offer game-changing insights. These insights can help in many ways in the complex decision-making processes.

To succeed, larger enterprises have relied heavily upon the algorithms, automation, and analyses achieved with the help of AI. Because this technology is becoming increasingly accessible and affordable, it helps smaller startups as well as consumers, giving them the tools to compete with larger players within their industry.

AI is playing an important role in empowering both consumers and fintech companies. AI-powered personal financial applications allow people to balance their budgets based on their specific income and spending patterns. AI acts as a robot advisor to individuals and organizations, to cut costs while boosting the bottom line.

Artificial intelligence is not limited to a behind-the-scenes role in the business world. AI-guided chatbots undertake a variety of internal and external communications, such as the self-service customer-facing tools employed by financial institutions. With the stiff competition in the fintech world today, it's no surprise that companies are adopting new technologies to stay one step ahead of the competition. Artificial intelligence allows fintech companies to eliminate human error while boosting productivity and increasing their bottom line.

## 4.4 BLOCKCHAIN

The digital economy is all about data. The two major breakthroughs in data science entering this century were Big Data and Blockchain. In recent decades, the increase of the data volume worldwide is followed by the variety. In the past, data were defined by text. But now, data can be text, image, video, and sound. Big Data is the name given to all the technologies that capture, store, analyze, search, share, transfer, visualize, query, and update data.

Data contain vital, private, and sensitive information about persons, organizations, and events. The protection of these data against unauthorized access or manipulation is important. Until recently, institutions, organizations, or companies built their own silos of data and information-management protocols. When data are managed privately, it is easier to ensure security. However, when data are in the cloud, the security measures need to be enhanced. In 2013, the Target data breach cost Target $18.5 million dollars to settle.[12] In 2015, hackers obtained personal details, Social Security numbers, fingerprints, employment history, and financial information of about 20 million individuals in a U.S. government database.

A traditional database is inherently unsafe. For example, Dropbox reset passwords for 68 million accounts in response to a 2012 breach.[13] On August 31, 2014, a collection of almost 500 private pictures of various celebrities was posted on the imageboard 4Chan.[14] The images were hacked due to a security issue in the iCloud API via phishing attacks.

The ultimate solution to data security does not lie so much in data protection, but in an effort to make it unhackable. Blockchain is such a solution, which provides a secure, immutable, distributed way of handling data.

Blockchain is also known as the Mutual Distributed Ledger (MDL). It is a structured database. MDL categorizes data into three types: *identity data, transaction data, and content data.* Using Identity MDL, Transaction MDL, and Content MDL, one can create all kinds of applications that were not possible with the conventional database.

Blockchain technology simplifies the management of trusted information, making it easier for entities/persons to access and use critical public-sector data while maintaining the security of this information.[15]

Blockchain technology uses *blocks of data.* Once these blocks form a chain, they are linked so that any change will escalate throughout the blockchain and therefore become more secure. Verification and management using automation and shared protocols protect the data from unauthorized access. In addition, the blockchain database is distributed. Any change in one of the copies will make it distinctly different from the other copies.

Blockchain can help fintech-type companies, government agencies, and others to digitize and manage existing records within a secure infrastructure, allowing agencies to make some of these records "smart." Rules and algorithms allow specific data in a blockchain to be shared with a third party, once predefined conditions are met and the third party identity is verified.

Some countries are more advanced in applying such technology. For example, Estonia is rolling out a platform called *Keyless Signature Infrastructure* (KSI) to safeguard all public-sector data. KSI creates hashes of the original data. The hashes are stored in a blockchain and distributed across a network of government computers. Whenever an underlying file changes, a new hash value appends to the chain. An unauthorized data change will produce a hash not acceptable by the blockchain.

The transparency of the history of each record detects and prevents unauthorized tampering. Government officials can monitor the "who, what, and when" of any change. The health records of all Estonian citizens are managed using the KSI platform, which is available to all government agencies and private-sector companies in the country.

Besides data protection against unauthorized access and change, *data sharing* is potentially the most vulnerable data path. Currently, data sharing is not reversible. Once a party receives data, he possesses the data. In some circumstances, it can present a risk. For example, when you hand out your credit card information, you must trust the other party not to use it for any other purpose besides the intended transaction.

To solve this problem, MIT developed a project called *Enigma*.[16] Enigma is a P2P network, enabling different parties to jointly store and run computations on data while keeping the data completely private. Enigma borrows blockchain technology and uses a modified distributed hash-table for holding secret-shared data. An external blockchain is utilized as the controller of the network, manages access control and identities, and serves as a tamper-proof log of events. Like blockchain, users can share their data with cryptographic guarantees regarding their privacy. When used in the credit card transaction, the merchant submits the transaction to receive payment and yet he does not have the credit card information for any other unauthorized use.

Besides managing data, blockchain technology, as a decentralizing file storage on the Internet, brings clear benefits as well. Today, HTTP downloads only one file from a single computer at a time, instead of getting pieces from multiple computers simultaneously. A P2P approach could save 60% in bandwidth costs. Distributed data throughout the network saves bandwidth and also protects files from getting hacked or lost.

## REFERENCES

1. "Internet of Things (IoTXE "IoT") connected devices installed base worldwide from 2015 to 2025," *https://www.statista.com/statistics/471264/iot-number-of-connected-devices-worldwide/*.

2. "Wireless sensor network," *https://en.wikipedia.org/wiki/Wireless_sensor_network*.

3. "IBM XE "IBM" reveals Proof of Concept for blockchain powered IoTXE "IoT"," Stan Higgins, *https://www.coindesk.com/ibm-reveals-proof-concept-blockchain-powered-internet-things/*.

4. *https://www.zhongan.io/en/aboutus.*

5. *https://www.walmartfoodsafetychina.com/our-work/policy-support.*

6. "GoogleXE "Google" 's next-generation AI training system is monstrously fast," Nick Statt, *https://www.theverge.com/2017/5/17/15649628/google-tensor-processing-unit-tensorflow-ai-training-system.*

7. *https://patents.google.com/patent/US5847981A/en.*

8. *https://azuremarketplace.microsoft.com/en-us/marketplace/.*

9. *https://www.tensorflow.org/.*

10. *https://caffe2.ai/docs/getting-started.html?platform=windows&configuration=compile.*

11. "In AI Technology Race, U.S. Chips May Be Ace-In-The-Hole Vs. China," Reinhardt Klause, *https://www.investors.com/news/technology/ai-technology-u-s-chip-stocks-vs-china/.*

12. "Target will pay $18.5 million in settlement with states over 2013 data breach," Samantha Masunaga, *http://www.latimes.com/business/la-fi-target-credit-settlement-20170523-story.html.*

13. "DropBox's 2012 breach was worse than the company first announced," Russell Brandom, *https://www.theverge.com/2016/8/31/12727404/dropbox-breach-passwords-hacked-encrypted*.

14. "4chan Chronicle/The Australian Hack," Wikibooks, *https://en.wikibooks.org/wiki/4chan_Chronicle/The_Australian_Hack*.

15. "Using blockchain to improve data management in public sector," Steve Cheng et. al., *https://www.mckinsey.com/business-functions/digital-mckinsey/our-insights/using-blockchain-to-improve-data-management-in-the-public-sector*.

16. *https://www.enigma.co/*.

# 5

# *Big Data and Artificial Intelligence*

## 5.1   WHAT IS ARTIFICIAL INTELLIGENCE?

The mention of artificial intelligence (AI) evokes images of science-fiction. In the 1970 movie, *2001: A Space Odyssey*, the AI machine commanded the space ship. It disobeyed the crew and caused disaster. We always harbor doubt in our mind: If AI becomes more intelligent than human beings, how do we control it? Today, such a fantasy is quickly becoming a reality. As human intelligence has barely changed in the last tens of thousands of years, the intelligence of AI is evolving exponentially over the recent years. Sooner or later in this century, AI will surpass human intelligence. This event is called the *Singularity*.[1] It is speculated that singularity may happen in 40 to 50 years, in the not-too-distant future.

Depending on its capability, AI is also classified as *Artificial Narrow Intelligence* (ANI), *Artificial General Intelligence* (AGI), and *Artificial Super Intelligence* (ASI).

ANI refers to the AI which can perform only very specific tasks, such as playing chess, or voice and facial recognition. AGI is almost human-like, and the intelligence of ASI will be superior to that of humans.

Today, despite the progress made, we are still a long way from achieving AGI, not to mention ASI. Singularity is the point at which ASI becomes a reality. That is the point of no return because AI will be able to continue to evolve on its own – without human input. When singularity is achieved, AI may do things beyond the comprehension of the human race. The intelligence gap between humans and AI will be in favor of AI and will grow beyond human control.

The founder of Tesla and SpaceX and the richest man on earth, Elon Musk, has said that he thinks AI poses a threat to humanity. The famous physicist Stephen Hawking also said that the emergence of AI could be the worst event in the history of our civilization. Both of them have a greater understanding of AI than most of us.

The fact that AI can make decisions independent of human help is scary. What if the decisions go against the best interests of humanity? How can we prevent this from happening? How can we undo the wrongs committed by AI? The answer is, we cannot. Even if the AI does not have bad intentions, it can be trained by a human who maliciously wants to harm others. After all, if a person can learn to do evil, so can AI.

Regardless of what the future holds, the development of AI is accelerating, driven by business and national interests, and cannot be stopped. AI is already altering the world and raising important questions for society, the economy, and governance.

For example, questions are raised regarding the conviction of criminals by AI.[2] It is no longer a philosophical question about how AI will impact us, it is a real situation in which a person's fate is decided by AI. Therefore, it is imperative and urgent for policy makers to resolve the issue by ensuring that AI development remains under certain measures of control, in answer to the question "How can AI be developed within the moral and ethical guidelines?"

Three reasons can be ascribed to the greater advancement of AI technology during the past decades:

1.  Computing and data storage are becoming more powerful and less expensive thanks to the progress in semiconductor technology. With 50 billion transistors on a single chip, you can do a lot of computing in a small space. Today, one can carry the functionality of a 1950s NASA-sized computer in the pocket.

2.  More and more data are generated and made available for deep learning. The more knowledge we feed the AI machine, the faster it learns.

3.  More investment is pouring into the development of artificial intelligence. Global investment in AI has grown from $13 billion in 2015 to $68

billion in 2020.[3] Companies investing in AI are seeing handsome returns. AI applications are found in many industry sectors, such as healthcare, sales and marketing, security, finance and investment, e-commerce, robotics, etc.

## 5.2   HOW IS ARTIFICIAL INTELLIGENCE CREATED?

AI is created by an AI machine and Big Data. The AI machine consists of hardware, memory, and algorithms. The hardware is the computer. Today, more and more AI is powered by the neural computer rather than the traditional computer. Neural computers imitate the functionality of the human brain. An algorithm is the deep-learning or machine-learning software. Most of the hardware today resides in the data center or in the cloud. Data are collected from everywhere. They are sent to the AI machines through the Internet.

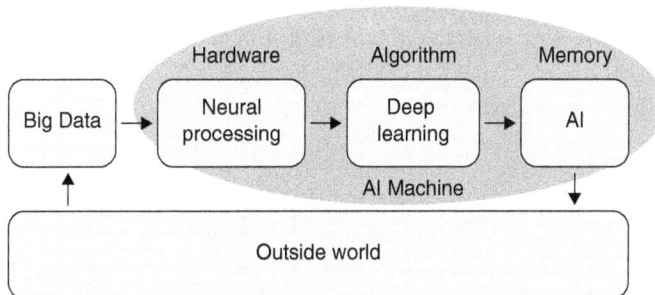

**FIGURE 5.1** Architecture of the AI machine.

The more data AI machines receive and learn from, the more intelligent they become. In 2009, the worldwide data generated was 0.5 zettabyte (ZB). Each ZB is $10^{21}$ bytes. In 2021, it was 40 ZB, an increase of 80 times. By this rate, in 2025, the data generated in 2025 will be 160 ZB.[4]

Conventional computer architecture faces difficulties in processing AI algorithms and handling huge amounts of data. AI computer architecture is evolving into a neuron-like system. It is called a *neural computer*.

Its processing units can comprise a Central Processing Unit (CPU), a Graphics Processing Unit (GPU), Field-Programmable Gate Array (FPGA), and Application-Specific Integrated Circuits (ASIC), all semiconductor chips.

The special kind of ASIC used in the AI machine is called the *Intelligent Processing Unit* (IPU).

A GPU is a chip to speed up multidimensional data processing for efficient performance on data such as an image. FPGA has reconfigurable logic blocks and interconnection hierarchy to perform parallel and serial sequential processing. The FPGA behaves in a fashion similar to connections between neurons in which they can create, break, and reroute connections between neurons. In addition, it has better energy efficiency and low-latency processing. Therefore, FPGAs have been widely adopted for neural network acceleration.[5]

These chips use traditional architecture, but they imitate neural processing. There are also newly developed chips which are built like neurons. Intel developed a neuromorphic system using their Loihi chips, which mimics the computing processes of eight million neurons. The University of Michigan also demonstrated a memristor array chip allowing localized AI.

These newly developed neural AI processors are capable of carrying out a large number of calculations in parallel and speeding up memory access by storing an entire AI algorithm in a single AI chip. This kind of computer architecture is also known as the *neuromorphic AI system*, which resembles the neuronal network in the brain.

The neuromorphic system is composed of Neural Networks (NN), also known as the Artificial Neural Networks (ANN). ANN mimics the human brain through a set of algorithms. It, in turn, comprises many node layers. Node layers include the input layer, hidden layers, and output layer. Each node, also called the artificial neuron, connects to another and has an associated weight and threshold. If the output of a node is above the specified threshold value, that node is activated, sending data to the next layer of the network. Otherwise, no data is passed along to the next layer of the network. Once all the outputs from the hidden layers are generated, they are used as inputs to calculate the final output of the neural network. When a network has more layers, it is "deeper," thus the name "deep learning."

In the multilayer ANN, because the output of one layer is passed into the next layer of the network, a single change can have a cascading effect on the other neurons. Therefore, when the NN is deeper, the final output will be influenced by the cascading effects from more inputs. The result will be more accurate.

The nodes in ANN can be constructed as feed-forward or feed-backward. In the feed-forward nodes, the data pass to the next node layer, directed from the inputs to outputs. In the backward nodes, data are sent back to the nodes in the previous layers, directed from the outputs to the inputs. This allows the construction of an error-correction loop.

AI machines perform two main tasks: learning and execution. In the learning phase, the AI system receives data and learns what that data is and how it should behave. The result of this learning is stored in its memory. In second task, execution, the AI system is fed data and it then processes that data to produce an appropriate response.

## 5.3  MACHINE LEARNING

*Machine learning* (or *deep learning*) is a branch of data science in the discipline of computer science. It is the algorithm which trains the AI machine using input data, by imitating the human brain. It is based on statistical methods to classify data and then makes predictions based on the classified data. The predicted results can drive decisions.

The terms machine learning (ML) and deep learning are interchangeable in most cases. However, some tend to make the distinction that deep learning is more advanced machine learning in that it automates the learning process, enabling the use of larger data sets. On the other hand, machine learning is a more general term relating to human-fed specific data for the machine to learn, sometimes also called supervised learning.

As the AI learning algorithm advances, deep learning will be more prevalent. In essence, the machine learning algorithm performs error detection/correction; optimization repeats the process until the optimized accuracy has been met. The final output is the decision.

The term *supervised machine learning* means that the algorithm uses human-labeled datasets to train algorithms that classify data or predict outcomes accurately. As input data are fed into the model, it adjusts its weights until the model has been fitted appropriately. One well-known application of supervised learning is to classify spam-like emails into the spam folder from the inbox.

Unsupervised machine learning is more advanced. It analyzes unlabeled data-sets to discover hidden patterns without human intervention. The algorithm can discover similarities and differences in the data set.

When the data set is partially labeled and fully unsupervised learning is not possible, the machine learning becomes *semi-supervised*. As the name implies, semi-supervised learning operates between supervised and unsupervised learning. It uses the labeled part of the data set to classify the unlabeled part of the data set. In most of the cases, when the data set cannot be fully labeled, semi-supervised learning is more efficient than unsupervised learning.

There are also cases when there are not enough models to train the AI; then, a model by trial and error can be used. It is sometimes known as *reinforcement learning*.

Today, the people training and using machine learning models are typically experienced developers, but the future ML systems should be more people-oriented, without the need for any coding skills to perform the same tasks. This has happened in the past. A compiler hides the complexity of low-level machine code, so that the programmers deal with more human-readable language. A database management system hides the complexity of data storage, indexing, and later retrieval, so that data engineers can use an easy-to-understand declarative query language. Likewise, future ML systems steer toward hiding complexity and exposing simpler abstractions. These new systems will not require users to fully understand all the details of how models are trained and used for obtaining predictions, but will provide them a more user-friendly interface that is less demanding and more familiar. Such a technique is known as *declarative ML*. In declarative ML, users declare only their data schema (names and types of inputs) and tasks rather than having to write low-level ML code. The successes of machine learning come from the improved understanding of the process of producing real-world ML applications. Building a working ML application becomes more like teaching kids to learn rather than doing software engineering work.

Before this can be done, researchers must extract common patterns from a set of tools, systems, and platforms. This allows quick improvement of models through more standardized processes. Where implementing an ML model once required years of work for highly skilled ML researchers, now can be achieved by writing a few lines of code. The availability of accelerator hardware also plays a major role in determining the success of ML algorithms, as does the availability of easy-to-use software packages tailored to ML algorithms.

Like any development effort, developing a machine learning project needs to start with identifying the business need, collecting data, building the project itself, and finally deploying and monitoring the result. The success of the final project depends on the success of each step in the procedure. Currently, the lack of standard interfaces between tools and modules makes the modularized approach and the architecture design choices difficult.

Despite many similarities between human learning and machine learning, there are still some substantial differences. Something which is easy for humans can be difficult for artificial intelligence. For example, humans have more creativity, can understand abstraction, and are capable of analytical reasoning, inference, etc., but the capability of artificial intelligence is limited in such areas. On the other hand, artificial intelligence can perform facial recognition out of millions of samples, but humans cannot. Over time, the capability of artificial intelligence will continue to grow, but human intelligence will not do so in the same way.

## 5.4 BIG DATA

Big Data uses parallel database management systems to handle huge volumes of unstructured data. There are many programming languages for parallel data processing, such as XML, JSON, and Avro. On a higher level, the database management platform for Big Data is often referred to as the *Data Lake*. The Data Lake can combine and synthesize all types of data from multiple sources. These data can be structured (the traditional relational database) or unstructured, such as texts, images, audio, videos, PDF, and binary data. This is distinctly different from the traditional data warehouse which contains only the structured data.

The Data Lake distributes data across multiple servers to be stored. Such a distributed parallel architecture can dramatically improve data processing speeds. It also catalogs information describing each dataset. Such information allows developers to gain understanding and confidence of the data and develop applications. The Data Lake platform can ingest data rapidly and transform it, tracking and documenting datasets.

There are many Data Lake platforms. HPCC is a typical example. It automatically partitions, distributes, stores, and delivers structured and unstructured data across multiple servers. Users can write data processing pipelines and queries in a declarative dataflow programming language called ECL. HPCC also has machine learning algorithms to analyze data, text, images, and videos, and sensor data. It can identify patterns in historical data and use the information to make predictions about the future.

Another platform is Google's MapReduce. With MapReduce, queries are split and distributed across parallel nodes and processed in parallel. The results are then gathered and delivered. The MapReduce framework was adopted by an Apache open-source project named "Hadoop."

A data lake allows an organization to shift its focus from centralized control to a shared model, to respond to the changing dynamics of information management. This enables quick segregation of the data into the data lake, thereby reducing the overhead time.

Big Data is like a gold mine to be explored. Using Big Data, one can effectively integrate predictive analytics and data mining into the full analytics lifecycle. For example, medical research organizations can extract a vast amount of medical data and information from their Big Data to speed up their research. Businesses can use Big Data to accurately predict outcomes and apply analytics to optimize their action steps. Big Data always works in conjunction with AI. Many Big Data functions overlap with the functions of AI. Often, AI and Big Data are two sides of the same coin.

## 5.5 AI APPLICATIONS

Currently, AI is already widely used. AI enables banks to become more competitive in related industries like real estate. The $55 billion property management industry is using AI to increase returns, lower costs, and improve the overall owner and tenant experience for the 50 million rental properties and 100 million tenants in the U.S.

Ecosystem players like mortgage bankers, payment systems, insurers, private banks, and wealth management are now working together with technology-led property management companies to serve their clients better.

AI can improve the financial market in many ways, of which one is by increasing security. Due to AI's capability of machine learning and pattern recognition, AI can analyze large volumes of security data and help to detect abnormal patterns of fraudulent behavior, suspicious transactions, and potential future attacks, to keep sensitive information safer. AI can also cut processing times by processing data more accurately and quickly, and reducing human error, by validating and double-checking data. The silicon valley startup, Pixmettle,[6] is developing enterprise AI-based tools which will help to detect frauds proactively and at a very high accuracy. There are many AI-powered applications, and the list is growing fast, some of which are mentioned below.

## E-commerce

AI is used in e-commerce to deliver a personalized shopping experience. The recommendations are based on the shopper's purchasing history, background, and experience. A visual search also allows a customer to buy something similar to the image of their search item.

## AI-powered assistance

AI assistants, like the chatbot can replace humans in the initial dealings with customers. A chatbot uses natural language processing, which can hear, understand, and talk to customers. More often, when you dial a service phone number, a chatbot answers the phone. It directs you to different parties depending on your answer. According to the 2017 survey by SITA,[7] a Geneva-based aviation technology firm, 52% of airlines were planning to use AI programs and 68% of airlines intended to adopt AI-driven chatbots in the next three years. AI-powered chatbots are growing in popularity within numerous service industries.[8]

## Fraud prevention

AI can detect unusual spending patterns and alert the customers. It can also detect fake reviews.

## Speech recognition

AI uses natural language processing to convert human speech into a written format. Many mobile devices incorporate speech recognition into their systems to conduct a voice search. Speech recognition is also used in language translation.

### Computer vision and facial recognition

Computer vision can decipher digital images and videos and use the information to take action. Facial recognition is the most-used application of computer vision. There are many other applications of computer vision; for example, in social media, computer vision can tag photos and recognize people, places, and objects. In the medical field, computer vision can spot features in radiology imaging. Of course, autonomous vehicles use computer vision to drive.

## Autonomous vehicles

AI can replace human drivers to drive cars autonomously. It collects information on the road and the environment to drive a car like a human driver.

## Surveillance

AI's facial recognition capability enables surveillance or ID functions. There are airports using such technology to board passengers without the need to check travel documents – the doors open only to recognized faces.

## Healthcare

AI has many uses in healthcare. It can spot prescription errors. It can identify hidden patient risks across various diseases and clinical events. It can also recommend appropriate action for each patient. There are also AI-powered Internet hospitals, some in the form of a healthcare kiosk. They offer convenience services, online medical services, and telemedicine. Micro-level healthcare can prevent those diseases which were once incurable. With AI, healthcare organizations can improve quality, cost, and the overall patient experience.

## Medical imaging diagnosis

AI can be trained to analyze medical images, such as x-ray, ultrasound, and magnetic resonance. It can detect alterations which are imperceptible by human eyes. It can also detect problems using a database which is much more extensive than the doctor's experience.

### Recommendation engines

You will find that on the online shopping site, recommendations often pop up based on your purchase history. This is also done using AI algorithms.

### *Automated stock and commodity trading*

You will find many stock brokers offering AI-assisted portfolio management. Based on your goal, risk tolerance, and financial situation, such a program designs an ideal portfolio for you to optimize the results, There are also AI-driven high-frequency trading platforms making trades per technical analysis and/ or fundamental financial data of the company or market, without human intervention.

## Robotics

AI-powered robots are used in warehouses and factories to move and manage inventories and goods, and in hospitals attending patients, or in dangerous environments to replace human workers.

## Process optimization

AI analyzes data from a factory and optimizes processes. It can reduce waste, improve product quality, and avoid breakdown.

## Human resource

AI can help to sieve through candidate applications to find their suitability for a certain job. It can profile a candidate based on their resumes.

## Drug R&D

AI can help to develop new drugs at a much faster rate than what is possible today. It can analyze the DNA of disease-causing virus or bacteria to find potential drug compositions.

## Agriculture

AI can identify the conditions of soil, its nutrition content, and crop diseases, so that pesticides can be applied to specific areas only. AI can detect where the weeds are growing. This makes the application of weedicide more efficient. Agriculture bots can replace humans in the harvesting of crops.

## 5.6    THE AI MARKET

In 2020, the global AI market size was \$62.35 billion.[9] It has grown 270% in the past four years. It is expected to expand at a compound annual growth rate (CAGR) of 40.2% in the next few years. At such rate, the global AI market will reach \$120 billion by 2025. Among different applications, the healthcare and medical market has a 20% market share.

The fundamental driving power of AI comes from semiconductor chips. Many companies are racing to build special-purpose chips to push the capabilities of artificial intelligence technology to a new level, such as those geared to help AI understand languages and pilot autonomous vehicles. Cerebras created a huge single-chip AI computer, $46,225^2$ millimeters in size, and packed with 2.6 trillion transistors. Intel, Google, Qualcomm, NVIDIA, and Apple all created processors that are designed to run AI software. Their advancements could push AI to create many more application markets than we can even conceive of today.

According to the 2019 AI index report by Stanford University,[10] Singapore, Brazil, Australia, Canada, and India experienced the fastest growth in AI hiring from 2015 to 2019. The report shows that during the last four years, for example, Brazil has shifted into high gear as one of the top five countries in the world with the fastest growth in AI hiring. Brazil's government has big plans for AI.[11] Brazil is rapidly emerging a leader in AI-enabled businesses. Brazil's future economy is banking on a big contribution from AI technologies, and the country is leading the rest of Latin America.

It is estimated that by 2035, AI will boost annual growth rates in the developing countries by about one full percentage point of GDP. PwC estimated that by 2030, AI will add up to \$15.7 trillion to the world economy.[12] For example, Brazil, already the largest Latin American economy, would boost their economy by \$432 billion by 2035, around an increase of 0.9%.

One area that is particularly ripe for AI innovation is the financial services sector. Brazilian fintech companies creating workarounds to the many bureaucratic hurdles and old ways of doing things are now booming in Brazil. Other fast-growing AI sectors in Brazil include ecommerce, on-demand delivery, logistics, and digital media and entertainment.

Two important applications for AI are tackling the traffic congestion issues in Brazil's massive cities and reaching people across a vast land mass, the 5th largest in the world. AI has an opportunity to make local and cross-country delivery of products quicker and more efficient, which would mean reduced pollution, lower costs, and less traffic.

## 5.7  GOVERNMENT'S ROLE IN AI

AI systems have the ability to learn and adapt as they make decisions. Their advanced algorithms, sensors, and cameras incorporate experience in current operations, and present information in real time so humans can understand.

Investments in financial AI in the United States tripled between 2013 and 2014 to a total of $12.2 billion. In the fintech application, high-frequency trading by AI has replaced much of human action. AI can spot trading inefficiencies or market differentials on a very small scale and execute trades that make money according to investor instructions. AI-powered trading has much greater capacities for digesting information. For example, detailed financial data of thousands of companies as well as their long-term and short-term technical price trends and actions are digested in a fraction of seconds before placing the trade. The price patterns and technical indicators can easily be translated into probabilities. AI can even predict the price by analyzing institution consensus on a particular stock and stock price technical analysis. Since stock trading is a probability game, such prediction can enhance the ratio of winning trades to losing trades and improve the reward-to-risk ratio.

The economic payoffs of AI are substantial. In order to boost economic development and social innovation, governments need to increase investment in AI and data analytics. Such investment will pay for itself many times over in economic and social benefits.

Governments need to formulate the regulations necessary to deal with rise of AI. It is vital, in the sense that only through highly regulated development can society derive the benefits and avoid the harm from AI.

The U.S. Congress has introduced the "Future of Artificial Intelligence Act," a bill designed to establish broad policy and legal principles for AI. It proposes the creation of a federal advisory committee to oversee the development and implementation of AI. Soon after, several government agencies have formed their advisory committees on AI: for example, the National Security Commission on Artificial Intelligence, led by former Google CEO Eric Schmidt; The U.S. Department of Commerce, which established the National Artificial Intelligence Advisory Committee to advise the President and other federal agencies on AI research, competitiveness and ethics;[13] the Pentagon, which also announced that the military will work on Big Data and AI for military purposes under the Global Information Dominance Experiment.

The legislation can provide a mechanism for the federal government to promote investment and innovation to ensure the competitiveness of the

United States, and at the same time, guide the AI development to reduce the potential dislocation of AI and social structure and ethics-related issues, such as national competitiveness, workforce impact, increase in income disparity, required education to train enough talent in the AI development, ethics-related issues, data sharing vs. privacy, accountability, bias in machine learning, investment efficiency, job impact, etc. This legislation is a step in the right direction

## 5.8  EUROPEAN APPROACH TO AI

The EU has an aggressive approach toward developing AI. In April, 2021, the European Commission published an AI development strategy to foster excellence in AI, to strengthen Europe's potential to compete globally. It is aiming to boost research and industrial capacity and ensure fundamental rights.[14] It is a program undertaken to shape Europe's digital future and to build a resilient Europe for the Digital Decade.

Europe is taking a comprehensive approach to aim at excellence and trustworthiness. It is to ensure that AI will be developed based on rules that safeguard the functioning of social order, people's safety, and fundamental rights.

In terms of the financial resources, the Commission plans to invest €1 billion per year in AI through the Digital Europe and Horizon Europe programs over the next decade. The private sector will contribute additional investments of a similar amount. The newly adopted Recovery and Resilience Facility makes €134 billion available for digital technology. This will be a game-changer, allowing Europe to amplify its ambitions and become a global leader in developing cutting-edge, trustworthy AI.

Initiatives such as the EU Cyber-security Strategy, the Digital Services Act and the Digital Markets Act, and the Data Governance Act guarantee the access to high-quality data, an essential factor in building AI systems.

At the same time, a European legal framework for AI addresses fundamental rights and safety risks specific to the AI systems. The Commission aims to address the risks generated by specific uses of AI through a set of regulatory rules which define the framework of AI development. These rules can potentially provide Europe a leading role in setting the global standard.

## 5.9    FUSION OF AI WITH BIOTECHNOLOGY

AI and biotechnology form a special pair of technologies that reinforce each other. On the one hand, AI accelerates the evolution of biotechnology, including genetic engineering. On the other hand, biotechnology will change AI in the most drastic way – fusion of man and machine. AI and biotechnology benefit mutually with each other's progress.

In the recent decades, progress in biotechnology is greatly accelerated by the rapid increase in computing power and more recently the emergence of AI, automation, and data analytics. This is especially true in the sub-branch of biotechnology – genetic engineering. A deeper understanding of the relationship between genetics and disease has led to the emergence of precision medicine.

In the future, advanced genomics, gene editing, synthetic biology, and new gene and cell therapies can cure genetic diseases and help the healthcare industry not only to treat, but also to prevent many incurable diseases. The biotechnology revolution has the potential to address many urgent global challenges, from climate change to pandemics, chronic diseases, food security, nutrition, and environmental degradation. Bioengineering can also revolutionize agriculture as well. CRISPR can change the DNA of plants to make them more weather- or disease-resistant, enabling farmers to grow more with better quality. Its economic impact in health care, agriculture, and consumer products will be significant. All of this progress will be accelerated by employing AI.

From the other perspective, biotechnology also takes the twist to make biologically based AI possible. In the U.S, Elon Musk created Neuralink, a startup company in California to conduct research on the interface between the brain and AI. In August, 2020, Neuralink demonstrated such a link between a pig and an external computer. The pig received an implant of a coin-sized device into her cerebral cortex. In the demonstration, as the pig sniffed around, impulses detected by the implant were transmitted to a computer, then transduced into musical notes; which chimed in sync with the pig's feeding.

The ERAINS project, by the European organization called the Human Brain Project (HBP),[15] has developed brain simulation software to simulate neural networks, called NEST 3. Its aim is to understand brain functions and develop brain-inspired AI. It is used in neuroscience and robotics studies.

In the simulation model, scientists can modify neurons and the connections between them. NEST makes it easier to construct complex network models in the computer to observe how complex networks behave under different conditions. It focuses on the dynamics, size, and structure of neural systems, rather than on the exact morphology of individual neurons. This allows researchers to perform simulations with more data and to explore a wide range of model variants, and makes it easier to validate models, contributing reliable and reproducible research, and therefore enabling exploration of how the properties of the network elements influence its activity.

China has achieved a breakthrough in Brain–Computer Interface (BCI) chip research, with its first BCI chip "Brain Talker," designed for decoding brainwave information. BCI is a system allowing a person to control a computer using his or her brainwaves, without requiring any movement or verbal instruction.

Brain Talker can identify minor neuronal information sent by the brain wave from the cerebral cortex, efficiently decode the information, and greatly quicken the communication speed between the brain and the machine. The chip can find wide use in the fields of medical treatment, education, home life, and gaming in the future.[16] Such a chip can accelerate the development of AGI.

Both experiments represent a giant step toward the eventual integration between life form and computer or other computer-powered devices. It is not certain which direction these researches will take. However, it is foreseeable that content in the brain can be ported to a computer and vice versa in the not too distant future. When this happens, AI can actually be created inside of biological matter – the human or animal brain. It has been estimated that the human brain contains roughly 100 billion neurons.[17] Even a cat's brain contains 250 million neurons. As a comparison, today's ANN may have hundreds or thousands of neurons.[18,19] Once such a feat is realized, AI capacity will accelerate much faster, independent of the progress in the HPC hardware and software. It will be an important step toward singularity. One can create a "superpig" as an AI machine.

Brain mapping is another task that the exascale computer can do. The purpose of brain mapping is to create an accurate brain map that lays out connections between neurons and the locations of the associated dendrites, axons, and synapses which form the communications channels of a brain. Such a map is called a *connectome*, a wiring diagram of all the neural connections in the brain. Connectomics is a study to capture, the map and understand the organization of neural interactions within the brain.[20] A connectome allows researchers to understand brain structure, how it is changed by learning or degenerative diseases, such as Alzheimer, and where the memory and conscience originate.

Researchers at the DOE's Argonne National Laboratory are working to develop a brain connectome. Since there are more connections in our brain than the stars in our galaxy, such a task is not possible until the arrival of exascale computers. In the case of Argonne National Laboratory, the exascale computer is the Aurora 21, created by IBM, NVIDIA, and Intel – the very first exascale computer.

China also has its own connectome project. In 2015, the Laboratory for Functional Connectome and Development (LFCD) in the Chinese Academy of Sciences successfully developed the Connectome Computation System (CCS), designed for mapping connections within the human brain[21] using image data from MRI (Magnetic Resonance Imaging).

The rapid progress in computing and AI makes it possible that one day, a human brain is fully understood and can be used by AI. Such a person with an AI-programmed brain becomes a biological AI. It can continue to update its Big Data through man–machine interface and acquires new intelligence. It will become another step in human evolution.

## 5.10 AI AND BLOCKCHAIN

Blockchain and AI are two complementary technologies in the data application. While AI boosts the intelligence of Big Data, blockchain provides security to Big Data. Blockchain makes the data more secure so that AI thoughts are private, like humans, in the sense that you cannot poke into someone's brain to read what he thinks, at least for the time being.

There are two perspectives on merging AI and blockchain technologies. One is to embed blockchain technology in AI. Such an approach makes the AI decisions trustworthy and authentic. One can believe that the decisions are truly derived from the intended Big Data, rather than being tempered. Blockchain helps AI provide more actionable insights, manage data usage and model sharing, and create a trustworthy and transparent data application environment. In healthcare, future gene therapy requires huge amount of genetic data to perform, and since such personal genetic data can be highly sensitive, it is foreseeable that such therapy will be performed by AI secured by blockchain.

The other perspective is to power blockchain applications by AI. This will bring intelligence, making smart contracts smarter. It allows a higher degree of business automation possible. AI models embedded in smart contracts executed on a blockchain can execute transactions which require a high degree of judgment rather than simply a "yes or no" decision; for example, the decisions in resolving disputes, in operating remote collaborative robots, etc.

The clinical trial of new drugs in the pharmaceutical industry executed by the applications of blockchain and AI can combine advanced data analysis with a decentralized framework to enable data integrity, transparency, speed of feedback, patient tracking, consent management, and data collection. It not only automates the trial process but also provides feedback and insight into the deficiency and the route to improve the new drug. At the same time, it maintains data privacy,

In processing transactions, blockchain and AI enable trust and speed up transactions. Loan applicants grant consent for access to personal records stored on the blockchain. Approval or disapproval can be obtained using trusted data and automated processes in seconds instead of days.

# REFERENCES

1. *https://didyouknowscience.com/what-is-the-singularity-concept-in-artificial-intelligence/.*

2. *https://www.weforum.org/agenda/2018/11/algorithms-court-criminals-jail-time-fair/.*

3. *https://www2.deloitte.com/us/en/insights/focus/cognitive-technologies/ai-investment-by-country.html.*

4. *https://www.statista.com/statistics/871513/worldwide-data-created/.*

5. *https://pubmed.ncbi.nlm.nih.gov/33577458/.*

6. *http://pixmettle.com/*

7. "How travel companies are using AI to acquire, engage, and retain customers," *http://travelwirenews.com/how-travel-companies-are-using-ai-to-acquire-engage-and-retain-customers-2-580212/.*

8. *https://thechatbot.net/ai-chatbots-airline/.*

9. *https://www.grandviewresearch.com/industry-analysis/artificial-intelligence-ai-market.*

10. *https://venturebeat.com/2019/12/11/ai-index-2019-assesses-global-ai-research-investment-and-impact/.*

11. *https://venturebeat.com/2020/01/12/brazil-is-emerging-as-a-world-class-ai-innovation-hub/.*

12. *https://www.bbvaopenmind.com/en/technology/artificial-intelligence/blockchain-and-ai-a-perfect-match/.*

13. Department of Commerce Establishes National Artificial Intelligence Advisory Committee | U.S. Department of Commerce, *https://www.ai.gov/naiac/.*

14. *https://digital-strategy.ec.europa.eu/en/policies/european-approach-artificial-intelligence.*

15. *https://usps.com/holdmailcode.*

16. *http://www.xinhuanet.com/english/2019-05/18/c_138069590.htm.*

17. *https://www.verywellmind.com/how-many-neurons-are-in-the-brain-2794889.*

18. *https://www2.deloitte.com/se/sv/pages/technology/articles/part2-artificial-intelligence-techniques-explained.html.*

19. *https://www.yourdatateacher.com/2021/05/10/how-many-neurons-for-a-neural-network/.*

20. Connectome – Wikipedia, *https://en.wikipedia.org/wiki/Connectomics.*

21. China's Connectome Computation System maps our brains | Datenna, *https://en.wikipedia.org/wiki/Datenna.*

# CHAPTER 6

# WHAT'S NEW IN THE DIGITAL ECONOMY?

## 6.1 USE OF BLOCKCHAIN TO SECURE IoT DATA

As previously discussed, IoT is the interface between the digital world and the real world. IoT-attached objects become part of the Internet. IoT collects data through sensors and sends the data to the Internet. By 2025, there will be more than 70 billion IoT-connected objects worldwide. Each IoT-enabled object will generate data. Data are valuable, and sharing the data will create explosive growth in the knowledge-based economy. Since data are an important resource of the digital economy, IoT plays an important role. To transmit data between the point of collection – IoT – and the point of processing – such as cloud or edge-computing centers – privacy and security are of major concern. Whenever there is an exchange of valuables, there is a market. This is where blockchain comes into play – to secure the data originated from IoT.

*IOTA* is designed to close the gap between the world of IoT and the blockchain. IOTA[1,2] is the brainchild of the IOTA Foundation – a German company. IOTA is a public, permissionless, distributed ledger using a new data structure called Tangle, to replace the block. Tangle is based on the *Directed Acyclic Graph* (DAG). In mathematics, DAG is a topological ordering that is in one direction only and has no return.[3] IOTA may be mistaken as a blockchain technology, but it is not. It is a distributed ledger technology.

Tangle has no blocks, no chains, and no miners.[4] Each data transaction functions as a block. Without the need to create blocks, there is no fee for the block creators. Therefore, the Tangle data structure is a truly feeless distributed ledger. Without blockchain, the transactions are linked in such a way that each participant must have approved two past transactions to make a new transaction. This is shown in Figure 6.1. The very first transactions are called genesis transactions. They are created by the tokens.

In the bitcoin network, many transactions are mined into blocks. The blocks form a chain. However, in DAG, each transaction is considered a block. Each validated transaction links to another validated transaction to form a chain, just like the blocks form a chain in the blockchain. There is no need to build blocks, which makes it more efficient. However, in DAG, links are two-dimensional, the networks grow forward and laterally. It is more like a net instead of a chain (Figure 6.1). IOTA has the algorithm to control the width of the Tangle network. The net is acyclic, therefore, such a structure is called a Directed Acyclic Graph. Transactions can be linked to up to eight previous transactions, in contrast to the blockchain in which each block can be linked to the only tip of the chain. The process of building a DAG involves the following steps: create transaction, sign, and select tip (unconfirmed transaction), do Proof of Work (only needed for spam protection and not for consensus), send the transaction to a node, and confirm the transaction. So, the transactions pass three stages: as tip, unconfirmed, and confirmed. Once it is confirmed, the transaction becomes a permanent part of the DAG.[5]

Today, more than 95% of the data are not shared because the owner of the data does not have any economic incentive to share them. The most noticeable shared data are intellectual properties, such as movies, music, and books. There are blockchain applications already aiming at such a market. IOTA wants to expand the data market beyond such an IP market to cover the data which do not have obvious values. The IOTA Foundation has called it the *machine economy* and the *data economy*.[6]

DAG, like blockchain, can offer security of data transfer. Therefore, an obvious market is to provide the security of data transfer. A company is willing to pay to guarantee that the data it collects from the fields are secure and there is no need to worry about theft or data hack. By deploying IOTA for its data collection, the company can be sure of the security of its data. In the same way, IoTs can transfer fully secure messages between different objects and devices using IOTA. The voting machine is also an ideal application for IOTA.

IOTA is also useful in the shared economy. For example, a bicycle with IoT can be a part of the DAG network. Likewise, a solar panel installation in a

DAG network can sell its surplus electricity in the open market. The potential for IOTA is huge.

IOTA is collaborating with Taipei city to make Taipei, Taiwan, into a smart city.[7] On completion of the project, it will turn Taiwan's capital into a functional and operational smart city. This includes an ID built-in, which will prevent identity theft and every other criminal identity related to manipulating with identification documents. In December 2017, IOTA also entered a partnership with world-renowned companies such as Samsung, Microsoft, Cisco, Fujitsu, and Volkswagen to develop the data market.

With the coins to trade data, a huge amount of locked data could be unleashed for widespread use. This will have an unimaginable and profound impact on everything we know of today. It is no wonder that the IOTA market value has leaped to fourth place of $12 billion in a relatively short time.

*IoT Chain* (ITC) is another distributed ledger built on DAG for IoT applications. It can handle over 10,000 transactions per second. What is unique about ITC is that it can run raspberry pi-level low-performance IoT devices. It is essentially an IoT operating system using DAG. It also has tokens for the settlement of smart devices using rights, ownership transfers, and other value transfers in the entire IoT ecosystem. The IoT Chain has the potential of becoming a new variation of the blockchain. The DAG can process thousands of transactions per second; therefore, it can be used for large-scale applications. It beats Ethereum's solution of scaling, called *sharding*, a database partitioning technique to divide a very large database into smaller components that are easy to manage.

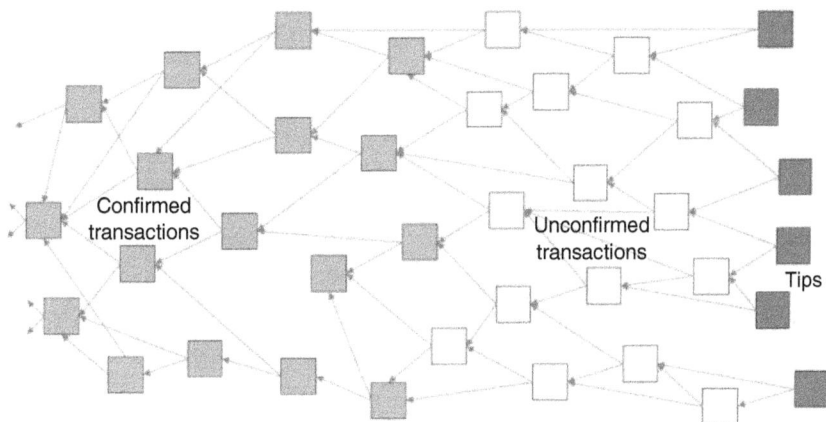

**FIGURE 6.1.** Tangle data structure.

## 6.2  BLOCKCHAIN AND CREDIT CARD

The credit card companies do not want to be left behind by blockchain technology. Blockchain technology may seem to be a threat to these companies because it provides P2P transactions, bypassing intermediates; however, they can also be big beneficiaries in using the new technology to streamline their operations. The credit card system is prone to fraud. Credit card information can be easily stolen to create fraudulent transactions. The reported credit fraud loss reached $27.85 billion worldwide in 2018.[8] Credit card companies see blockchain as a remedy to this problem. The payments industry as a whole is undergoing a paradigm shift. Moreover, the industry is big: the global consumer payment market reached $47 trillion in 2014, the first year that the share of digital payment volumes exceeded that of paper-based payment methods.

Financial institutions are keen to attain the *Straight-Through-Processing* (STP) concept.[9] STP is a scheme to optimize the speed of transactions. It allows the transfer of electronically entered data from one party to another in the settlement process without manually re-entering the same data repeatedly over the entire sequence of events. One of the benefits of STP is a decrease in settlement risk and time.

To achieve this, it is necessary to streamline the process of transactions across multiple points. By allowing information to pass along electronically, it requires the manual entry of data only once at the source. Multiple parties can receive the same information simultaneously if needed. STP will eliminate human intervention from financial transactions, thus reducing the cost of transaction as well. A true STP will save tremendous cost in credit card processing.

Blockchain technology, ideal for digital transactions, has the potential to implement STP and to transform the global financial network. The technology could accelerate the velocity of money, thus improving the efficiency in the economy. It also provides a path for legacy banking systems to interoperate, greatly improving efficiency. The use of distributed ledgers has the potential to disrupt the payment industry in the near future.

Major credit card companies, such as VISA, MasterCard, American Express, and major banks and financial service firms are all embracing blockchain technology due to a potential reduction in costs and improved product offerings.[10]

VISA operates a proprietary transaction-processing network, called VISANet. VISANet facilitates authorization, clearing, and settlement of payment transactions worldwide while offering fraud protection for account holders and rapid payments for merchants. It is capable of handling 24,000 transaction messages per second.

VISA is kicking off its blockchain development. It considers fintech as a unique opportunity at a time when the payments industry is undergoing a digital transformation. Visa partnered with the blockchain company BLT Group to streamline the cross-border transfers between banks. VISA Europe also partnered with Epiphyte to explore the possibility of using blockchain technology for international remittances.[11] The project created a prototype smartphone wallet app to enable the processing of remittances directly from a VISA card to a destination payment location over the bitcoin blockchain.

Recently, VISA issued the popular bitcoin debit card, the Coinbase Shift Card. VISA has also invested in a blockchain development platform, *Chain. com*, which serves an enterprise market. The incorporation of blockchain technology into the VISANet operation can potentially be very beneficial to VISA. Other credit card companies are not far behind.

Kreditech is a Germany-based fintech company.[12] It uses non-traditional data sources and machine learning to provide financing to people with little or no credit history. It is based on the conviction that not all the people without credit history carry high financial risk. By the use of its proprietary credit decision technology, Kreditech is doing good business helping people in financial need, and taps into a largely untapped market of the financially underserved population.

In summary, the blockchain-based networks and traditional technology-based alternative payment solutions will continue to merge. The payment service market landscape will be dramatically different a decade from now.

## 6.3  CROSS-BORDER RETAIL BUSINESS

Cross-border trade used to be the arena of business-to-business. The amount of cross-border retail purchase is negligible. This is because of the hassle of shipping, customs, currency exchange, and most of all, the guarantee of receiving money. Now it is changing. With the e-commerce boom, retail customers can order products directly from overseas. Cross-border e-commerce is booming, and there is no end in sight. Cross-border e-commerce trades will more than double over the next five years, reaching $424 billion by 2021. It will make up 15% of all online purchases in 2021.

China is the driving force behind such tidal change. Its share of the online cross-border market will grow to 40% by 2021, with the ease of placing orders online for overseas products, Chinese consumers are ever more attracted to buy foreign gadgets that are not available in China, because cross-border shopping not only offers customers better prices, it can also provide a degree of protection from fake or counterfeit goods by buying directly from the well-known merchants.

When Jack Ma, the founder of Alibaba, met with Trump in 2017, he promised to use Alibaba's online platform to sell American goods to the Chinese consumers. In the "Small Business Summit" held in Detroit by Alibaba in June 2017, attended by thousands of small business owners across America, Jack Ma laid out a plan for American small businesses to reach Chinese consumers directly.

Major U.S. brands and retailers have been successfully selling to Chinese consumers through Alibaba's Tmall, and the cross-border e-commerce platform Tmall Global, for years. However, this is the first time such a platform is available to small businesses. With infrastructure like the e-commerce platform, there are no more barriers of the distance or even borders for doing retail business.

However, today, besides the free-trade agreement between nations, the cross-border retail business is still full of regulatory and logistics issues. Alibaba is in discussion with the World Trade Organization to roll out a global trade platform – eWTP – which could expedite, simplify, and substantially increase the volume of cross-border e-commerce transactions. It could help millions of small businesses that previously missed the benefits of free-trade agreements, largely due to the excessive costs of compliance and the confusing assortment of rules, regulations, and red tape.

When small businesses have direct access to consumers, they can bypass middleman (exporters, importers, wholesalers, etc.). By doing so, they can reap the benefit of cost savings. Jack Ma proposed eWTP, the e-World Trade Platform, at the 2016 G20 meeting in Hangzhou. It is the first international e-commerce platform aimed at small and medium-sized enterprises or SMEs. For the first time, SMEs have the same facility to reach worldwide consumers as the giant companies using this platform. Its objective is to enable small and medium-sized businesses to reach consumers worldwide without going through intermediates.

Alibaba launched the first eWTP, the Digital Free Trade Zone (DFTZ), in Malaysia in February 2017.[13] It is an online free-trade zone, employing technology to reduce the barrier to trade. It enables Malaysian SMEs to expand their business and export globally and positions Malaysia as a regional hub for e-Commerce logistics and as the preferred gateway of choice for global brands and marketplaces in ASEAN. In another example, Alibaba collaborated with Philippine telecommunication company Globe Telecom to offer real-time cross-border remittance services using blockchain technology for individuals and small- and medium-sized enterprises. The new service allows users to send and receive the money within seconds across the border.

The spread of eWTP worldwide requires agreement among the countries. The technology is already available today. The domestic e-commerce technology can be easily adapted for the international DFTZ. However, due to the issues of foreign exchange, customs duty, and cross-border transactions, additional capabilities are required on the platform. Blockchain technology is ideal for such applications. Ant Financial, an Alibaba subsidiary, is currently exploring blockchain technology to simplify and streamline its financial processes.

By reducing national barriers to trade and applying new technologies, Ma hopes that any small business can utilize a smart road of smart hubs to sell their goods and services around the world. Ant Financial made a bid to acquire MoneyGram in 2017 for $880 million, to become the worldwide transaction settlement platform for eWTP. Unfortunately, the Committee on Foreign Investment in the United States (CFIUS) blocked the merger in early 2018. Nevertheless, even without the merger, MoneyGram and Ant Financial forged a new strategic business cooperation to explore and develop initiatives to bring together their capabilities in remittance and digital payments to provide their respective customers with user-friendly, rapid-response, and low-cost money transfer services. This move would give Alibaba an immediate access to the establishment, which handles cross-border currency transfers in nearly 200 countries.

## 6.4 COUNTERPARTY PLATFORM DAPPS

Many things we do involve agreement between parties, consciously or unconsciously. These agreements are contracts. Blockchain smart contracts are ideal to perform many of these functions with ease and security. For example, musicians, or any kind of intellectual property creators, can sell their work online using such smart contracts.

The Counterparty platform is a P2P, distributed, open-source financial platform built on top of the bitcoin blockchain. It can run smart contracts. By doing so, Counterparty instantly benefits from having a trusted and a secure mining network without the need to re-create its own. It pays bitcoin miners small fees to register Counterparty transactions. It is considered as a second-level protocol. Real-world assets can back up the digital assets on the Counterparty platform. Some interesting applications are:

- **Betting:** Counterparty turns the bitcoin blockchain into a betting platform, which can predict the market. Users can place bets on the information broadcasted. The Blockchain protocol escrows funds automatically and stores them securely in the bitcoin blockchain. Funds placed on bets are inaccessible until the bet is resolved or expires. Broadcasters can set a fee fraction to receive for their betting feeds as an incentive to run their broadcasts.
- **Token-Controlled Access (TCA):** Token-Controlled Access is access to private events, such as music events, parking tickets, etc. based on the ownership of tokens. In real life, tickets are tokens. People buy tickets to cinemas, flights, etc. Counterparty tokens are publicly tradable and have a monetary value.
- **Proof of Publication:** Using broadcasts, users can publish time-stamped information onto the bitcoin blockchain and such a timestamp cannot be deleted or altered. This makes it possible to verify the publisher's claim of the time of publication of a piece of information such as a patent. It will find wide use to protect patents, trademarks, and any other time-sensitive information.
- **Artist work coin:** In the music world, the use of blockchain technology makes it possible to use music coins such as the Tatiana Coin to buy songs directly from the singer. Singer-songwriter Tatiana Moroz released one of the earliest digital artist tokens. People can redeem the Tatiana Coin for her products and services.[14]
- **Crowdfunding:** Crowdfunding platforms powered by blockchain technology remove the need for the trusted third party. They allow startups to raise funds by ICO. One can issue a Counterparty asset in a crowdfunding event to raise funds for a project. Doing so will inspire more trust than the regular crowdfunding, because it is bounded by a smart contract. Swarm, Konify, and Lighthouse are three decentralized crowdfunding platforms.[15]
- **Voting:** Counterparty supports voting using user-created tokens. One can broadcast the subject for voting with terms and conditions, and let users vote on its outcome with full transparency by using tokens.

- **Instant messenger:** GetGems [16] has introduced cryptocurrency in a secure, fast bitcoin Wallet with all of the messaging features of Telegram, the world's most encrypted stand-alone instant messenger. GetGems makes handling bitcoin as simple as sending a text message.
- **Distributed computing:** FoldingCoin developed a platform to harness home computing power for medical and scientific projects. FoldingCoin rewards the participants with cryptocurrencies based on the computing power contributed. [17]
- **Game:** The gaming company Everdreamsoft [18] has developed Spells of Genesis as a blockchain-based trading card game on the Counterparty platform. Spells of Genesis is a mobile game mixing the collection and strategic aspects of Trading Card games with the addictiveness of Arcade games. While working as a core of the whole game economy and background story, bitcoin and other cryptocurrencies will become an in-game means of exchange. The gamers can exchange and trade game items easily and freely within or without the app.
- **RealEstate Coin:** RealEstate Coin allows one to invest bitcoin into U.S. commercial real estate. This app token gives common investors the opportunity to crowdfund acquisitions of net-leased commercial real estate, and secure payouts from the monthly lease payments of the tenant.

## 6.5   AML & KYC

The blockchain is ideal to provide the integrated decentralized monitoring efforts of financial transactions.[19] Anti-Money Laundering (AML) and Know Your Customer (KYC) practices have a strong potential for adaptation to the blockchain.

Currently, financial institutions must perform a labor-intensive multi-step review/ credit check process for each new customer. Using blockchain can reduce the costs of KYC substantially through cross-institutional client verification using blockchain. At the same time, blockchain can increase monitoring and analysis effectiveness.

Likewise, an anti-money laundering system built on the blockchain can leverage the cryptographically secure, decentralized, and immutable nature of the technology to identify and stop suspicious transactions effectively. Smart contracts will allow financial institutions to parse data securely through an AML engine on the blockchain automatically, providing high efficiency and minimum friction.

Each financial institution participating in the system serves as a node within the private permissioned blockchain network and uses the network directory and smart contracts to record transactions on the blockchain.

Since relevant information is stored in the blockchain and made available to each node, all related participants can detect suspicious activity. Anyone detecting suspicious activity can issue a warning to stakeholders and the transaction, and flag and stop the activity for further investigation. This is like turning all citizens into informers. The blockchain network updates itself immediately with the record of such an alert in an immutable and tamper-proof manner.

In April 2017, the Japanese government passed a law obligating all bitcoin exchanges in Japan to implement KYC and AML mandates. The startup Polycoin[20] has an AML/KYC solution that involves analyzing transactions. Those transactions identified as being suspicious are forwarded to compliance officers. Another startup, Tradle,[21] is developing an application called Trust in Motion (TiM), which allows customers to take a snapshot of key documents. Once verified by the bank, this data is cryptographically stored on the blockchain.

## 6.6  O2O BUSINESS

O2O (Online to Offline) is a new and emerging business model, which connects online business to the traditional brick and mortar stores. In the O2O business model, although customers make purchases online, delivery of the product or service takes place at physical locations. Both the online and offline retailers are adopting an O2O strategy to stay competitive. Today, most of the large retailers, such as Walmart, Target, Macy, and many others, allow you to shop online. You can even order online at the kiosk in the store if you do not find the product you want in the store. At the same time, the online retailers are buying into brick and mortar stores. For example, Amazon bought Whole Foods in 2017. The line between online and offline retailers is blurring. The O2O business is also known as the Omni-channel market.

In China, Alibaba formed a new partnership with retail conglomerate Bailian, which operates 4,700 stores across China. It acquired a major stake in the department store chain Intime Retail Group[22] for $2.6 billion, and also made a $4.6 billion investment in electronics retailer Suning.[23] In November

2017, it invested $2.87 billion for a major stake in China's top hypermart operator, Sun Art Retail Group.[24] Through this move, Alibaba Group obtained 36.16% in Sun Art Retail Group Limited by acquiring shares from Ruentex. Auchan Retail is also increasing its stake in Sun Art. The transaction gave Auchan Retail, Alibaba Group, and Ruentex approximately a 36.18%, 36.16%, and 4.67% economic interest in Sun Art, respectively.[25] In doing so, Alibaba has established offline outlets in multiple retail markets, from food supply, consumer, and department stores to electronics. *JD.com*, counting Walmart as its major shareholder, likewise financed Chinese supermarket chain Yonghui.

In a demonstration of the O2O concept, Alibaba featured an Augmented Reality mobile game that drove foot traffic to locations owned by Suning, Intime, KFC, and Starbucks, as well as malls in Beijing and Shenzhen and Shanghai Disney Resort. The AR games use GPS-enabled smartphones to allow users to move around the neighborhood and complete different tasks, which can be shopping or dining. Users receive instant information such as in-store promotions, in-store pickups of items ordered online, and collaboration on consumer data. The interactive shopping experience grabs customers' attention and curiosity, and transforms shopping into gaming.

Rivals in China such as *JD.com* are also highly active with O2O. *JD.com* has opened 1,700 physical appliance stores and plans to have 10,000 brick-and-mortar stores by the end of 2017. In early 2018, JD showed off its 7Fresh stores. The stores use an array of new technologies, such as autonomous shopping carts and Big Data analytics, which help to provide a personal store experience for the customers. The autonomous shopping carts guide the customer through the store autonomously, allowing them to shop hands-free and without having to focus on their purchases. A mobile app and digital payment technology will take care of the scanning and payment procedures. 7Fresh targets 1,000 stores across China, within 3 to 5 years. It will compete with Alibaba's technological supermarket, Hema, which already has 25 stores at the end of 2017.

Baidu also invests in the O2O business for food-delivery, ticketing, and entertainment with a $3 billion investment in group-buying site Nuomi and leading a $1.2 billion fundraising round in Uber. Baidu plans to invest $3.2 billion from 2015–2018 into O2O services. Analyzing customers' purchase habits and building up more robust user profiles allow the search engine to sell the information to advertisers, influence consumer choices in O2O spending, and receive a cut of each transaction conducted online and completed offline.

Other Internet giants such as Alibaba and Tencent also see the massive possibility of future revenue streams from O2O businesses. Tencent has been investing internationally, diversifying into hundreds of companies focused on gaming, mobile money, and artificial intelligence. Such deals include a $90 million funding round for the Indian healthcare information provider Practo, which provides an online search tool for consumers to find healthcare professionals, and leading a group of investors paying $8.6 billion for a majority stake in Finnish gamemaker Supercell in June 2016, further cementing its role as a global leader in gaming.

Tencent took a billion-dollar stake in a combined $4.5 billion private equity investment into Chinese car-hailing app Didi Chuxing. This is in addition to alliances with U.S.'s Lyft, India's ride service Ola, and Southeast Asia's ride-hailing startup Grab, and the acquisition of Uber's Chinese network. Tencent also has plans to expand into Hong Kong, Taiwan, Macau, Japan, South Korea, Europe, and Russia. Chinese players going overseas meet challenges different from those in their own turf; as a result, they do not always fare well outside their home ground. Business success overseas requires catering to the peculiarities of international markets and their consumers.

The Offline business is fighting back to go Online. However, the Online to Offline business is moving faster than the Offline to Online business. This is because there are technology innovations involved in the online retail business, which the brick-and-mortar stores cannot pick up fast enough. As a result, brick-and-mortar stores are struggling to compete with e-commerce.

## 6.7 THIRD-PARTY PAYMENT

In the United States and Europe, fintech has been driven by startups or financial institutions. On the other hand, China's Internet giants have largely been the sources of capital for its fintech firms. Ant Financial, which operates the Alipay payment platform, was a spin-off from Alibaba. In a nation where the most of the consumers historically pay cash, China is moving from cash to digital payments using smartphones, bypassing credit/debit cards. Fintech and blockchain technology greatly accelerate such a transition with the needed security. Therefore, China and Western Countries are taking different routes in the fintech development and deployment.

According to The Federal Reserve Study,[26] the U.S. credit/debit card transaction volume is $3.16 trillion and $2.56 trillion, respectively in 2016, totaling $5.72 trillion, while the U.S. mobile payment volume is around $112 billion.

In China, the non-bank third parties handle the payments from the buyer to the seller. Hence the term third-party payment. The third-party payment system has its roots in e-commerce, where the platform owner acts as an escrow. When the buyer pays, the e-commerce company tells the seller to ship the product. When the buyer receives the product, the e-commerce company releases the payment to the seller. The third party transfers the payment from the buyer's bank account to the seller's bank account. This method is necessary because few people in China have a credit card. China had only 0.29 cards per capita at the end of 2015, in stark contrast to an average of 2.35 credit cards per capita in the United States.[27]

Compared with traditional payment methods and credit card payment, third-party payment has its obvious advantages: convenience, cost saving, and accessibility using cell phone.

Research shows that it is very easy to hack the card number, expiry date, and security code of a credit or debit card using the so-called Distributed Guessing Attack. Neither the network nor the banks are able to detect attackers making multiple, invalid attempts to get payment card data.[28] The third-party payment system is inherently more secure than the credit/ debit card payment system, because the payer does not show his payment information. Rather, the payee must present his account information to receive the payment. This is just the opposite of the credit card payment system.

To make a payment by using a third-party payment system, the payee asks the customer to transfer the payment amount into the payee's account. The payment information is shown as the QR code either printed on the receipt, shown on the POS screen, or sent to customers' payment app in the cell phone. Once the customer confirms the destination and the amount of the payment, he authorizes the payment. You may wonder, in this case, that the risk is transferred from payer to payee. This problem can be easily managed by setting the payee's account to allow withdraw only to his designated account.

Certain unique features of China's e-commerce environment have further contributed to the popularity of e-commerce in China. The threshold for applying for credit cards from a bank is high in China. Even for those who have credit cards, many are wary of using them for online purchases for fear of leakage of personal information. Banks have also imposed stringent maximum transaction limits on online transactions effected through credit cards.

People have the impression that the third-party payment is free of service fee. It is not exactly true, although its cost is indeed much lower than that of credit cards. When the third party works with banks, banks charge transaction fees. Therefore, Tencent and Alipay alike, which used to provide free payment transfer services, have now started charging customers a small fee. Such a fee is still relatively inexpensive: 0.1% fees for a transaction amount over $3,000.

The dominant domestic online marketplaces for consumers are Taobao (Alibaba), Tmall, and *JD.com*, which handle payment transactions between buyers and sellers as third parties. As e-commerce proliferated, the third-party payment platforms also grew. At the same time, as mobile phone penetration got deeper, mobile payment apps started to appear to make the payments easier. Soon the convenience of this third-party payment system migrated from e-commerce to the physical stores. Today, most of the brick-and-mortar stores, street vendors, mom and pop shops, supermarkets, and restaurants have also joined the mobile payment system.

The Chinese third-party payment market in 2016 reached $5.5 trillion, which is roughly the same size as the U.S. credit/debit card payment market. The rapid spread of mobile payment platforms in China is pioneered by Alipay, TenPay, JD Pay, and UnionPay's Quick, ICBC's e-wallet, 99bill, and others.

The earliest entrant was Alibaba, which launched Alipay in 2004 to serve its Taobao e-commerce platform. Alibaba's Alipay was the most-used third-party payment platform. In part, the Chinese flourishing e-commerce market and its adoption of Internet and mobile payments can also be due to the presence of a massive domestic retail market.

Alibaba's Alipay is now the largest online payment gateway in China, accounting for half of the Chinese third-party online payments; Tencent's TenPay currently ranks second. Apple also launched Apple Pay in China in February 2016.

These e-commerce firms were not content with providing the payment service only. The fiercely competitive market served as a driving force to create new and innovative market applications. These firms were obligated to act under market force or foresee big opportunities in using similar technology to create new markets. Soon, they used the third-party payment platform as a springboard to enter other fintech businesses, such as online lending, e-insurance, credit rating, wealth management, stock trading, bike sharing, and many others. Once it started, the trend spread like wildfire to all the possible imaginable applications. This is how the Internet and e-commerce giants—Tencent, Alibaba, and *JD.com* entered the arena of fintech.

Alibaba hired off the payment service branch as Ant Financial, which manages Alipay. Alipay works with the traditional banks and credit card companies, including VISA and MasterCard.

Merchants and customers using Alipay could easily park their excess cash in Yu'e Bao to earn an attractive interest that banks were unable to offer. This natural extension of Alipay's payment service to money market fund service resulted in exponential growth. In June 2013, Alibaba launched the money market fund Yu'e Bao, run by Tianhong Asset Management, another Alibaba affiliate. By the end of December 2017, Yu'e Bao's market fund assets reached $233 billion, the largest in the world. Its closest competitor is JP Morgan's U.S. Government Fund at $140 billion.[29]

In addition, to serving its e-commerce platform, Alipay also expanded to more than 460,000 Chinese businesses. Recently, it is making inroads into the international markets by signing up overseas merchants and accepting foreign currencies. It has long dominated China's mobile payment market until its competitor Tencent came up with a more innovative mobile payment system, TenPay. Alipay saw its share of the market fall from 71% in 2015 to 54% by the end of 2016, while TenPay's share rose from 16% to 37% during the same period.

In June 2015, following the success of Yu'e Bao, Ant Financial launched MYbank, a new online-only bank in China. The online-only bank does not have a physical branch office. All the transactions are online.

Chinese mobile device manufacturers such as Huawei and Xiaomi are also moving into fintech and mobile payment partnerships, e.g., UnionPay. The regulatory environment has been generally facilitative to the vertical collaboration – from e-commerce, gaming, chat, and search engines to financial services. The offline-to-online interaction is also popular in China.

Tencent's meteoric rise in the fintech arena is thanks to its social media app called WeChat. WeChat users are able to transfer money between each other, as well as pay for services such as taxis, digital subscription, food delivery, and restaurant bills using an embedded function called WeChat Pay or TenPay.

TenPay takes advantage of the huge user base of the WeChat app ecosystem. With 890 million users as its customer base in the online messaging service, WeChat entered the mobile payment market a decade later. Anyone with a WeChat account can send and receive payments to anyone else with a WeChat account. The app allows users to keep funds in its wallet for peer-to-peer payments and in-app purchases. TenPay also has signed up physical stores – the off-line merchants, including Starbucks, which has 2,600 stores in China. By doing so, WeChat transformed itself from a social media platform into a payment platform in 2013 and launched a personal online investment fund in January 2014. One year later, WeBank, China's first online-only bank, also launched the same product.

WeChat Pay is targeting coverage of more than 10 million small merchants or stores in China. It has an innovative function called the Digital Red Envelope, or Hongbao in Chinese. The traditional Hongbao is a red envelope containing gift money in cash that the elderly give to young kids for Chinese New Year or a wedding gift. The ability to transfer money online via WeChat accounts revolutionized Hongbao tradition. Using WeChat's Hongbao function, one can send Hongbao electronically instead of face-to-face delivery. It became widely popular. In 2016, 64 billion Digital Red Envelops were exchanged over the six-day holiday period. An added benefit to the merchants, the mobile payment system collects the data gathered from spending habits and financial information. It, in turn, allows merchants to target their specific customers.

Facing threat from Tencent, Alibaba is not standing still. It is building its own physical network of stores, both domestically and overseas. It has already signed up more than 2 million brick and mortar shops in China with 10 million merchants on Taobao using Alipay. Ant Financial,[30] a spin-off from Alibaba, provides more financial services offerings than the money market fund giant Yu'e Bao to attract customers.

Apple launched Apple Pay in China in May 2016,[31] with 30 million bank cards signed up on the first day. However, its market share did not grow as expected due to several reasons. First of all, Apple Pay is a latecomer. The mobile payment market was already well saturated and dominated by two big players in fierce competition. In addition, Apple Pay uses NFC (Near-Field Communication) vs. the QR codes, used by both Alipay and TenPay, which introduced QR code system in 2011–2012. Soon afterward, the use of QR codes spread quickly in major Chinese cities.

There is an underlying reason that NFC cannot duplicate the success of the QR code in China. NFC payment requires dedicated NFC-equipped smartphones and the point-of-sales terminals in the store. It is unreasonable to expect millions of Mom and Pop shops and street vendors to sign up for the NFC equipment, while one can easily print a QR code on a piece of paper. QR codes are inexpensive to create and only need a camera-enabled smartphone to scan. QR codes provide pertinent and relevant information and deliver it quickly and efficiently.

Besides payment, QR codes also serve a channel of communication from store to customers. QR codes direct customers instantly to the website link, SMS, or text messages of the physical store. Increasingly, Chinese retailers have started using QR codes on billboards, posters, and flyers to offer discounts and product information. By scanning the codes, smartphone users can use mobile payment options to purchase the product or service immediately – promoting impulsive purchase.

Once on the website, store owners can deliver any information they want, such as the product information, promotion, coupon, discount, product display, restaurant menu, price list, the location of the other franchise stores, membership, upcoming events etc. Customers can enter the virtual queue for train tickets or seats in a restaurant, or make purchases or order from QR code. Receipts often contain QR codes, which open the portal to a wealth of information about the store or business, including ads, coupons, promotions, etc. QR codes can allow easy access to events and consumers can download various calendars to their phones, ensuring they have the information needed to attend the event. Tipping digital content is quite popular in China, and content creators on WeChat's mobile publishing platform use QR codes to collect tips with payment transactions processed by WeChat Payment.

Recognizing this growing trend, The People's Bank of China (PBOC) recently revealed plans to regulate QR-based payment technologies[32] and has authorized the China Payment & Clearing Association to draft standards for mobile purchases linked to QR codes. Favorable regulation will likely support the development of virtual credit cards, providing further stimulus for fintech firms focused on digital payments.

QR codes are popular for both offline and online platforms. Any QR code on the WeChat messaging app can be decoded with the touch of a finger. In the United States, Amazon has begun to experiment with QR code-scanning mobile payments at its Amazon Go locations.

Besides the choice of technology, the failure of Apple Pay to crack the Chinese market has another reason. As a third-party payment service, both Alipay and TenPay are cross-platform services that are open to users on iOS and Android and any type of phone. The Android mobile operating system has 75% market share in China as compared to 24% of Apple's iOS. This allows them to reach a much wider market using the smartphone apps. Apple Pay only works with the iPhone; that automatically excludes the majority of the Chinese market who use Android phones.

There is a large presence of a new segment of digitally perceptive consumers – the Gen-Y and millennial – who account for 45% of consumption. They are driving the online retail market and leading the charge in China's mobile payments adoption, with 66% of post-1990s millennial shopping and 54% banking via their mobile devices. A rising number of young Chinese consumers end up accessing financial services for the first time through fintech-developed platforms, rather than traditional banks.

Although third-party payment transaction still involves banks, it cuts traditional banks off from relationships with merchants and retail customers. The banks merely process the transactions for the third party, without establishing a relationship with the payment parties. It deprives the banks the potential of other mainstay businesses, such as loans, deposits, and investments. The emergence of such new payment platform offers significant opportunities for fintech companies to gain substantial scale but can have a potentially devastating effect on the banking status quo in China.

Fintech firms, such as online-only banks like MYbank and WeBank, with streamlined lending processes and innovative credit rating assessments, have broadened financial access for a large segment of the population often ignored by the traditional banks in China.

The traditional banks are fighting back with their own fintech transformation. For instance, ICBC, the world's largest bank by assets, has been adapting quickly to the fintech revolution. ICBC embarked on research of advanced technology and the cultivation of technical talents by establishing seven innovation labs in ICBC's head office, for artificial intelligence, cloud computing, the blockchain, biometric identification, Big Data and Internet finance, and blockchain-based financial trading system. It is ramping up efforts within the payments space to capture customer data. It successfully launched an e-commerce platform, e-Buy mall, which has grown to become one of China's largest e-commerce platforms. ICBC relied on its capabilities as a bank to facilitate e-commerce, payments, and forex. Its quick payment tool, ICBC e-Payment, already had 60 million customers in September 2015. ICBC also launched an e-based finance product system that offers payments, financing, and wealth management services, with the largest local online revolving loan extending $259 billion to more than 70,000 SMEs.

Other banks have also collaborated with fintech firms to launch digital initiatives. For example, the Postal Savings Bank of China (PSBC), China's largest lender by branch network with 40,000 branches, is working with Ant Financial's MYbank and Tencent in Internet and mobile finance. Through such collaboration, both parties benefit. Banks will be able to reach a new segment of customers and the online banking capabilities of the large e-commerce players. Fintech companies can establish a brick and mortar branch office without physically building it, allowing them to venture into the O2O business.

The Chinese Government has an open policy to promote financial inclusion of China's 234 million unbanked people living in rural areas and in the poorest neighborhoods. The collaboration between the online-only banks and the traditional banks fulfills the desire of government policymakers.

Before there was an online third-party payment system, an offline third-party payment system has also been in existence. It works like a bank but without a branch office. Its physical presence is a kiosk or an ATM-like machine. Lakala, founded in 2005, is China's largest off-line financial service provider.[33] It boasts 60,000 self-service payment stations in China at convenience stores, supermarkets, shopping malls, community centers, hospitals etc. People can pay utility bills, buy train or airline tickets, buy movie or show tickets, book hotels, and even buy wealth management products at Lakala kiosks. It also offers a mobile payment platform and POS devices like those used in restaurants and cross-border payment services.

In a few short years, China's third-party payment system evolves from the mere online shopping payment system to an omnipresent payment system replacing cash entirely. The U.S. payment ecosystem is also shifting toward mobile. However, such a shift requires a fundamental overhaul of the current credit/debit card infrastructure and unseats the existing benefactors. This will also depend on the incumbents, e.g. giant credit card companies, to come up with an innovative solution for the mobile payment yet without giving up their exclusive positions in the existing system. The introduction of fintech may have a huge impact on the mobile payment system.

On June 21, 2010, the central bank of China issued the administrative rules governing payment services by non-financial institutions. These rules are the first set of regulatory measures China has adopted toward non-bank third-party payment processors. It will fundamentally affect China's third-party payment service, an important feature and an integral link of e-commerce, and possibly of e-commerce itself.

## 6.8   MOBILE WALLET AND PAYMENT TRANSFER

The mobile wallet is a new form of payment using mobile devices, i.e., cell phones. Such a payment system is prevalent in China and is getting more popular elsewhere. Such a trend is evident, and sooner or later, it will replace credit cards and cash, as it has already happened in China.

The mobile wallet is an app in the mobile device to store the information of payment method, which can be a credit card or a link to a bank account. In China, most of the mobile wallets use a third-party payment system. In the United States, some popular mobile wallets are Apple Pay, Google Pay, and Samsung Pay. Many financial institutions, such as Chase, Capital One, PayPal, and Wells Fargo Bank also have mobile payment apps. Even some retail stores, like Walmart and Starbucks, offer such a service.

Likewise, Europe has also seen development of the mobile wallet system. There are many competing wallets operated by various types of domestic and international entities in different countries. The organization Mobey Forum Digital Wallet Working Group has evaluated 49 major mobile wallets by comparing their strategy, features, functionality, and technology.[34] A total of 34 banks operate 26 of them. These include iDEAL of Netherlands, MobilePay of Denmark, BKM Express of Turkey, Swish of Sweden, and Vipps of Norway. The other 23 mobile wallets are non-bank operated. While bank-operated wallets mostly serve the domestic market, the non-bank wallets are more successful across Europe. They include Neteller, Skrill, PayPal, SEQR, Masterpass, Yoyo, and Amazon Pay. Twenty-seven of these mobile wallets are credit card-based, while the remaining are Automated Clearing House (CH) network-based, which transfers funds between banks.

The advantages of the mobile wallet are ease of use, without the need of carrying multiple credit cards. Many of the sponsors of mobile wallets also provide rewards as incentives to the customers. Some mobile wallets also provide P2P solutions. At the merchant POS, some mobile wallets use Near-Field

Communication (NFC) solutions. Others use QR code, Bluetooth, or even Barcode.

Square, one of the pioneers in the payment solution technology arena in the United States, offers a square-shaped reader plugging into the audio jack of a smart phone and turning it into a credit card reader to accept contactless payment, including Apple Pay. In doing so, it can turn a smart phone into a POS (Point-of-Sale system). It also offers a virtual gift card in the form of a QR code stored in the customer's smart phone. When the merchant, which accepts such a gift card, scans the QR code, it receives the payment from the gift card.

CashApp is another of Square's innovative money transfer products. It allows person-to-person money transfer via the app or website. In 2015, such an application was expanded into business, which allows individuals as well as business owners to send and receive money, and to buy and sell Bitcoins. By 2019, six short years after its launch, with 15 million active digital users, CashApp already ranks number 6 in the United States, behind JPMorgan Chase, Venmo, Bank of America, Wells Fargo Bank, and Citibank.

One of the major concerns with using the mobile wallet is security. Like credit cards, the payments go through the mobile network and can be hacked. Blockchain technology can address such a safety issue.

## 6.9   EUROPEAN SECURITY SETTLEMENT PLATFORM

T2S, short for TARGET2-Securities, is a securities settlement platform to centralize settlement in central bank funds across all European securities markets. It is the twin sister of TARTET2 – Eurosystem's cash transfer system. T2S is to integrate highly fragmented securities settlement mechanisms across the borders of many different countries in Europe.[35] By doing so, it can reduce the costs of cross-border securities settlement, which is many times higher than the cost of domestic settlement. It will also increase competition among providers of clearing and settlement services in Europe.

T2S is changing the European post-trade landscape, not only by offering an integrated settlement service in central bank money for securities transactions but also because it has brought post-trade harmonization. Harmonization aims to achieve a common set of rules and standards across countries. The combination of TARGET2 and T2S forms the cornerstone of an integrated financial market in the European Union.

The T2S settlement platform integrates the liquidity and balance sheet management, asset servicing, and collateral management into a single operating platform. Thus, the implementation of T2S does not end at the cross-border securities settlement, but it is a critical step forward toward the final goal of having a unified market for financial services in the European Union.

The Eurosystem launched the project in 2008, before the invention of blockchain, and the platform entered operations in 2015. The Eurosystem owns and operates the platform. Before T2S, the Central Securities Depositories (CSDs) and custodians in different countries handled the post-trade activities, such as clearing and settlement of the cross-border security transactions. However, each country has different regulations, which complicates things. They interface directly with the market participants. The fragmented system incurs the high cost of cross-border security trade settlement. Therefore, the cross-border security trade volume is small.

After implementation, the T2S platform unifies the rules and standards and connects all the CSDs across Europe. The T2S platform can also facilitate post-trade activities. Thus, banks will be able to streamline their operations and produce cost savings.

With T2S, the cost of cross-border settlement cost is lower and it is foreseen that the cross-border investment volume will increase dramatically. Therefore, the T2S platform will have a positive impact on financial stability and economic growth in the EU.

The T2S platform was initiated a year before the appearance of blockchain technology or MDL technology, and developed during the period when MDL was still obscure. When T2S was ready for deployment, MDL technology emerged. T2S was forced to look into the new technology and adapt it accordingly. However, at this late stage of the T2S deployment, there are many unknown challenges to the operation of implementing blockchain onto T2S. There are many debates on whether to upgrade or amend to incorporate MDL technology now or later, and how to restructure the T2S platform using blockchain.

Meanwhile, incorporating the still evolving MDL technology into T2S at this moment could be operationally difficult, expensive, and risky, because it involves some fundamental changes to the recently developed T2S platform. Critics have warned that hasty implementation of an unproven technology may pose a risk to the capital market. In addition, the regulatory impediments of blockchain's adoption into T2S are far from clear. The implication of implementing MDL technology in T2S is more than just cross-border trades. The interface between the cross-border MDL-based systems and the domestic traditional database systems poses a major challenge.

The European Central Bank (ECB) has already invested a lot of money into T2S development and deployment. Incorporating MDL technology amounts to redeveloping the T2S platform over again. This truly presents a huge dilemma. The success of the T2S project is critical for the further integration in the EU's financial markets. To break through the complexities of development, testing and migration have been a daunting task because of too many conflicting interests.

The ECB has considered a range of blockchain models currently under development. These differ on a number of dimensions, including the validation mechanism, network architecture, permissions, the level of data sharing and replication, and the cryptographic tools of choice. The possible mass adoption in the market also needs to weigh functional, operational, governance, and legal aspects. Since the blockchain technology is still evolving, it is not mature enough to meet the high requirements in terms of safety and efficiency for such huge application. The safety of financial markets requires better consideration.

Therefore, for the time being, the ECB has decided to put off a DLT solution. However, it remains open to considering innovative solutions in the field of blockchain when such technologies are proven and mature enough to be the cornerstone of the Eurosystem financial infrastructure. ECB entered a joint research project with the Bank of Japan to study the possible use of DLT for market infrastructure. The project can help define how new technologies can change the global financial ecosystem of today and ensure that central banks are adequately prepared. In addition, ECB also established a DLT task force. Its objective is to assess the potential impact of DLT on harmonization.

## 6.10 CREDIT RATING SYSTEM

Most people do not appreciate the importance of the credit rating system to the overall economy. At a personal level, if one does not have a good credit rating, they may have a difficult time obtaining a loan or even a credit card. A rating downgrade can negatively impact company finance. On a larger scale, the credit rating can have a detrimental impact on the country's economy. During the East Asian economic crisis of 1997, the economy of many countries suffered an exacerbated blow due to the lowering of their credit rating by rating agencies.[36] These are some visible examples. However, the impact of the credit rating system is relevant to more than just when there is a financial problem. A good credit rating system works to accelerate the economy like enzymes in a biological body act as catalysts to accelerate chemical reactions. Likewise, a bad credit rating system can hurt the economy. Credit rating is to the economy like a temperature check is for the body. You will not pass the airport temperature checking station, if you have a fever.

The flow of capital in an economy is like the flow of blood in the body. Billions saved as money in savings deposit in the banks are channneled into entities to produce economic activities. The credit rating can determine where this capital will go. Entities with good credit score get capital with a lower borrowing cost. However, it does not mean that these entities will produce more economic activities for the capital they receive than other entities with a lower credit score, especially if the score is not accurate. An inaccurate credit rating system can reduce the capital efficiency and increase the overall business cost, just like bad infrastructures. On the other hand, a sound credit rating system can enhance the efficiency of resource allocation and promote economic growth.

Most of the consumer finance instruments, such as credit cards, are unsecured. Although the individual amounts are small, the aggregated amount is large. For example, in 2016, the U.S. credit card debt is $1 trillion,[37][38] while the total consumer debt is $3.9 trillion, and it is rising.[39] The growth of the debt means the expansion of bad debts. It is very important to find ways to establish and strengthen the control capacity and collection capacity.

Financing such large consumer debt without driving up the cost of financing is a major challenge. When the consumer debt demand increases but the financing channels are unable to meet the demand, financing cost will go up. Opening up the financing channels, such as the issuance of bonds, asset securitization, and other financing means maybe not as easy because each financing channel has different tolerance to the risk, which should be accurately gauged. This is where the credit rating comes in.

The construction of a sound credit system is far from easy. Current consumer finance company data and data integration are insufficient to build a sound credit rating system because of the lack of data coverage, data quality, missing standards, missing data, and rapidly changing personal credit. Deviation in data collection and integration can occur during the process of data separation, in addition to other issues.

Moreover, an entity's creditability is more than just its credit history and related data. It is essential to establish an effective credit score model by associating the credit history with the risk. The credit risk also needs to be quantified to remove the bias associated with the subjectivity.

Traditionally, banks have their own credit score model. Banks need to build up their historical data and find suitable forecasting models. However, due to the immense scope of the credit rating, banks are not able to do it effectively and accurately. A complete and effective credit-scoring model requires the overall composition of the targeted entity as well as the circumstances when the data are collected. If the development of the credit system is not comprehensive enough, the risk and cost for the banks are high.

An ideal credit agency acquires data from multiple sources; builds massive data handling, mining, and processing capability; determines the reliability of each data source with the anti-fraud and filtering model; and carries out data cross-validation. After acquiring enough data, building the credit score modeling is no less challenging, because the credit data are not always coherent and consistent. Until now, the tools available for data collection, mining, and processing are limited.

Fintech can help credit rating in two aspects: the first is the acquisition and processing of data and the second is the creation of a comprehensive model by deploying Big Data technology and artificial intelligence. Fintech will play an important role in this arena in the future.

Compared to traditional credit companies such as FICO, fintech companies with Big Data technology have the advantage in the breadth and depth of the data, can gather more dimensions of behavioral information, and can discern a previously undetected pattern, which will, in turn, give a more comprehensive rating. With the Big Data mining and analysis techniques, the data collected have less asymmetry. Through Big Data collection and data mining, consumer finance companies can identify their customer needs and customer portraits. Thus, they can more accurately target marketing and form consumer credit judgments. They can also correlate borrowers to different consumer finance platforms and determine customers' repayment intention and ability under different economic environments. A stress test will reveal customers' financial capability under different circumstances, such as unemployment, or a health problem.

Applying artificial intelligence and machine learning, such as random forest, neural network, or gradient-boosted decision tree (GBDT), can improve the modeling accuracy. Credit scores based on artificial intelligence can make credit management work more efficient, objective, and focused. Such a score can determine the entity's creditworthiness under certain circumstances.

The current state of the credit rating system in China is still immature and this has caused high social financing costs, lending efficiency, and the industry's ability to assess risks, inhibiting the economic vitality. Both the government and the industry have recognized its importance. They are devoting great effort toward developing a credit rating industry by using new technologies in recent years, such as Big Data and artificial intelligence.

In 2009, the China Banking Regulatory Commission (CBRC) issued guidelines for the supervision of the internal credit rating system for credit risk of commercial banks. In 2013, the Chinese State Council issued the Regulations on the Administration of Credit Industry. By the end of 2014, the central bank credit center had already accessed 1811 data institutions and covered 350 million people and business entities. With the gradual establishment of a modern credit system helped by fintech, a credit rating industry is emerging.

In September 2015, the State Council issued the plan for Big Data Development. In a series of policies, regulations, and guidelines, the PBOC and CBRC encouraged financial institutions to innovate consumer credit products.

In 2016, the Chinese government is taking a consolidated approach to develop an extensive nation-wide Social Credit System (SCS). The SCS is akin to the combination of credit rating systems in the United States – FICO, Vantage score, CE score, Moody's rating for bonds, S&P credit rating, Better Business Bureau (BBB), and many others that are even more comprehensive. One difference is that in the United States, the private companies provide scores, but in China, it is the government which provides SCS.

SCS focuses on honesty in government affairs, commercial integrity, societal integrity, and judicial credibility. The scope embraces both personal and business credit and the trustworthiness rating. Such a rating can easily translate into "trust" for the blockchain validation. In an era when the daily business dealings involve totally unknown parties, such a trust system becomes essential. SCS intends to remove the "Trust" barrier. However, there are critics condemning such a system as a Big Brother.[40] SCS will come online by 2020.

The Chinese credit rating industry is by no means limited to the government. The Government has also granted licenses to eight private enterprises to develop their credit scoring systems. Among the licensees are e-commerce companies Alibaba, Tencent, and Ping An Insurance, and five credit rating companies: Pengyuan Credit Services, China Chengxin Credit Information, IntelliCredit, Credit Arm, and Yin Zhi Jie.

Independently, in September 2016, China's National Internet Finance Association (NIFA) also launched its Internet Financial Industry Information Sharing Platform (IFIISP). NIFA, run by the central bank and with 400 member traditional financial and Internet finance companies, including heavyweight companies such as Ant Finance, JD Finance, Lufax, and Yirendai, was established to regulate Chinese fintech firms and control risks in the sector. The IFIISP provides credit data on a customer by sending requests to all other member companies and collating the results without divulging the source data to protect competitive insight. The NIFA took a giant step forward in developing a proper credit score system with IFIISP.

Even so, China's P2P regulations remain relatively less burdensome than those in developed markets, whether by design or by omission. However, as the system evolves, the government sees greater need to tighten the regulations. In 2001, President Bush signed the Patriot Act, which required certain ID verification for the customers to open a bank account. In 2016, China followed suit, with concerns over money laundering and fraud, to set up new regulations that required in-person verification to open a bank account. Since the online-only banks do not have a physical branch, they need to collaborate with traditional banks. Thus, traditional banks have gained an additional source of business from the online banks.

Chinese legislature is including a more substantive data protection framework. The new framework includes the PBOC's additional requirements for non-bank payment institutions around effective protective measures, risk control systems, and KYC measures, and storage of sensitive information. The Chinese government will likely continue to take a leadership role in setting the agenda on data privacy and protection as this will increasingly become a central pillar of the financial services marketplace – critical in enabling the fintech sector to operate and prosper.

In addition, some private enterprises have already moved ahead with their own versions in credit rating. As e-commerce companies have already generated a huge amount of customer and supplier data from their own platforms, they set up their own credit rating system. For example, the scoring platform called "Sesame Credit Management," developed by Alibaba's Ant Financial, analyzes data generated from 300 million customers and 37 million small businesses on Alibaba's shopping platforms. Customers with a higher credit scores enjoy special privileges. Other similar systems are built by Tencent using the data from their own social media app, WeChat and WeChat Pay. They also offer the credit rating services to other financial services providers. For example, Jubao uses social media data generated on WeChat and Weibo to assess customers' creditworthiness. Meanwhile, JD Finance is collaborating with U.S.-based ZestFinance in a Joint Venture to develop services of credit risk evaluation and to extend consumer access to credit in China.

With such a torrent of activities, China is setting up a world-class credit rating system quickly. In a few more years, when these systems are up and running, people will feel more confident in transacting with unknown parties and push China's fintech market even further. People will also be more cautious in avoiding actions that will spoil their credit rating. The credit rating system will support risk-adjusted loan growth to bolster consumer spending, further supporting the growth of fintech.

Currently, China's consumer expenditure is only 39% of the GDP, vs. United States 68%, France 55%, and Germany 63%. [41] Stimulating household consumption is one way to boost GDP growth. Fintech will help.

Chinese fintech firms are leveraging Big Data from e-commerce, messaging, search, social media, and other Internet-based services to personalize the customer experience, provide new services, and leverage operational efficiency. Customer data can be used to support other online revenue streams, such as lending, insurance, investment, and wealth management.

Right now, the development of most of these systems is progressing in parallel. As China's mobile financial market matures, the interoperability across mobile wallets and other banking services will receive more importance to improve efficiencies, democratize the ecosystem, and level the playing field between new entrants and incumbents. Such an open-architecture policy would start a race to offer the most innovative solutions, as players attempt to differentiate themselves from the pack.

## REFERENCES

1. *http://iota.org/.*

2. *http://iotatoken.com/IOTA_Whitepaper.pdf.*

3. *https://en.wikipedia.org/wiki/Directed_acyclic_graph.*

4. *https://iota.readme.io/docs/what-is-iota.*

5. Tangle | IOTA Beginners Guide (*iota-beginners-guide.com*).

6. "IOTA data market place," David Sonstebo, *https://blog.iota.org/.*

7. *https://globalcoinreport.com/iota-miota-is-trading-up-while-testing-digital-ids/.*

8. *https://www.prnewswire.com/news-releases/payment-card-fraud-losses-reach-27-85-billion-300963232.html.*

9. "Straight Through Processing," *https://www.investopedia.com/terms/s/straightthroughprocessing.asp#ixzz51TkRyllZ.*

10. *https://www.nasdaq.com/articles/how-visa-is-embracing-both-the-blockchain-and-cryptocurrency-2020-12-07.*

11. *https://www.nasdaq.com/articles/how-visa-is-embracing-both-the-blockchain-and-cryptocurrency-2020-12-07.*

12. *https://www.kreditech.com/.*

13. *https://mydftz.com/dftz-goes-live/.*

14. *https://www.tatianamoroz.com/tatiana-coin/.*

15. *https://techcrunch.com/2014/10/17/bitcoinbitcoin-2-0-crowdfunding-is-real-crowdfunding/.*

16. *http://getgems.org/#/.*

17. *https://foldingcoin.net/index.php*

18. *https://www.everdreamsoft.com/.*

19. "BlockchainXE "Blockchain" for AML XE "AML" – harnessing blockchain technology to detect and prevent money laundering," Floyd DCosta, *https://internationalbanker.com/technology/blockchain-aml-harnessing-blockchain-technology-detect-prevent-money-laundering/.*

20. *https://polycoin.io/.*

21. *https://tradle.io/.*

22. "AlibabaXE "Alibaba" Takes Big Step Offline With $2.6 Billion Intime Deal", Bloomberg News, *https://www.bloomberg.com/news/ articles/2017-01-09/alibaba-others-to-privatize-intime-for-up-to-hk-19-8- billion.*

23. "AlibabaXE "Alibaba" to invest $4.6 billion in China electronics retailer Sunning", Gerry Shih, *https://www.reuters.com/article/us-alibaba- suning-appliance/alibaba-to-invest-4-6-billion-in-china-electronics- retailer-suning-idUSKCN0QF0VP20150811.*

24. *https://www.cnbc.com/2017/11/20/alibaba-invests-2-point-9-billion-in- chinas-sun-art-retail-group.html.*

25. *https://www.businesswire.com/news/home/20171119005069/en/ AlibabaXE "Alibaba" -Group-Auchan-Retail-Ruentex-Form-New.*

26. "Federal Reserve payments study 2016", *https://www.federalreserve.gov/ newsevents/press/other/2016-payments-study-20161222.pdf.*

27. "Average Number of Credit Cards Per Person: 2017 Card Ownership Statistics," *https://www.valuepenguin.com/average-number-credit-cards- per-person.*

28. *https://techxplore.com/news/2016-12-seconds-hack-credit-card.html.*

29. "China's giant Yu'e Bao money market fund riskier than US rival, Fitch says", Gorgina Lee, *http://www.scmp.com/business/money/markets- investing/article/2124465/chinas-giant-yue-bao-money-market-fund- riskier-us.*

30. *https://www.antfin.com/index.htm?locale=en_US.*

31. "Apple pay is coming to China in 2016," Rich McCormick, *https://www. antfin.com/index.htm?locale=en_US.*

32. "China's centralbank to standardize QR code payment," *http://www. chinadaily.com.cn/a/201712/27/WS5a43be15a31008cf16da3d82.html.*

33. "Company overview of Lakala Payment Co. Ltd.," *https://www.bloomberg. com/research/stocks/private/snapshot.asp?privcapid=35020357.*

34. *https://www.mobeyforum.org/european-digital-wallet-landscape/.*

**35.** "T2S XE "T2S"," European Central Bank, *https://www.ecb.europa.eu/ paym/t2s/html/index.en.html.*

**36.** "The Procyclical Role of Rating Agencies: Evidence from the East Asian Crisis", G. Ferri, et. al. *http://onlinelibrary.wiley.com/doi/10.1111/1468-0300.00016/full.*

**37.** "US credit card debt skyrockets, approaching $1 trillion," *https://www.rt.com/business/335249-us-credit-card-debt/.*

**38.** "2017 Credit Card Debt Study: Trends & Insights," *https://wallethub.com/edu/credit-card-debt-study/24400/.*

**39.** "Average Credit Card Debt in America: 2017 Facts & Figures," *https://www.valuepenguin.com/average-credit-card-debt.*

**40.** "Big Data XE "Big Data" meets Big Brothers as China moves to rate its citizens," Rachael Botsman, *http://www.wired.co.uk/article/chinese-government-social-credit-score-privacy-invasion.*

**41.** "Household final consumption expenditure (% of GDP)," World Bank, *https://data.worldbank.org/indicator/NE.CON.PETC.ZS.*

# CHAPTER 7

# FINANCIAL SERVICES INDUSTRIES

## 7.1 FINTECH

The completely new branch of technology, called *financial technology* or *fintech* for short, is derived from the innovations of the Internet, blockchain, Big Data, 5G, cloud and edge computing, and artificial intelligence. Fintech creates a proliferation of new applications delivering financial services directly to the end customers. It merges many of these new technologies into financial services, such as mobile payments, money transfers, loans, fundraising, asset and wealth management, digital currencies, and many others. It is envisioned that fintech will provide financial services to billions of people around the world, circumventing the current financial establishment. Blockchain, as one of the fintech-enabling technologies, can transform the financial services industry by making transactions faster, cheaper, more secure, and transparent.

Although not all fintech applications use blockchain, blockchain-based fintech is an important subset in this domain. The drastic rise of investment in fintech in recent years is due to the advancement of these new technologies, especially blockchain technology.

Throughout history, the advancement of transaction techniques – from the invention of money to the invention of paper money – has continuously triggered a revolution in the financial industry. Money and finance are essentially the data flow that indicates economic activities. The financial industry cannot exist without the record keeping, processing, and transaction operations of financial data.

The advancement in data flow greatly reduces the operating costs, enabling improved service in the financial industry. The invention of computers and modern communication technology has pushed financial technology to a new high in speed, cost, and efficiency. The arrival of blockchain and the other above-mentioned technologies will reshape the traditional business model and continue to bring cost reduction, speed and security of financial transactions, asset transfer, and business opportunities.[1]

The traditional financial industry has already seen a rapid change in the last five decades. Today, the change is accelerating. The new fintech companies are introducing more improvements in service and are meeting customer demands better. As smartphone technology becomes omnipresent, the birth of blockchain technology spurs the change, giving additional momentum to the development of financial technology.

Worldwide, fintech investment jumped from $20 billion in 2015 to a whopping $135 billion in 2020.[2] It is growing fast. There are over 12,000 fintech startups today with an average valuation of $4.4 million. There are 24 fintech startups that have reached unicorn status with a valuation of more than $1 billion in 2019. It is a phenomenon that rivals the early days of the Internet.

Fidelity National Information Service (FIS), one of the world's largest providers of financial technology information services,[3] published a survey report. The report shows that that 41% of the companies that participated in the survey are testing or implementing blockchain technology to increase revenue stream, 47% are using blockchain technology for collateral management, 42% use blockchain for regulatory reporting, and 36% have implemented blockchain technology for clearing and settlements.

As the word "fintech" implies, its development involves participation from both financial companies and technology companies. IBM, Google, Intel, and eBay are the big names investing in fintech. Manufacturing companies are also interested in fintech because it can streamline manufacturing-, financial transaction-, and supply chain-related activities. Many of the baseline technologies driving fintech are also driving Industry 4.0 – the next generation of manufacturing. Many governments have embarked on fintech projects for applications such as digital currency, land title registration, etc. It is truly a global effort from multiple sectors of the economy.

Fintech embraces all aspects of financial systems, including payment and transfer, lending and financing, retail banking, financial management, insurance, credit rating, markets, and exchanges. As a result, fintech is shaking up all sectors of the economy in a big way. Its disruptive technologies are challenging the traditional business model by offering everything – from peer-to-peer payments and loans to investment management and crowdfunding.

While fintech start-ups and technology providers wield huge influence, they currently lack the scale, experience, established client trust, and regulatory backing to embark on financial services on their own. At the same time, the financial institutions want to maintain and improve their position by keeping customers happy, increasing revenues and reducing costs, becoming more efficient, and maintaining a competitive, well-run business.

Although the financial industry started to take notice of the Bitcoin in its early years, around 2010, it did not show much interest in it initially, and looked upon the Bitcoin as an investment instrument. However, when the underlying technologies such as blockchain and MDLs were widely discussed, and other applications besides cryptocurrency such as the Ethereum platform were developed, the financial industries took notice.

The financial services industry has the highest ratio of IT spending versus revenue, from $200 billion in 2015 to reach $500 billion in 2021, most of which is spent on maintenance rather than on creating new services. Blockchain technology provides an opportunity to address this issue. Banks are exploring opportunities for business with these fintech start-ups through capital investment and joint development projects. By doing so, banks ensure that they are positioned to tap into fintech potential, and leverage the technology expertise of non-bank fintech players. They recognize that if they fail to do so, they risk becoming obsolete.

Innovation is emerging in many different business areas within the finance industry, such as retail, markets, lending, payments, messaging, security, and foreign exchange. The changes are expected in new and improved solutions, data management, security, and modular IT. The fintech platforms in development are both P2P and cloud-based. Cloud-based solutions are flexible and cost-effective, and can scale up to accommodate growing demands, thereby enabling businesses to build and adapt their operations more effectively and efficiently.

*Application programming interfaces* (APIs) enable the interaction between the user and the service as well as two or more online-connected services, providing the opportunity to build solutions that integrate and combine different services and data sources. Both banks and non-banks have demonstrated a high degree of adoption. New cloud and API technologies have been instrumental in enabling the fintech start-ups to disrupt established players and accelerate change.

Big Data analysis can detect fraud based on customers' spending pattern and geographic location. Artificial intelligence has made it possible to effectively analyze and interpret vast, complex sets of data, uncovering untapped patterns and trends.[4] It allows banks to create solutions that are more effective, optimizes business processes, and provides value-added services to meet client needs.

The generation, storage, and transfer of a large amount of financial data online prompt more security concerns. Biometric security techniques find wider adoption in smartphones and other mobile devices. Blockchain technology brings additional security to the system.

As fintech companies continue to introduce new digital capabilities, the banking sector is facing a paradigm shift. The banks that fail to keep up will fade away. Indeed, the financial service industry sees the potential for change in the banking industry as positive, and is reassessing the strategies and business models. A partnership has been forged between the blockchain technology companies and the financial institutions.

Recently, *DeFi* has become a popular term. DeFi is short for the Decentralized Finance. It is a financial service using blockchain applications. To most people, Defi and fintech are the same. For some, there are subtle differences. While Defi emphasizes "decentralized" financial service, fintech is a broader term for financial technology, whether centralized or decentralized, and whether using the blockchain or not. For example, central bank currency is certainly not decentralized. DeFi services are provided through Dapps (Decentralized apps), mostly run on the Ethereum blockchain. These applications include lending, trading, credit rating, trading, etc. We can consider DeFi as a subset of fintech.

## 7.2 BLOCKCHAIN AND FINTECH

Blockchain technology is being hyped as a solution for everything. The financial institutions, sitting on the cusp of a major technology revolution, are afraid of the negative impact it might have on them, while also trying to understand how they can benefit from it. The lure of blockchain is in its method of securely verifying and tracking transactions cheaply and automatically.

The threat posed by blockchain technology, from the financial institutions' perspective, comes from the much-hyped ability of blockchain to bypass a trusted third party to perform transactions. Blockchain enables non-bank entities to enter markets that are traditionally the domain of banks and other financial institutions.

Although Bitcoin's meteoric rise attracted much attention, it turns out that Bitcoin is only one of the many applications of blockchain technology. The applications built on blockchain do not have to resemble Bitcoin in any meaningful way. For an analogy, the Internet is built on the protocols called TCP/IP; however, there is a wide variety of applications built on top of TCP/IP. Many of them bear little resemblance. Over time, many blockchain applications may eclipse the Bitcoin.

Financial institutions also find that blockchain technology has characteristics that can greatly enhance its hold on the financial services. The key is the *Permissioned blockchain*. With the Permissioned blockchain, the financial institutions can build applications that solely meet their own requirements, and thus retain the ownership. This has greatly increased their interest.

Fintech service providers working with the financial institutions aim to capture customers by offering a more intuitive way to access products and services. As smartphone and Internet penetration continues to increase, the financial services industry is primed for technological adoption and breakthroughs in the workplace.

In 2020, the fintech industry was still in the early stage of development. The current development barely touches the capability of fintech's underlying technologies, including blockchain, Big Data, and AI. Companies are trying to identify opportunities for innovation. In the next decade, we will see greater development of the application platform and the proof of its concept, feasibility, and impact on existing systems, such as the supply chain system. Some will work as intended and others will not. Most important of all, the regulations and security will have to catch up with the technology development, before the technology moves in a direction that does more harm than good.

To properly set up the legal regulatory framework and guarantee data security, we need to understand better how the technology will evolve. So far, the regulations do not cover cryptocurrency. Different countries are taking different approaches. A case in point is the DAO crowdfunding and its subsequent hacking, which caused some anxiety in investors and raised many questions on its regulatory issues. It should be noted here that DAO hacking occurred not because of the weakness in the blockchain technology, but because of its implementation.

Because the blockchain eliminates errors and duplication, it is ideal for transforming a host of digital processes. Decentralization of trust has introduced possibilities to make processes such as cross-border payments, trading, and settlement faster, more reliable, and less costly. Data integrity, ensured by the chronological storing of data enforced with cryptography, reduces the risk. This, in turn, reduces the compliance burden and cuts regulatory costs with the KYC initiatives.

Even before the appearance of the blockchain, banks already saw an increase in competition from nonbanking entities, especially high-tech and e-commerce players in areas such as mobile payments and lending. The blockchain is likely to intensify such competition, as it will reduce technological barriers for digitally perceptive nonbanking entrants.

A blockchain-based system can allow companies to become market makers and open up cash in exchange for completing a cross-border transaction at a lower rate. Blockchain applications also open up alternative funding methods beyond the traditional channels controlled by the venture capitalists, private equity, or IPO. Likewise, blockchain applications also open up other lending channels.

Banks, while they cannot prevent other people from chipping away their business, will have to find other innovative and efficient ways to compete. They are also creating their own versions of blockchain applications and could make quick inroads into their traditional strongholds. The blockchain will create a new set of opportunities for banks to collaborate with startups in exploring niche business areas which integrate Internet of Things (IoT) and/ or smart devices to carry out autonomous transactions through smart contracts.

## 7.3  TECHNOLOGY-DRIVEN FINTECH

Fintech arises due to the emergence of several disruptive technologies in the first decade of $21^{st}$ century. Blockchain technology is one of them, and probably the most important one. Nevertheless, other technologies also have a profound impact on the development of fintech, such as mobile technology, Big Data, and artificial intelligence.

Since the invention of the iPhone in 2007, mobile technology is more than just communication using the cell phone. The cell phone becomes a mobile command center. It is the Internet on the go. It is a portal of the Internet in one's palm. Tens of thousands of apps are available to harness the power of mobile Internet. Many of them are driving fintech.

The technology-driven fintech revolution is evident in two prominent examples: Alipay and WeChatPay. In 2016 alone, these two apps handled $5 trillion of online payment in China, rivaling $8.2 trillion payment handled by VISA worldwide. Other businesses such as bike sharing sprang to life because of mobile payments. Renting a bike is as easy as scanning the QR code on the bike using a mobile payment app to unlock it. Two of the largest Chinese-based start-ups, Ofo and Mobike, have more than 13 million bikes combined and have each raised at least $1 billion.[5] The Alipay app offers investment opportunities in the online money market fund of $217 billion, the largest in the world. Such is the power of mobile technology in the financial market.

Likewise, e-commerce rising out of the Internet also transforms retail business. The e-commerce giant, Amazon, has a market cap of $570 billion, almost twice as big as Walmart ($290 billion). The Chinese e-commerce leader Alibaba, also has a market cap US$440 billion, not far behind that of Amazon. With the arrival of the blockchain, more changes are on the way.

Using a mobile phone to rent a bike is an example how technology is transforming the way transactions are processed and initiated. With the arrival of blockchain technology, all forms of the payment will change, including the newly arrived mobile payment.

Fintech startups are playing a significant role in altering the financial service market. This presents both a challenge and an opportunity for banks. Fintech start-ups and e-commerce giants have made a quick inroad into the payment market, bypassing banks. These new players are taking payments to the next level of performance in transaction speed and convenience. The biggest impact is on retail payments.

An increasing number of new non-bank financial service providers are exploring the foreign exchange and remittances market, a huge market dominated by the traditional banks. The blockchain platform enables exchange of money in real-time, reducing the exchange rate risk. Foreign exchange service providers have already entered the market, offering minimal costs and P2P business models such as WeSwap.[6] They bypass banking networks and are more efficient. On the other hand, the real overhaul of the foreign exchange market must come from governments. In Europe, initiatives such as SEPA (Single Euro Payments Area) and TARGET2 (Trans-European Automated Real-time Gross Settlement Express Transfer System) intend to make cross-country transfer as easy as domestic transfer.

Fintech startups are playing a significant role in altering the financial service market. However, the founders of fintech startups are usually technology-savvy entrepreneurs who do not have the expertise and the exposure in the financial service market. fintech startups can bring in-depth technology and expertise, but lack the banks' knowledge of the intricacies and practicalities of functioning payment systems and whether new concepts could be realistically applied in the real world. Banks will be able to offer guidance regarding regulatory requirements and security standards – an area that fintech startups have little exposure to. Banks also have access to a large pool of clients. In the end, banks and fintech startups realize that they need each other.

The Fintech Innovation Lab, administered by Accenture and sponsored by the Partnership Fund for New York City, Credit Suisse, Goldman Sachs, J. P. Morgan, Lloyds Banking Group, and many others, is a program designed to help startup companies to refine and test their value proposition. It also has partnership arrangements with many startup fintech companies.

Barclays encourages fintech startups with the Accelerator Program, which provides Fintech start-ups with funding, office space, and access to Barclays' APIs and data. California's startup accelerator company, Plug and Play, connects VCs and angel investors to the startup community. It counts Citi Ventures, Citi's venture capital subsidiary, as the financial supporter of the "The Plug and Play Fintech Programme."[7] London-based Level39 is another example of the accelerator of technology to Europe's most high-profile fintech firms.[8]

With Permissioned Blockchain technology, fintech will supplement the current banking system rather than replace it. For example, the bank account is still indispensable in order to use most of the fintech services. Banks must now prioritize the adoption of a new technology-focused strategy. Despite the fact that non-bank payment service providers are eroding the banks' traditional business, few want to take on the heavily regulated financial services on their own. Most of them seek partnership with the existing financial institutions to develop new fintech applications.

Adopting a fintech-friendly strategy can position banks in the driver's seat of the fintech revolution, ultimately enabling them to provide relevant, user-friendly solutions that present real value and meet the evolving needs of their clients. Banks have always invested in the development of sophisticated technology capabilities in order to improve the efficiency of their payment operations and quality of client service, and to reduce risk, lower costs, and establish a competitive advantage. Such a tradition will serve them well in the future.

Many established banks are investing heavily in fintech and focus on exploring the potential they have to offer the global payments arena. They develop strong relationships with fintech players to establish a fintech strategy to re-engineer the process of payments and other assets, such as securities, bonds, loans, etc., using blockchain and Big Data technology. They also identify key value-adding elements in financial services (such as risk, costs, transparency, and speed) for improvement.

Such a development for the banks requires substantial effort from the proof of concept to the deployment on a larger scale. Banks have to choose from a wide variety of technology applications that may or may not serve their interest. The process of choosing applications can be daunting because the technologies are evolving and their standards are migrating. Worst of all, the new regulations are not yet defined.

Traditionally, the financial services industry has had one of the highest ratios of IT spending as a proportion of revenue. In 2017 alone, the IT spending of the banks in North America, Europe, and the Asia Pacific amounted US$215 billion.[9] Such a spend was mostly on system maintenance rather than on the development of new services. The banks are hopeful that the deployment of fintech may provide some saving in IT.

The new technology is also becoming a great equalizer. The emerging market will leapfrog to adopt the newer generation of technology. The impact is demonstrated quickly in the retail payments sector, as it is evident in China. Banks must also adapt quickly to the mobile payment trend.

The technology equalization benefits not only the emerging market, but also the Small and Medium Enterprises (SMEs), who are traditionally underserved by banks. The emergence and growing popularity of non-traditional forms of finance, such as Supply Chain Financing (SCF) and P2P lending, can channel much-needed financing to this underserved sector. A growing number of fintech start-ups are also enabling SMEs to access payment services that were previously unavailable to them. The development of a new retail payment system exerts enormous influence over the future path of corporate payments. The traditional players and fintech pioneers are establishing collaborative partnerships to leverage the best elements of both parties, and thereby deliver optimal solutions.

Many countries have introduced real-time payment solutions. In Europe, MyBank is a payment authorization solution that enables users to authorize payments via the online banking portal of their own banks across Europe.

In the UK, a payment system called Paym enables customers of many UK banks to make payments directly to each other's accounts. Currently, the use of mobile payment is much less in the corporate and wholesale payments sector. However, the volume will increase in view of its many benefits.

The Chinese mobile payment market has already exploded to $5.5 trillion in 2016, almost 50% of China's GDP, and the same size as the US credit/debit card market.

Consumers in retail banking are also benefitting from the development of payment systems that run in real-time rather than via the traditional method of batch processing. This, in turn, has fuelled further innovation, enabling consumers to conduct payments without the need for credit or bank cards, instead of using service layers that run on top of existing real-time payment infrastructures (e.g., the UK's Zapp, which runs on top of the Faster Payments service).

The trend toward real-time payments poses serious technical challenges to the global banking infrastructure, the specific linkages to anti-money laundering (AML) and reporting databases, as well as customer accounts payable/receivable, and reconciliation. Without blockchain technology, it is almost impossible to conduct a huge volume of global transactions in real time without running into problems of money laundering.

One of the hurdles in the implementation of the new payment system is the lack of a standard. The establishment of a standard is an important enabler in the growth of national and international payments infrastructures. Common standards must exist so that new services can extend the existing systems without glitches. ISO 20022 (the universal financial industry message scheme)[10] and XML standards[11] (electronic data exchange standards for exchange of transactional information between trading partners) are finding wider adoption.

With so much effort going into the payment sector of fintech, a dramatically new landscape may emerge in the coming decade.

There is also a new initiative called Bank Payment Hubs (BPHs),[12] which brings together different elements of bank payment systems to better manage payment flows and improve flexibility. It also allows AML to integrate across banks and enables banks to better handle the demands of faster payments and manage risks. In addition, with BPH, there is improved transparency and availability of data, which can add value to both banks and end-client businesses in terms of process management, cash management, and cost savings. BPHs also move bank payment systems to industry standard messaging, enabling them to connect more seamlessly with outside channels and partners.

Fiserv,[13] a data processing Fortune 500 company based in Wisconsin, US, focuses on the financial services industry. It has been providing the tools such as billing and payment, ATM processing, auto loan solutions, and risk management, using the Prologue Financial general ledger software to serve financial institutions. A growing number of new banking platform providers are emerging, such as Bank of America Merrill Lynch (BAML)[14] and Aveloq,[15] offering ready-made platforms capable of plugging into new systems such as SEPA and Faster Payments. These ready-made platforms are application-friendly and extremely easy to implement. They substantially increase the speed of deployment of the new technology. Many banks are adopting such platforms, rather than building new platforms from scratch on their own.

## 7.4   GLOBAL FINTECH LANDSCAPE

Hot money is pouring into fintech. Venture capital funding for Bitcoin and blockchain startups reached $2.5 billion in 2016. Fintech investment is by no means limited in the Venture Capital industry; many top U.S. and European banks are exploring blockchain applications by either collaborating with startups or creating innovation labs to test their proofs of concept.

The areas of focus for banks and startups alike include cross-border payments, trading activities, custody services, and customer behavior analysis. Santander, for example, claims to have identified 20 to 25 use cases, with a focus on international payments and smart contracts. Barclays is reportedly focusing on 45 internal use-case experiments,[16] while Citibank has created its own version of Bitcoin, called Citicoin.[17] Startups focusing on non-financial use cases have seen a jump in numbers, with new entities entering the market each year. In fact, the number shows that nonfinancial-use cases outnumber financial ones, indicating that the applications are not confined to the financial ones, and many applications allow real-world assets be linked and traded in the blockchain.

Blockchain's disruptive nature comes from its ability to transform almost any process, from the basic documentation to settling complex contracts across geographies. This inherent capability is alluring to finance and banking decision makers, who believe its disruptive power is good for their industry.

Blockchain's transformative effect will extend to the global financial system. Currently, security trades take two to three days for payments and securities settlement. Employing blockchain technology with a decentralized ledger can greatly speed up the settlement process. It will have a transformative effect on the capital markets.

This benefit extends to very complex instruments, such as derivatives. There are many incentives for banks and financial institutions to deploy blockchain technology in capital markets, such as lower operational cost and faster trade settlement. Executing international trades will become as easy as domestic trades. Decentralizing the clearing process will eliminate a considerable amount of trading risk. Trust level will increase with all transactions recorded transparently on a distributed ledger. The real-time transaction would eliminate counterparty risk. Regulatory reporting becomes easier with easier access to transaction information for regulators.

The blockchain startup R3 has attracted 42 international banks and financial institutions.[18] R3 has enlisted 11 bank partners to develop a peer-to-peer distributed ledger. It has established industry standards and protocols for blockchain in banking. It also develops commercial applications for banks and financial institutions. R3's effort to create industry standards is a small but significant step toward creating interoperability of blockchain solutions across the financial system.

R3, which opened the first tranche of $200 million in financing exclusively to members of the consortium, symbolized a new trend for the mainstreaming of blockchain technology. The company already counts as its notable clients the government of Singapore, the Bank of Canada, and other national financial institutions. R3's proprietary ledger can develop applications and support the infrastructure network for financial services firms and technology companies to build their own ledger-based applications and services. Besides R3, other projects such as the Hyperledger Project, Post Trade Distributed Ledger (PTDL), and Digital Asset Holding, etc. are doing pilot runs for blockchain prototypes.

Due to the accelerated speed of globalization in the last two decades, especially after China joined the WTO, the world's existing financial system is getting more strained and adding a cost to trades and services. For example, from 2006 to 2016, the world export of manufactured goods grew from $8 trillion to $11 trillion, while both the world export of agriculture products and travel and other commercial services have increased 70% during the same period.[19]

The emergence of MDL technology comes at a time when the financial services industry is in need of further improvement. Innovations in digital technologies, MDL technology, and smart contracts have the potential to enhance capital market infrastructure significantly.

While London, New York, and Frankfurt have been the world's financial centers for centuries, China has leapfrogged ahead to become the center of global fintech innovation and adoption. The Chinese fintech hubs are concentrated in major cities such as Shanghai, Hangzhou, Beijing, and Shenzhen.

The speed, sophistication of development, and the scale of deployment of China's fintech ecosystem is breathtaking. A complete value chain for the blockchain sector has emerged in China, ranging from hardware manufacturing, platform and security, to application services, investment, media, and human resources. The number of blockchain technology companies in China exceeded 400 in 2018. These companies are exploring ways to apply blockchain in a wide array of areas.

Prompted by the huge e-commerce market and the growing appetite of consumers, China's technology leaders are revolutionizing many aspects of financial services. The Chinese fintech companies are not the most innovative; however, unlike the fintech activities in the West, China's fintech ventures into many industrial-scale applications with a huge user base. fintech's quick start in the past decade has resulted in several niches – online lending, insurance, etc. A handful of Chinese fintech firms went public in 2017, led by the first online-only insurer ZhongAn, which claims 523 million customers.

Multiple fundamental factors contribute toward triggering China's fintech development – the size of unmet banking needs, government regulatory support, a mature mobile payment platform, a huge number of mobile and Internet users, a large e-commerce market, a growing middle class with disposable income, and easy access to capital – a fertile breeding ground for fintech.

China mined 70% of the worldwide Bitcoin before the 2021 crackdown on Bitcoin mining. China also has the second largest fintech investment after the US and 8 of the world's 27 largest fintech companies, valued at more than $1 billion. fintech Innovators, a collaboration between fintech investment firm H2 Ventures and KPMG Fintech, announced Fintech100, the leading fintech companies in the world.[20] Chinese fintech companies took five of the top ten, including the top three spots. The US took three. Germany and UK took one each. The top three Chinese fintech companies are Ant Financial, ZhongAn, and Qudian.

The world's biggest Bitcoin miner, a Beijing-based company called Bitmain, controls nearly 30% of all the Bitcoin mining power worldwide. Roughly two-thirds of the world's processing power that is devoted to mining Bitcoin resides in China. Thousands of custom-designed computers fill these warehouse-like mines, humming non-stop to solve Bitcoin puzzles to receive Bitcoin awards.

Bitmain is more than just a Bitcoin mining company. It is also a multinational semiconductor company with state-of-the-art IC design capabilities. Bitmain offers products including chips, servers, and cloud solutions for blockchain and AI applications. According to Frost & Sullivan, Bitmain is among the world's top 10 and China's second largest fabless IC designer. Bitmain has successfully released four generations of AI chips. With advanced tensor acceleration for deep learning, Bitmain's AI chips can be used for a wide range of applications such as facial recognition, automatic driving, smart cities, smart governance, smarter security, medical services, and more.

There were 65 ICO events in China in the first half of 2017, collecting over $394 million, but the ban on ICOs brought that to a halt. On the other hand, the government is actively encouraging fintech development with favorable policies and investments. In doing so, China is trying to channel blockchain technology into the financial and industrial applications, away from cryptocurrency.

Fintech investments in China including Hong Kong surged to $10.2 billion in 2016.[21] Venture capitalists contributed $7.7 billion. In the same year, fintech investment in North America was $9.2 billion, out of which $6.2 billion was from VCs,[22] followed by the UK at a distant third.

China's interest in blockchain technology extends to more than just the Bitcoin. Some of China's biggest firms are betting on its technical capability to revolutionize their businesses. They are aggressively looking for solutions to their existing problems in the newly developed but huge financial markets, such as the $5.5 trillion-a-year-third-party payment market[23] or the $180 billion-a-year online lending market, which accounts for 75% of the worldwide market share in 2016.

China is also the home of four of the ten largest banks based on the value of assets in the world, according to the 2017 S&P Global Market Intelligence report.[24] Chinese banks are highly profitable, with an average ROE of around 17% vs. 9% for the US banks and 2% for the European banks. Because of the insufficient social security safety net and traditional habits, the Chinese tend to save more for the rainy days. The Chinese saving rate is at 46%. In 2015, China had $27 trillion in savings.[25]

China's largest fintech company – Ant Financial – is valued at about $350 billion, 6 times as big as Goldman Sachs, the biggest investment banker in the US. In 2016, it raised $4.5 billion, making it the largest single private placement in any fintech firm globally. At the end of 2020, it was preparing an IPO in the Shanghai and Hong Kong markets. Its IPO was set to break the record worldwide.[26] Even though its IPO was suspended due to regulatory concerns, it does not diminish the fact that it processes more financial payments than any other company in the world. It runs the largest mobile payment platform. It also runs the largest money market fund in the world.

The Chinese government openly supports fintech development with policy, funding, and government-organized consortiums as well as a relaxed regulatory environment to a certain degree – until it becomes a force that may destabilize the national economy, as it happened in the case of Ant Financial. The Chinese government has also officially included the scope of digital technology, including Internet, cloud computing, Big Data, artificial intelligence, machine learning, and the blockchain, into the 13th National Five-Year Plan.

Fintech development is in unchartered territory. The existing regulations do not cover many of fintech's potential influences on the society or economy. Interestingly enough, China and the West are adopting different approaches.

In China, the government allows the new technology and system to evolve freely before regulating them, while in the West, the existing regulations often prevent the new system from flourishing, and new regulations often take years to pass as legislation. The Chinese approach has the advantage of letting the technology flourish and dampening it before it exerts a negative impact. However, in the event of crackdown, it usually generates a negative image. Such a difference is embedded in the culture and is related to perception and reality. It is difficult to say which one is right.

A typical and the most well-known example of the fintech development and regulatory stance is the cryptocurrency project, Libra, by Facebook. Many US regulators and politicians expressed concerns soon after it was announced in 2019, including the U.S. House Committee on Financial Services and the Federal Reserve. They asked Facebook to halt the project, citing the lack of regulatory framework and monetary policy and issues related to privacy, national security, trading, money laundering, consumer protection, and financial stability. Politicians in the EU also raised the same concern. In 2020, Facebook rebranded Libra as Diem, in a scaled-down version to address the concerns raised by the U.S. regulators.

China's Ministry of Industry and Information Technology has organized a special government–industry working group to present a plan for promoting the development and adoption of blockchain technology. The Chinese government also launched the "Internet Plus" initiative in March 2015 to speed up the integration of Internet infrastructure, the development of chip technology and high-speed computers, and applications of cloud computing and Big Data as part of a wider effort aimed at incorporating Internet technology into different sectors of the economy.[27] The plan stipulates development targets and supportive measures for Internet and fintech industries. It aims to hasten the integration of Internet/IoT and other derivative technologies, such as Big Data and the blockchain, with different business sectors, including but not limited to traditional financial services.

The Chinese government operates more than 750 government-guided funds nationwide. In 2015, it appropriated a massive $231 billion to fund start-ups, of which $6.5 billion went toward promoting digitalization and smart technologies.

China also has a protected financial market, in addition to its relatively underdeveloped banking system. On average, there are 8 bank branches per 100,000 people in China vs. 28 bank branches in the US and Europe. Also, the Chinese credit/debit card market is relatively untapped. Interestingly, the Chinese credit/debit card market is about the same size as the electronic payment market in the U.S., while the Chinese electronic payment market is about the same size as the US credit card market.

Internet technology through the use of mobile phone has been an important growth engine of the Chinese consumer market. Such technology has created great companies like Alibaba, Tencent, etc. China sees all technologies derived from Internet technology as an opportunity to grow its economy. A major effort is devoted to the development of artificial intelligence, encryption, the decentralization scheme, Big Data, and finance. One of the important infrastructures of fintech is the data center. In the early 21$^{st}$ century, the data center for data flow has the same significance as a power plant did for electricity flow in the early 20$^{th}$ century. China is investing heavily in data centers.

Understanding the fintech industry in China may provide an insight into China's grand strategy to boost its economy by deploying the latest technologies in the financial industry, and how such adoption will revolutionize the everyday life of its citizens.

China's startups and tech giants pulled in a record $58.8 billion from investors in 2017. The top investments went into logistics and transportation ($16.8 billion), e-commerce ($12.7 billion), fintech ($4.8 billion), and Internet services ($2.5 billion). The largest single investment, worth $5.5 billion, went to Didi Chuxing, which raised a total of $9.5 billion in 2017. Didi Chuxing is more than a ride-hailing service. It also invests heavily in AI, for research on a self-driving car.

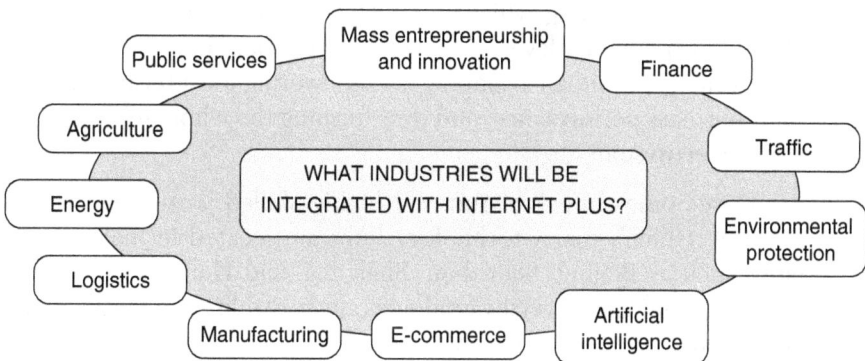

*FIGURE 7.1* China's Internet Plus Initiative.

Alibaba accelerated its drive into brick-and-mortar stores by opening a supermarket chain, Hema. When a customer shops at a Hema store, their preferences are saved in its app. That makes it easier to order online and get deliveries if you prefer to do it that way next time.

Cainiao, a partnership company created by Alibaba in 2013 with 15 delivery companies dedicated to e-commerce logistics, received $799 million in funding. Mobike, a bicycle sharing company, raised $815 million. In April 2018, Meituan-Dianping, China's largest on-demand online service company, bought Mobike for $2.7 billion.[28] *Ele.me*, an online food delivery company, raised $1 billion. *Ele.me* has 260 million users across 2,000 Chinese cities, ordering meals from 1.3 million restaurants. Also in April 2018, Alibaba bought controlling shares of *Ele.me* at its valuation of $9.5 billion.[29]

Bytedance, the new media firm behind the news app Toutiao and TikTok, saw its valuation jump to more than $20 billion. Toutiao alone claims 120 million users. Pulling together news from other sources, Toutiao has 120 million readers each day who spend an average 74 minutes flicking through the app – double the time spent on Snapchat. Toutiao's popularity derives from the use of machine learning to create customized newsfeeds based on in-app behavior and reading preferences, similar to what Cambridge Analytica is doing. In 2017, it spent $800 to acquire video-based social app – *Musical.ly*, another Chinese startup. *Musical.ly* has captured over 90 million users. It is a hit with North American teens, rising to the top of app store rankings next to Instagram and Snapchat. People can upload 15-second videos of themselves singing popular songs, dancing, or performing comedy skits. Some *Musical. ly* users have even found fame through the app, launching their own clothing lines.

Meituan-Dianping, which raised $4.4 billion in 2017, is the Chinese equivalent of Groupon. By leveraging AI technology and innovation within its platform strategy, Meituan-Dianping is empowering local businesses to improve their business performance, and transforming the whole service industry into a digital ecosystem.

Developing fintech requires a highly skilled workforce with an open mindset. China's major technology hubs are located in major metropolitan cities such as Beijing, Shenzhen, Shanghai, and Hangzhou, where a skilled workforce and top university graduates are available abundantly and the global connections are one hop away from international airports. Beijing hosts the country headquarters of many technology multinationals, both foreign and domestic, such as Microsoft, IBM, Cisco, *JD.com*, and Baidu. Shenzhen is home to tech giants such as Huawei, ZTE, and Tencent. Shanghai, an international financial hub, and Hangzhou are where Alibaba is headquartered.

Fintech firms are also located near some of the world's top-ranked universities for technology and engineering, such as Peking University and Tsinghua University. These educational powerhouses create an unparalleled and constant pool of new talents for the tech industry. These regions are continuously investing to nurture a conducive environment for fintech firms in China.

The Chinese fintech market was a product of the unique combination of several factors. In 2016, the Chinese online retail sales were approximately $900 billion, with a 26% increase year-on-year, with one-third of the population ordering online at least once a week. E-commerce is about 16% of the country's total retail sales. At the same time, China has an untapped market of underserved customers. The Chinese banks' priority is to serve the state-owned enterprises (SOEs) first. Small-to-medium-sized enterprises (SMEs) are normally at a disadvantage in securing needed financial services, such as loan, investment, insurance, and others from banks, so that they turn to alternative providers, which provide service at higher cost. The rise of fintech services caters to this huge market segment.

Chinese start-ups also enjoy a range of benefits from the Government, such as eligibility for annual tax deductions. Those qualifying as New High-Tech Enterprises (NHTE) pay taxes at a lower corporate rate of 15% compared to the normal 25%. Even fintech firms already financially backed by large Internet players have been able to secure funding from government-affiliated firms. For instance, when Alibaba's fintech affiliate Ant Financial raised $4.5 billion in a Series B funding round in April 2016, it attracted investments from state-controlled entities like China Investment Corp, CCB Trust, China Life, China Post Group and China Development Bank Capital.

Competition is heating up for funding Chinese start-ups. This led to a 252% expansion in fintech investments in the 12 months ending June 2016. Almost all the investment funds are from domestic sources.

In May 2016, China saw its first fintech angel fund, the FinPlus Fund,[30,31] backed by the Fugel Group. The angel fund intends to invest $0.15- 0.75 million in seed funding into individual start-ups, and provide corporate offices and access to Fugel Group's clientele. Other private investors include Chinese leasing provider, Bohai Leasing, which took part in a $207 million Series C funding round in 2015 in *Dianrong.com*.

Some foreign investors are venturing in as well. Foreign venture capital firms, such as Silicon Valley's Sequoia Capital, launched a China division in 2005. Although China has less extensive physical banking infrastructure compared to the US and Europe, its digital infrastructure is quite mature. Its online penetration rate is 54% as compared to the 89% in North America and 73% in Europe.[32] However, because of its large population, China has 750 million Internet users of whom 96% are mobile Internet users. The smartphone is the universal Internet access device in China. The accessible wireless networks in public in China's major cities are much more extensive than in the West. As a result, mobile online payment users reached 358 million by the end of 2015, with an annual growth rate of 65%. Fifty-eight percent of the population is using their smartphone to conduct financial transactions primarily through Alibaba's Alipay or WeChat Pay payment service. In Q2 of 2016 alone, there were 6.3 billion mobile payment transactions.[33]

**FIGURE 7.2** Chinese mobile payment market.

The leading e-commerce companies compete with each other to offer more and better services to their customers by digging into the consumption ecosystem. Such an ecosystem contains both financial and retail activity data – a treasure trove of valuable insights into the market as well as the technologies needed.

In 2016, China's e-commerce sales amounted to $900 billion, of which 47% came from global digital retail sales. Online purchases in China will soon reach 18% of the country's total retail sales value, compared with 8% in the US, 12% in South Korea, and 16% in the UK.

By 2020, mobile transactions will rise from 56% of all e-commerce sales to 68%. With the Chinese government encouraging citizens to shop online, and mobile broadband subscriptions projected to reach 90% by 2020, the adoption of e-commerce activities can go beyond urban metros and into rural areas.

Having domestic dominance with high levels of Internet and mobile penetration, China has the world's largest and most developed retail e-commerce market. It has created a unique, dynamic, and rapidly evolving ecosystem, which is a fertile ground for innovation in commerce, banking, and financial services. Such an ecosystem has drawn many technologies into its development whirlpools, such as Big Data and AI.

For the year ending in June 2016, Chinese fintech investments surged to $8.8 billion, the largest global investment in this sector. As this exponential growth continues, China's fintech is evolving into a completely new digital financial marketplace. The digitally perceptive Chinese consumers are ready to embrace fintech offerings, creating opportunities for fintech firms willing to take on digital transformation.

The proliferation of the Internet, communication, and blockchain technology creates new business models that did not exist before. The new business models aim to tap the $27 trillion personal savings of the Chinese consumers. fintech firms intend to channel this pool of savings into wealth management, insurance, and private banking.

To meet these needs, the Chinese technology giants are aggressively creating innovative platforms with both financial and non-financial solutions for their customers. They are also investing heavily in emerging technologies to support next-generation financial services, such as blockchain and artificial intelligence.

The competition among the e-commerce players to lure online customers is fierce. Over the past few years, the battle has spilled over to the fintech industry, with Baidu, Tencent, and several other tech giants offering short-term loans and wealth-management products through digital channels.

The major Chinese fintech firms are aggressively creating all-inclusive platforms. Ant Financial, for instance, offers customers using multiple products a package deal which includes not only financial services but also other types of services such as transportation, dining, medical services, and much more. This has already reaped initial success, as measured by the speed of customer acquisition.

More Chinese financial service players are developing their own digital and fintech technology, launching e-commerce platforms, e-payment tools, and online financing and wealth management services. The barriers are getting higher for newcomers. Not only they have to leverage new technologies, but also amass a huge user base and merchant information, the online banking capabilities, as well as the presence of a large number of brick-and-mortar outlets in order to survive. Those who meet only a part of the requirements must seek partners to collaborate, acquire, or be acquired.

Nevertheless, traditional banks are not out of the market. New regulations require in-person verification to open accounts. Online-only banks need to collaborate with traditional banks to use their established infrastructure.

Domestic state-owned and private investors funded almost all of the fintech activities in China. So far, foreign entrants have met with varying levels of success – limited by government restrictions on operations and investment, as well as cultural differences. In late 2017, China opened up the financial market to foreign institutions.[34] This is a positive development for China and global financial firms alike. It brings additional resources and technology to China and prepares the Chinese economy for further globalization. It will also provide Chinese firms with new capabilities in areas such as risk management and banking system automation. During Jack Ma's visit to the US in June 2017, he envisioned SMEs in the US selling directly to the Chinese consumers online, thus opening huge market access for SMEs in the US.

Foreign payment processing companies such as VISA and MasterCard have had to work through UnionPay when processing local transactions. Since June 2016, China started to accept foreign payment processors for domestic card clearing businesses.

Having tasted great success at home, Chinese fintech giants are looking to go global, both to diversify revenue streams and to reduce their dependence on the domestic market. Such a move is a giant step into unchartered territory. Chinese companies cannot expect to replicate and export domestic business models abroad. The peculiar conditions that make these companies successful in China may not exist in other countries. The key question is whether Chinese fintech players will be able to adapt to the conditions abroad and compete internationally. There are many entry barriers to cross, such as: to set up across-the-boundary transaction processing capabilities; to overcome international payment barriers; to face different regulatory environments; to build trust, brand name, and reputation; and to prevail over cultural differences. In addition, they may not count on government support or a favorable regulatory environment outside of China. The overseas market may not have enough underserved SMEs and consumers. They need to adapt to local cultural norms and expectations. They will also need to compete directly with the local or international fintech companies and financial powerhouses. The best and safest approach to do so is to collaborate with and invest in overseas partners.

However, armed with enough capital, experience, and the huge market at home, Chinese fintech firms will make inroads into the global market. Eventually, they will play an increasingly important role in the global fintech collaborations and drive additional technological innovation. Their experience abroad, in turn, will allow them to develop the market at home further to increase the Chinese consumers' contribution to GDP by at least 10% above today's level. What is evident is that the next phase of development in fintech innovation in China will have a major impact on global financial services in the future.

In the Asia Pacific region outside of China, segments of China's fintech industry, like payments and insurance, are already leading, with non-banks commanding a 35% or higher market share within the span of two years. The major companies making an inroad into the Asia Pacific region are Ping An, which leads digital insurance, and Alipay, TenPay, and UnionPay for payments/remittances.

Many Chinese fintech companies also form alliances to leverage each other's strength in technology, marketing, or database. For example, the China Ledger Alliance, comprising regional exchanges, created an open source blockchain protocol to support IoT development. Financial Blockchain Shenzhen Consortium, including members such as Ping An Insurance, a member of the global consortium R3 and Tencent, collaborates on research and group-wide blockchain projects, with a focus on capital markets technology, securities exchange, trading platforms, banking, and life insurance. It aims to create a securities trading platform prototype and develop credit, digital asset registry, and invoice management services.

The Qianhai International Blockchain Ecosphere Alliance aims to establish an efficient ecosystem for developing blockchain technology and its applications. The Alliance membership includes the world's leading global technology companies such as Microsoft, IBM, and Hong Kong's Applied Science and Technology Research Institute (ASTRI). It hopes to accelerate the commercialization of blockchain R&D and promote its application to support China's social and economic development.

Aggressive Chinese tech firms equipped with skilled IT infrastructure and application development are looking to go global. They are investing in global technology hubs, penetrating new product markets overseas to diversify revenue streams, and reducing domestic reliance. Baidu, Alibaba, and Tencent are expanding to serve outbound Chinese travelers abroad and expats, while seeking out new customers in emerging economies from Africa to South and Southeast Asia. They are particularly interested in the future possibilities of new O2O revenue streams. For example, Alibaba currently has more than 86% of its revenues coming from China but aims to generate half of all sales from overseas. The group is developing an international ecosystem that encompasses targeted marketing, logistics, payment services, and cloud computing.

Their strategy is to achieve globalization via international acquisitions and expansion. For instance, its AliExpress e-commerce platform is already doing brisk business in markets such as Russia and Brazil. Alibaba made its largest international investment to-date in April 2016 with $1 billion for the control of Lazada Group, Southeast Asia's largest clothing and electronics portal. In the summer of 2017, it invested an additional $1 billion, and in March 2018, it has doubled down on Lazada with an additional $2 billion investment, with a total investment of $4 billion.[35] To further increase exposure into Southeast Asia, Ant Financial took a stake in Ascend Money, a Thai online-payment provider.

In 2015, Ant Financial ventured into India with a $680 million purchase for about 40% of Paytm, India's largest mobile commerce platform with 122 million users and 23 million mobile wallet users, and another $100 million for online marketplace Snapdeal. In 2017, Alibaba invested an additional $177 million in Paytm E-commerce, a spinoff of Paytm.[36] These investments gave Alibaba a payments banking license in India and an immediate foothold in a country with an exponential growth in the online payment industry with a CAGR of 50% from 2007-2014.

To expand the business, Alipay has announced ambitions for one million offline partner merchants globally within three years, a move that will allow 120 million Chinese tourists traveling abroad every year to pay with Alipay even when they are abroad. The first of these cross-border payment partnerships was rolled out in 2015, allowing Chinese tourists with an Alipay account to shop and pay at 70,000 overseas merchants with the app. With 450 million active registered users and 200 financial institution partners, Alipay is collaborating with leading global payment providers to ensure that international merchants can be integrated into handling the Chinese payment platform at home.

Ant Financial and European retail merchant leaders, Germany's Wirecard and Concardis, established a partnership to serve the growing number of Chinese tourists in Europe. Alipay also entered an agreement with Ingenico to embed Alipay into Ingenico's payment portal, the largest in Europe. This allows European merchants to accept customers who use Alipay for their purchases. A global agreement with the insurance giant AXA allows Alibaba/Ant Financial to sell AXA travel insurance to outbound Chinese travelers.[37]

Likewise in the US, the partnerships with San Francisco-based ride-hailing service Uber Technologies, Airbnb, and Macy's allow for Chinese customers to use their Alipay wallet. Baidu has also created its own alliance with overseas merchants in Thailand, South Korea, Japan, Hong Kong, Macau, and Taiwan.

## 7.5  MAJOR GLOBAL FINTECH COMPANIES

KPMG, one of the world's leading accounting firms, compiled a list of the world's 100 top fintech innovation companies.[38] Asia-Pacific companies dominate the top ten in the list: Ant Financial (China), Grab (Singapore), JD Digits (China), GoJek (Indonesia), Paytm (India), Du Xiaoman Financial (China), Compass (United States), Ola (India), Opendoor (United States), and OakNorth (United Kingdom). Forty-two companies in the Fintech100 are from the Asia Pacific region. This is probably because the region is behind in the traditional finance service infrastructure in comparison to the West, and leapfrogs to adapt the new technologies without the need to work around the established financial establishment. Out of the Fintech100, 34 are located in Asia, 36 in Europe and the Middle East, 22 in North America, 7 in Australia, and 1 in New Zealand.

The Fintech100 companies raised over $18 billion dollars in 2019. This shows how hot the market is. These fintech companies already serve over 2.5 billion customers globally with innovative products and services. Chinese fintech companies led the Fintech100, but Indian companies are not too far behind. The top fintech Company, Ant Financial, planned a $30 billion IPO – the largest IPO in the world, before aborting the plan due to regulatory issues.

The fintech industry is no longer an isolated industry. It is converging with the traditional financial industry, as more traditional financial companies such as banks are adapting fintech. Fintech is also globalizing quickly, as the distribution of the Fintech100 shows.

The fintech market can fall into the following categories: electronic payments, online financing, supply chain management, consumer financing and P2P lending, e-insurance, online fund and personal finance management, and online brokerage.

China's financial services sector is ripe for change, exuberated by exponential growth in digital connectivity, the deep penetration of smartphones, the explosion of e-commerce, and a core of restless Internet giants.

Tencent, the leading value-added Internet service company in China, entered the fintech arena with a simple social media app called WeChat. It was originally only a messaging app. However, it morphed into a huge fintech app when it developed WeChat Pay function. By 2017, it claimed a whopping 1 billion users.[39]

In the 2014 Chinese New Year, when Tencent introduced the Hongbao (red envelope) function in WeChat Pay, it became an instant success. Two years later, Tencent's WeChat Pay platform handled 32 billion digital Hongbao transactions over the six-day Chinese New Year holiday. This compares to 4.9 billion transactions PayPal did for the entire year of 2015.

Tencent operates more than a dozen data centers across China. It is moving stealthily to open overseas data centers.[40] Its Silicon Valley data center opened in April 2017, followed by four more in Frankfurt, Mumbai, Seoul, and Moscow by the end of 2017 to cater to its expanding client base. Its plan is to have eight overseas data centers in total to serve online games, online finance, video, and other Internet-related industries. The new overseas data centers, located strategically in regional business or technology hubs worldwide, are part of Tencent's broader strategy to invest in the latest technologies such as cloud, security, Big Data, and artificial intelligence, to capture the next wave of growth. It also aims to serve its Chinese enterprise partners to deploy their services globally, as well as international companies expanding their businesses in China or in other parts of the world. The company's cloud revenue has already more than tripled year-on-year in 2016 due to the expansion.

Tencent, which expanded its popular WeChat messaging app into an ecosystem of Online-to-Offline (O2O) services over the past few years, pulled in users with its own web bank and its mobile payments platform WeChat Pay. It also joined China Rapid Finance, a consumer-lending marketplace, to offer other investment products.

Alibaba pursues the same strategy. It is expanding cloud services overseas. Alibaba's cloud sales soared by 126.5% to $675 million from 2015 to 2016. As a comparison, the size of the world's leading cloud service operators is $500 million, of Google; $1.6 billion, of Microsoft Azure; and $9.8 billion, of Amazon.[41] Alibaba's fintech subsidiary, Ant Financial, claims that over 100 million users have taken out loans. Ant Financial managed $96 billion for 295 million clients by mid-2016.

Baidu's Financial Services Group (FSG) had $3.7 billion in assets in 2017, which accounted for 12% of Baidu's total assets. FGS sells wealth management products and loans and offers web banking for customers. Those services are tied to its mobile payment platform Baidu Wallet, with 100 million activated accounts at the end of 2016 and 88% growth from 2015. Baidu also invested in Zest Finance, a U.S. fintech company that uses Big Data for credit scoring purposes.

*JD.com*, one of the two largest online retailers in China and a Fortune Global 500 Company, spun off its fintech arm, JD Finance[42]. At the end of 2017, its e-commerce platform had 266.3 million active customers. Despite being a retail company, *JD.com* focuses on the technology of logistics and developed the world's largest drone delivery infrastructure. Its delivery system deploys AI, autonomous technology, and robots. It has recently started testing robotic delivery services and building drone delivery airports, as well as operating driverless delivery by unveiling its first autonomous truck. *JD.com* has also launched a food supply tracking system using blockchain, in Beijing supermarkets and online stores.

Wanxiang Blockchain Labs, a subsidiary of the Wanxiang Group, is one of the world's largest automotive parts makers, working with Ethereum. It is the largest blockchain development backer in China. After purchasing 500,000 ETH tokens in 2016, they pledged $30 billion for the development of a smart city in Hangzhou - a nine-square-kilometer plot of land, with a planned population of 90,000 people. In such a smart city, blockchain would power everything from the city's electricity grid to its traffic control system.

The Wanda Group, the world's largest private property developer, operating hotels, theme parks, shopping malls, theaters, media companies, and department stores, also diversified into the fintech arena. In 2016, Wanda joined Hyperledger to build smart apps for its businesses. Hyperledger is a community for the development of blockchain applications. It is a global collaboration, hosted by the US-based Linux Foundation, counting leaders in finance, banking, Internet of Things, supply chains, manufacturing, and Technology as its members. Soon after, Wanda announced its blockchain platform Polaris, an open source platform, for smart supply chains, pharmaceutical management, finance, and invoicing. The company is also working with China's Ministry of Industry and Information to draft domestic blockchain standards.

There are also many other fintech companies specialized in the specific areas of financial services. To mention a few: Wecash[43,44] is China's first Internet credit assessment company that provides solutions for technology companies. FangDD offers an online platform through which homebuyers and home sellers can directly connect to each other. Jimubox is a Beijing-based marketplace-lending platform that provides small and medium enterprise loans and individual consumption loans to under-banked Chinese borrowers.

Such an interest is not limited to the financial or retail companies. Manufacturing companies also see an opportunity to unify the fragmented data flows through their large and complicated factory floors and supply chains by marrying a blockchain data layer with IoT devices. By doing so, they are bringing blockchain to the manufacturing floor.

Fintech approaches are spreading to industries as well. Although Industry 4.0 is different from fintech by targeting industrial applications rather than financial services, many of the basic technologies, such as IoT, Big Data, AI, communication, etc. are the same. The development of one will help the development of the other. There are also sectors of the market in which these two initiatives overlap, such as supply chain management.

A case in point, Taiwan's Foxconn, the world's largest contract manufacturer of electronics and best known for manufacturing Apple's products, is developing a highly efficient supply chain that could also track delivered goods.[45] Foxconn sees blockchain as a way for its suppliers to get easy financing. It formed a subsidiary called FnConn[46] in 2013 to provide loans and financing solutions to suppliers, including Foxconn's upstream and downstream supply chains. The company also supports other small and medium-enterprise (SME) customers in the computer, communication, and consumer electronics (3C) manufacturing industries. FnConn works to improve supply chain finance, support industry and economic development, and drive better integration across the financial services industry in China.

## 7.6   TECHFIN

Not to be confused with fintech, *TechFin* is simply technology-based financial services. In contrast to the traditional financial services centered on banks and other financial institutions such as insurance companies, venture capitalists, or private equity, TechFin refers to a new breed of financial services created by the proliferation and innovation of new technologies. The financial services offered by TechFin could not exist without the baseline technology. The technology-centric companies using the newly developed fintech dominate Techfin.[47]

Large Internet and e-commerce companies have amassed a huge customer base and market share to become powerful service providers in the financial market. The most well-known companies of this type are Amazon, Netflix, eBay, PayPal, Google, Apple, Square, *Hotel.com*, Uber, and Airbnb in the US, and Baidu, Tencent, Alibaba, *JD.com*, Juzhen Financials, Zhongnan Construction (a property conglomerate), CreditEase (microfinance and wealth advisor), Shanghai Insurance Exchange, Qtum, and many others in China, and MercadoCrédito and MercadoLibre in Latin America.

TechFin harnesses Big Data using AI and blockchain for achieving efficiency in financial services. The real disruptions, however, come from the companies offering end-to-end solutions that cut out existing players. We have seen this in many economic sectors such as Uber vs. taxis, Netflix vs. cable companies, or Airbnb vs. hotels.

Sovereign funds like GIC Singapore or private equity funds like KKR and Blackstone invested heavily in TechFin. TechFin companies receive more funding than fintech startups. Global investment in the sector grew from less than $10 billion in 2012 to more than $80 billion in 2018.

Alibaba, the e-commerce giant in China, entered the financial services sector with the creation of Ant Financial in 2016. It is estimated that the valuation of Ant Financial in 2020 before the aborted IPO was higher than $300 billion, ranking among the world largest banks.

The entry of these fintech firms is a paradigm shift in the financial industry, from money-centered financial service to data-centered financial service. It may be the single most important development in financial services in recent history.

TechFin creates new financial service markets using the new technologies. However, these new financial services are often shortcuts to the existing financial services. They embrace not only financial services but also retail business (such as e-commerce), and service business (such as tax and hotel). For example, Alibaba is not only an e-commerce company but operates many data centers worldwide.[48,49,50] Amazon AWS (Amazon Web Services) pioneered cloud computing in 2006, and currently has 49 data centers in 18 countries worldwide.[51]

The data centers in the early 21$^{st}$ century are akin to the power plants in the early 20$^{th}$ century. The power plant delivers power to each household while the data center delivers data to each individual. These data centers power TechFin companies and give them a boost in the provision of financial services. When financial services become more and more data-centric, sooner or later, traditional financial institutions will have a difficult time competing with the power amassed by TechFin companies, unless they too adopt the same strategy

These data centers allow TechFin companies to provide far more efficient financial services and improved decision-making. Consumers get the first taste of the targeted ads from Google Ads. With a search engine, Google Ads can deliver ads to the right customers. The same will be the case with financial services in the future. Such targeted and tailored financial services can be a boon for the small and medium enterprises (SMEs). TechFin companies also open the door of P2P business across national borders, which is the exclusive realm of B2P business.

## 7.7   BLOCKCHAIN TECHNOLOGY FOR BANKS

Financial institutions need to identify opportunities for innovation using blockchain. Financial service operations are vast and complex. To identify areas of traditional operations suitable for blockchain technology application with clear benefits and no negative impact requires serious investigation, because many implications of such change are not well understood.

Since blockchain is essentially designed to handle transactions and ledgers, all kinds of operations requiring ledger and transaction are natural candidates for the blockchain application. For example, in the shipping business, many operations such as documentation tracking, bills of lading, letters of credit, and the import/export process use transactions and create ledgers. Blockchain technology can fully automate these processes.

In the same way, in a supply chain-related operation, payments form a Chain of Custody (CoC), a chronological paper trail of transaction flow. It is what MDL/ Blockchain does the best. By using Identity MDL and Transaction MDL, banks can immediately reap the benefit of improved security of the stored identity, improve portability of data, and reduce the time taken for KYC efforts. The data in MDL are much more secure than in the traditional database.

The benefits of Blockchain applications are more than just data security. Since the bank has non-stop operations, any glitches caused by the database going down can be costly. The distributed nature of Blockchain ensures that the database never goes down.

However, for banks to make the transition from the traditional system to the MDL-based system is not easy. The most challenging task is not the construction of MDL. The real challenge is to manage the transition and to test it out against the real-world environment. Banks need to create plans to enable Blockchain technology to co-exist with their traditional systems. Only when Blockchain is mature and robust enough can it replace existing banking systems. It also needs a common protocol that enables interoperability.

Banks planning to move their processes to Blockchain need to start by assessing how interoperability can advance their Blockchain objectives. Since it is most likely that banks themselves do not have the expertise in blockchain technology, they will employ blockchain technology firms to do the development and implementation. Together, they will define protocols and standards upon which the future of blockchain applications will be built. By measuring the results against expectations, banks will be able to refine the application and use this knowledge for future application development.

Since the financial market is heavily regulated, regulations will be an important consideration in Blockchain implementation. It is essential to grasp the implication of the regulatory environment before development. For example, the current regulatory framework has no provisions to accommodate a technology that will eliminate intermediaries. Storing financial data on the distributed network in different countries will also face compliance issues. There is no legal framework for smart contracts today. New legal definitions are required to resolve the disputes arising from smart contracts. The same is true of the validation, safeguarding, and preservation functions that are performed not by the third party but by the blockchain platform.

If the legal framework of blockchain operations is established, financial institutional operations can be greatly simplified by replacing these functions with blockchain. By doing so, it can lower the barriers and costs of setting up trusted third-party services, and perhaps lead to increased demand.

Identity verification, authentication, and data management could streamline the many traditional operations of financial institutions. For insurance companies, the streamlining of digital authentication and better management of personal data and history disclosure could translate into more direct and efficient relationships between insurance companies and their customers. Over time, this could bring additional benefits by reducing identity and claim frauds.

In the KYC and AML processes, an identity MDL could transform service levels. Global leaders, including UBS, Deutsche Banks, JP Morgan, and Bank of America Merrill Lynch are testing blockchain applications to improve workflows and reduce costs.

Commercial trade financing will become easier when it comes to applying blockchain technology. A trade-financing workflow based on blockchain allows both the carriers to issue a bill of lading and banks to issue a letter of credit as digital assets on the same blockchain.

Decentralizing document verification allows companies to execute the most updated version of documents and verify their authenticity. The verified documents can be shared with third-party requestors.

Numerous potential applications were discussed in Chapter 6. Due to the limited scope of this book, we cannot cover all the possible applications, and new applications are being developed every day.

## 7.8    CROWDSALE AND CROWD PREDICTION

Permissionless blockchain technology is based on a large number of participants. Not only does the large mass make consensus possible, but it also forms a crowd. Any financial or social events based on the crowd can be managed by blockchain. The most well-developed blockchain technologies based on the crowd are crowdfunding, crowd prediction, and forecast.

Initial Coin Offering (ICO), also known as *crowdsale*, is a special form of crowdfunding. It is a new way for the digital currency startups to issue new coins to fund their venture. Typically, the startups release a percentage of the cryptocurrency to early backers of the project in exchange for funding. Because ICO is such a new phenomenon, there is no regulation on the ICO process yet and it is prone to be fraudulent. ICO companies essentially bypass the rigorous and regulated capital- raising process required by venture capitalists or banks.

ICO offers blockchain startups and projects an easy method of raising capital without the existence of intermediaries and mediators. Some ICOs have raised millions of dollars at very high valuation without a clear vision, user base, revenue stream, or even a working product. This would not be possible with traditional angel funding and venture capital firms without an active user base and a solid revenue stream.

It will not be long before the legislation and regulation of ICOs appear. Like IPO, in an ICO event, the startup firm creates a business plan for its project including the target money to be raised. It tries to sell its business plan to the potential investors. Instead of issuing shares of the startup company to the investors, it issues crypto coins. A successful ICO example is the Ethereum, which launched ICO in 2014 and raised $18 million.

With blockchain technology, betting is becoming much more than a simple wager. Say, if millions are predicting the outcome of an election, the prediction may become true. Crowd predictions have a high degree of accuracy in events whose outcome can be influenced by the crowd. Of course, there is no predictability for the events that the crowd does not have any control over, such as the weather.

Augur, a blockchain application development company, combines the magic of betting with the power of blockchain technology to create a forecasting tool using Ethereum blockchain.[52] Using the Augur application, anyone anywhere in the world can create a prediction market quickly and easily. Prediction markets have proven to be more accurate at forecasting the future than individual experts, surveys, or traditional opinion polling due to the so-called the "wisdom of the crowd."

Augur's prediction based on the predictable data can be very powerful. The probability of crowd prediction can have an impact in the real world. This is especially useful in predicting consumer spending patterns, election and economy trends, or even the stock market. After all, the stock market is driven by the same psychology as crowd prediction. If most investors bet on a stock price to rise, it will rise. It is obvious that investors will not buy the stock or even sell it, if they think the stock price is going down. In essence, investors are betting or voting with their money. Likewise market sentiment is the overall attitude of investors toward the financial market. The crowd psychology is revealed through the activity and price movement of the securities and market. Therefore, permissionless blockchain technology can be used for prediction and forecast. Blockchain technology finds applications in prediction and forecasting using the collected data.

Augur's platform can also be used in betting. It allows users to buy and sell shares, which are priced proportional to the probability of the outcome. For example, if you predict that the probability is 60%, you pay 60 cents to buy the share. If you are right, you get 1 dollar back. If not, you lose 60 cents. The concept is similar to the binary option, which predicts the stock price, except that the binary option does not have enough volume to influence the outcome.

As more people bet on an outcome, the probability of that outcome becoming true will rise. The probability may rise or fall during the course of prediction since crowd's prediction can change per real-world occurrences.

The one who initiates the subject of prediction is called the market maker. He can pose any subject for betting, such as the Dow Jones Index three months later. He provides the initial funding and receives trading fees in return.

People have been betting on horse races for a long time. Horse race betting can be fun and profitable if you know what you are doing. Bets are placed in many other markets as well: auto racing, baseball, basketball, boxing, football, golf, hockey, etc. All kinds of betting activities are crowd-based. They are well suited for the blockchain application. The collective intelligence of many people is superior to that of the smartest people in the world. It provides real-time predictive data and the transactions use real money – which incentivizes market participants to reveal what they think will happen, rather than what they hope will happen. All funds are stored in smart contracts – eliminating counterparty risk and allowing fast, automated payments to winning traders. Blockchain can also automate the deposit and withdrawal of funds. With no human intervention required, there is no human error. In summary, blockchain technology has automated the betting and prediction industry.

## 7.9 BUILDING MDL FOR FINANCIAL SERVICES

There is a wide variety of financial services. The possible applications of blockchain in financial services are practically unlimited. Services like private banking, capital market service, certificates of deposit, bonds, derivatives, voting rights associated with financial instruments, commodities, stocks, credit data, mortgage or loan, P2P lending, donations, airline miles, business license, business ownership/ incorporation/ dissolution, chain of custody, and many more can benefit from using blockchain technology.

In general, the trusted third parties in finance services provide three functions: validation, safeguarding, and preservation. In principle, any financial service which performs these three functions, can deploy blockchain technology.

Before starting a blockchain application development, the developers must have clear answers to the following questions:

- How can the blockchain be constructed to best meet the application requirements?
- What kind of consensus mechanism is the best? Is it Proof-of-stake, Proof-of-work, Proof-of-Concept, dBFT, or hybrid?
- What elements of the trusted third party are to be replaced by blockchain?
- How are transactions authorized?
- Is it going to be truly peer-to-peer or merely decentralized?
- Are all nodes equal and performing the same tasks, or do some nodes have more power and additional tasks?
- Are tokens needed?
- Is the blockchain application in question going to interface with other blockchains?
- Does it need sidechains?
- Is there a need to separate Identity MDL, Transaction MDL, and Content MDL?

- What technical choices are there on cryptography standards, peer-to-peer arrangements, guaranteed distribution approaches, partial cryptography, programming languages, communication protocols, etc.?
- Is it going to be a private or a public blockchain? Is it Permissioned or Permissionless?
- Is it P2P based or cloud based?
- How scalable does it need to be?

For example, if the application already has trusted third parties such as banks, regulators, or government, it does not need PoW to establish trust; or if the application requires scalability, PoW is not suitable. Only when these questions have definite answers can the framework design of the blockchain be defined.

After defining the scope of the MDL in question, the next task is to build the blockchain itself and a small suite of software providing an interface to MDLs for tasks such as selection and storage of documents, document encryption, sharing keys, viewing the MDL transactions, and viewing the MDL contents subject to encrypted limits. A suite of software is needed to test various options for MDLs. It should permit the testing of a variety of MDL configurations and simulated situations. The outputs are to be shared and revised with participants.

The InterChainZ project was a consortium research project, pioneered by London-based Z/Yen to provide a real learning experience on blockchains. The project intended to demonstrate how blockchains could work for financial services. The tool used is the online demonstrator of InterChainZ, an online MDL, which can be configured to explore how they might work in a different environments of use. The outputs are interlinked MDLs along with software, explanatory materials, and website information.[53]

Blockchains incorporate trusted third parties for some functions which can have significant potential in financial services, such as know-your-customer (KYC), antimony-laundering (AML), insurance, credit, and wholesale financial services. In addition, the encryption of MDLs produces immutable records.

InterChainZ demonstrated many potential applications, for example, data ledger, identity application, insurance policy placement, large-scale archive, and voting validation. It also works with partners on specific use cases. For example:

- **Validation:** It uses blockchain to validate identity. A third-party bank confirms the validation of the identity and financial information. Such a validation service is useful to individuals who need to comply with AML or KYC requirements.
- **Audit:** It uses blockchain for credit audit. In this demonstration, MDL functionality allows companies to validate their identity and finance report. A trusted third party reviews the information, confirms and adds it to MDL. The potential creditors or business partners are provided with a public key so that they can confirm the validation and view the information.
- **Insurance policy placement:** It uses blockchain to validate insurance history and relevant data of an individual or business. When he or it applies a new insurance policy, he or it shares the key with the insurance company. It saves the insurance company the need to verify historical data relevant to the applicant. New policy details are added to the MDL as an update. In the same way, one's credit history can also be validated easily.

Z/Yen also explored InterChainZ storage options and network architectures using both Content MDL and Identity MDL and tested the scalability of InterChainZ. InterChainZ MDL has the advantages of a centrally controlled ledger, simple approval rules, fast entry to the ledger, simple implementation and maintenance, reliance on the single trusted third party, and is not dependent on specific nodes to be available. Without the burden of PoW, InterChainZ can validate 3,000 to 5,000 transactions per second, almost as fast as credit cards.

## 7.10  DIGITAL CURRENCY

It is thought that cryptocurrencies are decentralized and there is no ownership. There is nothing to prevent the technology from being used to create centrally controlled digital currency, whether by a central bank or by private enterprise. Most of the countries in the world are experimenting with national digital currencies. Some are moving faster than the others. Even a company like Facebook announced its intention to create its own digital currency – Libra. However, central banks are taking cautious steps toward creating digital currencies because the technology is still evolving and the full implication is not yet clear. After all, hasty introduction of a national digital currency could cause unforeseen consequences.

One of the incentives for the advanced economies to consider a national digital currency is countering the growth of private digital money before it is too late. Payment apps like Venmo, WeChat, and Alipay are generating greater digital payment market share, undermining the national currency, challenging central banks and raising concerns about consumer protection and data privacy. This is especially true in China. Facebook's intention to create its own Libra currency alarmed the governments, who feared that future private digital currency may rival national currencies in circulation, power, and influence, undermining the authority of national governments. This prompted policymakers to explore a solution before users adopt an alternative over which the government has limited control. We are seeing that the European Central Bank coordinated digital currency research and development. The U.S. Federal Reserve also showed its intention to develop the digital dollar.

In China, the mobile payment is a precursor to digital currency. The size of the mobile payment market dominated by the third-party payment systems, may threaten its financial systems, since the third-party system has not been regulated by bank rules. China piloted a national digital currency in April 2020, partially to counter such a trend. It also serves to help to promote and enhance Chinese currency globally and influence the global payments infrastructure in the future.

A national digital currency has many advantages, such as modernizing domestic payments systems, and facilitating cross-border trade and remittances.

The national digital currency is also known as the Central Bank Digital Currency (CBDC). It is simply the digital form of a country's fiat currency. Instead of printing paper bills and minting coins, the central bank issues electronic tokens, whose value is backed by the full faith and credit of the government. CBDCs are the liability of the government. They are 100% replaceable by cash.

Contrary to Bitcoin, the CBDC is not decentralized. The Central bank is its authority, which controls the issuing and circulation of the currency.

However, in many ways, it works similar to the Bitcoin. For example, digital currencies can be stored in the electronic wallet, which can be an app in the mobile phone or the PC. Payment can be made from wallet to wallet. Face-to-face payment does not require a network. CBDC can be transferred via NFC. The transaction is updated when the phones have access to a network. For remote payment, distance is not a limitation. Payment can be made from wallet to wallet across the globe. Such a feature makes cross-border payment extremely fast and easy.

The transaction cost is also much lower than the current remittance system. The Bank of England estimates that it can boost GDP by up to 3% by lowering transaction costs. It is also an equalizer for the huge unbanked population in the developing countries.

The advantages also bring risks. Fast money transfer across boundaries, without passage through government-regulated banks, makes the financial system less stable. Central banks would need to significantly ramp up their operational capabilities to manage a digital currency, from managing reserves and deposits, to protecting user privacy, preventing digital counterfeiting, and mitigating cyber attacks and other operational risks.

In addition, when a centralized digital currency is more widely adopted, the authority of its issuer, whether a country or an enterprise, increases. When such digital currency becomes global, the power of its issuer can be quite significant. The Chinese DCEP and Facebook's Libra are cases in point. Today, much of the global payments infrastructure is using the dollar which is under U.S. jurisdiction. If alternative systems were developed, the U.S. could lose its currency dominance and the power that comes with it.

## REFERENCES

1. "Business opportunities for Swiss FintechXE "Fintech" companies in Russia," Switzerland Global Enterprise, *https://www.s-ge.com/sites/default/files/cserver/mig/sites/default/files/censhare_files/paper-fintech-opportunities-russia_3.pdf.*

2. *https://fortunly.com/statistics/fintech-statistics/.*

3. *https://www.fisglobal.com/.*

4. "How AI is transforming the future of FintechXE "Fintech"," Rich Wordsworth, *http://www.wired.co.uk/article/how-ai- is-transforming-the-future-of-fintech.*

5. "Cash is already pretty much dead in China as the country lives the future with mobile pay," Evelyn Cheng, CNBC, *https://www.cnbc.com/2017/10/08/china-is-living-the-future-of-mobile-pay-right-now.html.*

6. "Innovation in payment," BNY Mellon, *https://bravenewcoin.com/assets/Industry-Reports-2015/BNY-Melon-innovation-in-payments-the-future-is-fintech.pdf.*

7. *http://www.citigroup.com/citi/news/2014/141202c.htm.*

8. *https://www.level39.co/news/welcome-level39-2/.*

9. *https://www.statista.com/statistics/554889/it-expenses-of-banks-by-region/.*

10. *https://www.iso20022.org/.*

11. *https://www.gs1.org/edi-xml/xml-advanced-remittance-notification/3-0.*

12. "What is payment hub," Lisa Perales, *http://blog.powertopay.com/what-is-a-payment-hub.*

13. *https://www.fiserv.com/index.aspx.*

14. *https://www.bofaml.com/content/boaml/en_us/home.html.*

15. *https://www.avaloq.com/.*

16. "How Barkley stole the blockchain spot light in 2016," Bailey Reutzel, *https://www.coindesk.com/barclays-stole-blockchain-spotlight-2016/.*

17. "Citibank is working on its own digital currency XE "digital currency" – Citicoin," John Biggs, *https://techcrunch.com/2015/07/07/citibank-is-working-on-its-own-digital-currency-citicoin/.*

18. *https://www.r3.com/.*

19. "Trend in world trade," WTO, *https://www.wto.org/english/res_e/statis_e/wts2017_e/WTO_Chapter_02_e.pdf.*

20. "The Fintech100 – Announcing the world's leading fintech innovators for 2017," *https://home.kpmg.com/xx/en/home/media/press-releases/2017/11/the-fintech-100-announcing-the-worlds-leading-fintech-innovators-for-2017.html.*

21. "Accelerating Fintech in China," Joshua Bateman, *https://techcrunch.com/2017/10/08/accelerating-fintech-in-china/.*

22. "Global Fintech VC investment soars in 2016," Lawrence Wintermeyer, *https://www.forbes.com/sites/lawrencewintermeyer/2017/02/17/global-fintech-vc-investment-soars-in-2016/#7e2fe2d82630.*

23. "Internet trend 2017," Mary Meeker, *http://www.kpcb.com/internet-trends.*

24. *https://en.wikipedia.org/wiki/List_of_largest_banks.*

25. "With $27 trillion in savings, Chinese are set to change the world," Eda Corran et al., *http://www.smh.com.au/business/china/with-28-trillion-in-savings-chinese-are-set-to-change-the-world-20150625-ghy4x1.html.*

26. *https://marketrealist.com/p/when-is-ant-group-ipo-date/*.

27. "How is Internet Plus altering China," *http://www.china.org.cn/business/2016-07/11/content_38851412.htm*.

28. "China's Meituan Dianping acquires bike-sharing firm Mobike," CNBC, *https://www.cnbc.com/2018/04/04/meituan-dianping-acquires-bike-sharing-firm-mobike.html*.

29. "AlibabaXE "Alibaba" Takes Control of Ele.me, at $9.5 Billion Value," Shelly Banjo et al., *https://www.bloomberg.com/news/articles/2018-04-02/alibaba-buys-ele-me-in-deal-that-implies-9-5b-enterprise-value*.

30. *https://finplusgroup.com/*.

31. Finplus, *http://www.finplus.me/*.

32. "White paper: China internet statistic," *https://www.chinainternetwatch.com/whitepaper/china-internet-statistics/*.

33. *https://www.chinainternetwatch.com/12815/mobile-payment-2014/*.

34. "China makes historic move to open market for financial firms," Bloomberg News, *https://www.bloomberg.com/news/articles/2017-11-10/china-to-allow-foreign-firms-to-own-51-of-securities-ventures*.

35. "Alibaba doubles down on Lazada with fresh US$2 B investment and CEO," Jon Russel, *https://techcrunch.com/2018/03/18/alibaba-doubles-down-on-lazada/*.

36. "Alibaba to invest US$177 m in India's Paytm," Simon Mundy, *https://www.ft.com/content/5cbb69bf-a2ae-3288-8500-27656a12067b*.

37. "AXA, AlibabaXE "Alibaba" and Ant Financial Services announce global strategic partnership," *https://group.axa.com/en/newsroom/press-releases/axa-alibaba-ant-financial-services-announce-global-strategic-partnership*.

38. *https://home.kpmg/xx/en/home/insights/2019/11/2019-fintech100-leading-global-fintech-innovators-fs.html*.

39. *https://www.statista.com/statistics/255778/number-of-active-wechat-messenger-accounts/*.

40. "Tencent Cloud to Open Five More Overseas Data Centers in 2017," *https://www.prnewswire.com/news-releases/tencent-cloud-to-open-five-more-overseas-data-centers-in-2017-300445849.html*.

41. "Guess Who's King of Cloud Revenue Growth? It's Not Amazon XE "Amazon" or Microsoft," Barb Darrow, *http://fortune.com/2017/09/27/cloud-computing-revenue-growth/*.

42. "China's JD.com isn't in a rush to list its finance arm," Christine Tan, et al., *https://www.cnbc.com/2017/09/03/jd-com-ceo-richard-liu-on-a-future-jd-finance-ipo-and-beating-alibaba.html*.

43. *http://wecashgroup.com/*.

44. "Wecash Completes US$80 Million Series C Financing Led by China Merchants Group, Forebright Capital and SIG Ventures," *https://www.prnewswire.com/news-releases/wecash-completes-us80-million-series-c-financing-led-by-china-merchants-group-forebright-capital-and-sig-ventures-300443456.html*.

45. "Foxconn reveals plan for blockchain supply chain domination," Michael del Castillo, *https://www.coindesk.com/foxconn-wants-take-global-supply-chain-blockchain/*.

46. *www.fnconn.com*.

47. "FintechXE "Fintech" vs Techfin," Kunal Patel, *https://www.finextra.com/blogposting/14499/fintech-vs-techfin*.

48. "AlibabaXE "Alibaba" scouting locations for a second European data center," Misha Savic, *https://www.bloomberg.com/news/articles/2017-09-28/alibaba-is-scouting-locations-for-a-second-european-datacenter*.

49. "AlibabaXE "Alibaba" cloud is opening its first data center in India," Jon Russell, *https://techcrunch.com/2017/12/20/alibaba-cloud-india/*.

50. "China's AlibabaXE "Alibaba" opens Silicon Valley data center," Laura Luo, *http://www.datacenterdynamics.com/content-tracks/colo-cloud/chinas-alibaba-opens-silicon-valley-data-center/93479.fullarticle*.

51. *https://aws.amazon.com/compliance/data-center/*.

52. *https://augur.net/*.

53. *http://www.zyen.com*.

# CHAPTER 8

# TRADING AND LENDING

## 8.1 SECURITY TRADING

The potential for improved efficiency in trade settlement makes a strong use case for blockchain in security trading. When executed peer-to-peer, trade confirmations become almost instantaneous without the need for third-party clearance. This means intermediaries such as the clearing house, auditors, and custodians can be removed from the process.

Numerous stock and commodity exchanges are prototyping blockchain applications for the services they offer, including the ASX (Australian Securities Exchange), the Deutsche Börse (Frankfurt's stock exchange), and the JPX (Japan Exchange Group). The first mover in the area is Nasdaq's Linq, a platform for private market trading (typically between pre-IPO startups and investors). In a partnership with the blockchain tech company Chain, Linq announced the completion of its first security trading as early as 2015.

More recently, NASDAQ announced a blockchain project for proxy voting on the Estonian Stock Market. The Australian Securities Exchange (ASX) has been testing blockchain in equity trade settlement and clearing. Nonetheless, Australia's equity market being relatively small and unsophisticated, blockchain adoption is more straightforward. Markets such as NASDAQ must take a more cautious approach.

A number of financial institutions are participating in working groups as a means to develop blockchain further. An example of such a group is the R3 Consortium, which comprises banks looking to adopt blockchain technology for financial services. Several high-profile asset managers are exploring blockchain as a mechanism to speed up transactions in illiquid assets.

The same Straight-Through-Processing (STP) concept applied to credit card processes applies to security trading as well. Blockchain has the potential to disrupt capital markets. Potentially, it could save between $15 billion and $20 billion by 2022 by streamlining cross-border payments, securities trading, and regulatory compliance.

There are some challenges to overcome before this can be realized. It will require standards and regulations agreed on by the industry, regulators, and governments. The scale of this challenge is huge. However, once the challenges are overcome, blockchain technology has the potential to impact markets globally, including emerging economies which are in the early stages of developing their market infrastructures.

For the security trading application, the system must be capable of recording transactions in an immutable ledger where transactions are signed cryptographically and are impossible to forge. Blockchain technology can meet this requirement. Domus Tower Blockchain,[1] developed by a startup in San Francisco, is intended for applications such as securities trading.[2]

Domus Tower Blockchain can process over 1 million transactions per second on Amazon's Web Services, with the potential to scale to more than 10 million transactions per second. Data are stored in a *Merkle Directional Acyclic Graph* (Merkle DAG), a variation of DAG, whose data structure is similar to Merkle tree. The data transmitted to the blockchain are digitally signed and verified before being written to a block. Its advantages over the traditional security trading platforms are that it is faster and more secure.

As a blockchain technology platform, Domus Tower provides an immutable, permanent record of time-stamped transactions. All transactions are audited cryptographically in real time with a Merkle root. Every transaction is signed in real-time with a public/private key signature that is impossible to forge. The append-only, time-stamped structure of a blockchain makes it much easier to scale. These qualities allow the Domus Tower platform to excel over the traditional database security trading systems, while still working in the same frame as the securities industry today, where parties know each other and trust data feeds. It also excels over the Permissionless blockchain platforms, which face scaling and transaction speed problems.

Domus Tower Blockchain can create linked blockchains where the assets of an account on one blockchain must match the liabilities on the account of another blockchain. It is a centralized, Permissioned blockchain.

All transactions in the Domus Blockchain require a digital signature. The cryptographic digital signature is verified before the data is written to a block. The "Merkle root" guarantees an immutable history of all signed data stored in all the prior blocks of the entire Merkle graph. Since the Domus Blockchain is a Permissioned blockchain, it does not use PoW/PoS or Byzantine Fault Tolerance. It operates in an environment where participants trust each other. Only the agents who have access to the blockchain can write transactions to that chain.

Domus Blockchain performs a series of micro-services, which perform a specific task. Micro-services operate on simple data-driven interfaces. The major components include a "signature verifier," "transaction batcher," "block maker," and a "client." The Domus Blockchain achieves high scalability. It does not use a vote-based approach to writing transaction data.

## 8.2 COMMODITY TRADING

Today, commodities are traded in the future exchanges using future contracts. Buyers promise to buy tons of coffee, for example, by signing a future contract with the supplier for the future delivery of a certain lock-in price. However, from the signing of the contract to the actual delivery, many things can change.

Trading commodities using blockchain smart contracts can have all the benefits of blockchain advantages. Mercuria, the Swiss-based commodities giant with an annual turnover of $91 billion, successfully tested an oil trade using blockchain technology.[3]

Using blockchain to trade commodities can save billions of dollars a year in commodities trading by eliminating paper documents and moving to a digital equivalent with blockchain. However, the implementation may require a drastic change in the way that commodity trading is conducted.

There is more than one approach to commodity trade using blockchain technology. The most direct approach is to use smart contracts, which still settle the trades in the fiat currencies. A more radical approach is to digitize the commodity assets. For example, a certain number of tokens can be the digital equivalent of one ton of coffee of a certain quality. These tokens represent the ownership of one ton of coffee of this quality, and they can be used to redeem the coffee. They can trade for other cryptocurrencies or fiat currencies.

ACChain has digitized Pu-erh tea and has plans to digitize the world's grain supply.[4] For such digitization to happen, IoT must be a mature technology. We will illustrate by an example of soybean transaction: Brazil ships 100 tons of soybean to China. When the shipment arrives at the port of destination, the IoT with sensors will first verify the tonnage, moisture content, and color of the soybean to ensure all the physical parameters are within the specifications of the smart contract. If all the conditions meet the contract terms, the smart contract will trigger the payment event. It is not up to the buyer to accept or not accept the merchandise. Under certain unsatisfied conditions specified in the contract, the smart contract will automatically apply a discount to the price of the soybean. In the worst case, the smart contract will reject the shipment, and will not trigger the payment. Likewise, smart contracts for any commodity – ore, petroleum, wheat, rice, fruit, etc. can apply similar criteria.

It is easy to establish the specifications for degradable products, such as fruits and fresh produce for shipment, so that if there is a refrigeration problem during the shipment, the smart contract of shipping will apply a certain penalty to the shipper.

When smart contracts using blockchain for commodity trading become prevalent, they can be easily standardized. These predefined smart contracts are executed by all the relevant counterparties with the conditions for execution clearly spelled out.

During contract execution, the events trigger actions such as transactions initiated, information delivered, etc. For the digital assets on the chain, the smart contract can settle the account atomically, in other words, as agreed by all parties. To settle the assets off the chain, the smart contract needs to include off-chain settlement instructions. Smart contracts guarantee a very specific set of outcomes. Energy and commodity trading on blockchain will drastically change the way trading is performed and will result in a great saving in the transactions in billions of dollars.[5]

## 8.3    ENERGY TRADING

Energy is a special form of commodity, and so is energy trading, especially the trading of electricity. With the wider use of renewable and clean energy, such as rooftop solar energy installations, micro-generation of electricity is becoming a huge trend in the power generation business. Households are not only consumers but they also become small energy suppliers. However, household energy supply is erratic depending on the weather and consumption amount. It is very difficult to balance the supply and demand in each unit of the micro-generation. In such a blockchain-based platform, energy is treated as an asset. This is why blockchain technology is ideal to manage such a situation.

Currently, the surplus energy generated by households is sold back to the grid at a much lower price than that of electricity from the grid. The application of blockchain technology to the micro-generation of energy becomes a great equalizer. Smart meters register electricity produced and consumed in the blockchain. It then allows for consumption of the surplus energy in the neighboring household, which pays to the original producing household. The credits can be redeemed against the grid for future energy use. In this way, the surplus energy is consumed near the household that produces energy, without the need to travel a great distance.

The blockchain enforces these contracts in real time automatically and without supervision, allowing creation of a utility market with minimal effort. It is foreseeable that communities can install a small-scale public power generation utility in the neighborhood and become self-sufficient in energy consumption. It can cut down transmission loss dramatically.

Not only can the large-scale application of blockchain smart contracts in the micro-generation of energy provide the households with better energy selling price but will also avoid long-distance energy transmission, smooth out the energy utilization across the grid, and encourage the installation of localized micro-generations. In a sense, for the first time since the invention of the large-scale electric power plant, electricity generation can be decentralized.

The blockchain allows the purchase and sale of electricity according to users' personal preferences and needs. By doing so, it provides monetary benefits by optimizing for the most favorable energy transactions at any given time, and it increases independence from the grid in case of power supply issues. In order to develop and enable P2P trading of electricity, micro-generated electricity needs to be verified, with the generation time and the amount recorded. This is to monetize the energy as the price of electricity varies over time based on supply and demand. The monetization is done using tokens, which can be traded and audited in a blockchain.

The term "P2P trading of electricity" may be misleading. Because of the small amounts of surplus electricity generated by domestic suppliers is intermittent, instead of sourcing electricity from a single household, consumers will have to buy and sell electricity across an open market, swapping their energy supplier on a minute-by-minute basis. Households can buy electricity based on their own personal preference, such as clean energy, nuclear, or best price. Essentially, it is a bazaar of the energy market on the grid.

In the U.S., the software foundry company ConsenSys is developing a range of applications for the electricity market. One of their projects, called the Transactive Grid,[6,7] is in partnership with a distributed energy outfit, LO3.[8] The project uses Ethereum smart contracts to automate the monitoring and redistribution of micro-grid energy. Ethereum-based smart contracts automatically redistribute the energy.

Likewise in Europe, 26 European energy trading firms jointly conducted P2P trading in the wholesale energy market on a platform called Enerchain. A German blockchain technology company Ponton developed the platform.[9] This platform enables traders to buy and sell directly without brokerage and exchange. However, the blockchain-based energy trading is not limited to P2P. It can be B2B as well. Ponton's Enerchain platform also works for B2B.

The large power grid operators are also looking into the potential for blockchain technology to simplify the power grid management processes. The complex task of electricity distribution is managed by many specialized organizations. A Transmission System Operator balances the energy to keep the grid load and frequency stable. A Distribution System Operator monitors the loading on the grid and keeps it stable at the local level. They need to coordinate any supply and demand imbalance and disruption, such as outages, congestion, as well as micro-generation in the local grid. There are also aggregators who pool many power plants to balance the power in the grid, to make sure that the flow is continuous and constant. Ponton has also developed a blockchain technology-based platform for real-time grid management, called Gridchain, which is ready for field-testing.[10]

## 8.4  ALTERNATIVE TRADING SYSTEM

Any platform matching buy-and-sell orders but not regulated as an exchange is an *Alternative Trading System (ATS)*. It is not new but exists in many different forms: a multilateral trading facility, electronic communication network, cross-network, or call network. While the exchanges trade security, commodity, foreign exchange, and financial derivative products, most ATSs are trading other products. Usually, the ATS is registered as broker–dealer and focuses on finding buyers for the sellers and vice versa to conduct transactions. It does not set rules governing the conduct of trading. However, it does play an important role in providing an alternative means for liquidity. This is especially true for the securities not qualified for stock exchange listing, or the unlisted ADRs.

Theoretically, ATS involves willing parties of buyers and sellers. The rules of public trading do not apply. Yet, the boundary between the ATS and the exchange is blurry. It can happen that institutional investors use an ATS to find counterparties for transactions of the equity, which is on public stock exchanges. Alternatively, a small group of selected investors, e.g. banks, mutual funds, private equity, and pension funds, participate in the purchase of a large block of securities in a private placement by invitation. A private placement may be intended to conceal trading from public view since ATS transactions do not appear in the order books of the national exchange. Since such a trade involves publicly traded security or assets, it may violate public interest. Cryptocurrency trading is also an example of ATS trading. Therefore, regulators have recently stepped up enforcement actions against alternative trading systems. The SEC introduced Regulation ATS in 1998 to protect investors and resolve any concerns arising from alternative trading systems.

With the advancement of blockchain technology, more and more trading happens outside of exchanges. ATS growth becomes unstoppable. The Delaware-based Delaware Board of Trade Holdings (DBOT) specializing in the blockchain trading platform is the first company to seize the opportunity to develop the technology for ATS. DBOT became the first and the only blockchain-based ATS fully licensed by the SEC. The Seven Stars Cloud Group (SSC), a Chinese-based Artificial Intelligence and Blockchain-Powered Fintech Company for the delivery of digital asset securitization solutions, acquired a controlling ownership stake in DBOT in 2017.[11]

DBOT's technology will be used to power the SSC's blockchain-based NextGen X platform, which focuses on the trading of financial products including ETFs backed by digital assets that can be tokenized and settled (including digital currency options) via "plug and play" and the blockchain-based *Initial Exchange Offerings* (IEO) network.[12] Its plug and play nature allows it to be adapted to different ATSs.

IEO is a term newly invented by SSC to differentiate the fact that the offering to be traded is backed by physical and digital assets rather than the promise of a plan. SSC's NextGen X will apply blockchain and artificial intelligence to create a "hybrid solution" for supply chain finance, risk management, and asset-backed digital securitization. By creating "financial superintelligence," it will be able to rate financial risk and price assets before monetizing into issuance and trading through the IEO. SSC plans to establish ATSs in the U.S., UK, Germany, China, Korea, Africa, Singapore, the UAE, and Japan, and will expand issuance and trading volume via 30 targeted local and regional exchanges and ATSs.

## 8.5    PEER-TO-PEER LENDING

ROSCA stands for Rotating Savings and Credit Association. It is a popular type of P2P lending. This traditional form of P2P lending has been practiced by billions of people all over the world, dating back to ancient time.[13]

A ROSCA is organized by a group of trusted parties, or members, who agree to contribute a fixed amount of money at a fixed interval, called "round." At the end of each round, the pot contains the sum of everyone's contribution. Members bid on this amount in a reverse auction manner, where the lowest bid wins. The winning bidder then receives his bid. The remaining will be split equally among all of the participants as a form of interest payment. If a bidder's desire to get the money is strong, he will have to enter a lower bid to ensure that he would win. In effect, he is paying higher interest.

For example, a ROSCA consists of 10 members; each member contributes $1,000 to the pool. Every month, there is a pot of $10,000. In each round, there is only one winner. The winner of the bid is by the lowest offer. For example, the winning bid is $9,000. The winner then borrows $9,000. The remaining $1,000 is returned to each member in equal share as a form of interest. Since the winner has contributed $1,000 ten times in the last 10 rounds, he is essentially paying $1,000 interest to borrow $9,000.

Each user is guaranteed to win one round in turn. A winner will have the next opportunity to bid only after all the other members receive their winning bid once. This ensures a Pareto optimal outcome, where everyone is better off as they would have been had they saved the money alone.

ROSCAs are seeing growing popularity in the U.S., primarily within immigrant populations. It is also becoming popular in places where informal credit is the norm, such as in China. Community systems worldwide are another reason why blockchain is great for leveraging reciprocal finance.

The traditional ROSCA requires trust. The scope of ROSCA is limited to a small group of people who know each other and trust each other to be participants. Therefore, its scope is limited. With the arrival of blockchain technology, suddenly, people find that the ROSCA scheme can be extended far beyond the familiar circle because trust is no longer an issue. Blockchain provides a perfect platform for ROSCA application.

ROSCAs can be a successful supplement to regular financial services — another tool in the toolbox. Reciprocal aid is a perfect fit for blockchain technology, providing people around the world access to more advanced financial tools. Most of all, ROSCA is a self-financing model. All the profits are distributed to the participants. The idea for ROSCA is to have a community of like-minded people with financial goals.

Anyone can start a ROSCA with the ROSCA blockchain application, and set rules: the number of maximum participants, the time period of the round, and the amount of contribution. It can also be dissolved when all the participants receive the bid.

All kinds of platforms with the ROSCA concept, like eMoneyPool, Monk, Puddle, Moneyfellows, ROSCA Finance, Partnerhand, StepLadder, WeTrust, etc. are springing up. One of the most successful platforms, WeTrust raised $6.5M market capital in an ICO in April 2017. Its market capitalization tripled within ten days of coin issuance. As a peer-to-peer financing system, the platform has to be Permissionless.

The rapidly growing market of P2P lending is loosely regulated, and plagued by fraud and defaults. The worst P2P lending fraud happened in China 2014-2015,[14] when 900,000 investors lost over $7.6 billion in a Ponzi P2P lending scheme of Ezubao. As a result, people lost confidence in P2P lending. Half a year after the exposure of the fraud, nearly one-third of all online lending companies in China were in financial trouble and 40% of them (1,600 P2P lenders) exited the market by April 2016. That left the larger, more established online lenders to dominate the largest online lending marketplace in the world.

There are also other types of P2P lending. Using a different business model, China Rapid Finance (CRF) is one of China's largest consumer lending marketplaces in terms of the total number of loans granted. Much like the e-commerce marketplace, where the platform operator offers online space for buyers, CRF operates the marketplace without taking credit risk by using machine learning and proprietary technology to select qualified borrowers. For first-time borrowers, the cap of the loan amount is limited. After the customers establish their credentials, the cap of the loan amount increases. Its board of directors includes reputable global financial executives with extensive experience.[15]

The China Banking Regulatory Commission (CBRC) newly proposed restrictions for banks which would pave the way for P2P lenders to enter the wealth management market and deliver financial advice in an innovative way.

The Chinese P2P market cooled down and the surviving P2P lenders sought to collaborate with banks to restore their reputation and re-establish their credibility, even though they were not involved in the scam. For example, a collaboration between *Dianrong.com* and the regional Bank of Suzhou set up a P2P loans platform targeting SMEs. The Shanghai-based P2P lender China Rapid Finance (CRF) collaborates with China Construction Bank to create a P2P platform providing investors access to CRF's P2P offerings via the bank. Other collaborations are between P2P lenders, such as Jimubox, RenRenDai, Minshengyidai, and China Minsheng Bank for the bank to manage and safeguard investors' funds. Even CreditEase, a leading Beijing-based fintech conglomerate with a nationwide network in 255 cities in China, made a similar arrangement with China CITIC Bank.[16]

Fintech experts believe that artificial intelligence and blockchain technology can prevent fraud. It prompted many P2P lenders to seek blockchain solutions. To prevent the scam from happening again, the Chinese central bank PBOC also introduced new regulations to oversee P2P lending and online payments in China, such as the imposed credit limits, requirement of a principal guaranteed by the platform, etc.

The Ezubao event is a temporary setback for P2P lending. New regulations and platforms with new technologies are gradually restoring consumer confidence in P2P lending. Once the confidence returns, the market is expected to grow at an annual rate of 50% again, because there is an undeniable demand.

Non-banks, which appeared on the scene in the last decade due to the flourishing e-commerce, have an upper hand in China, especially when it comes to competitiveness in offerings, digital functionality, experience, quality, innovation, and even trust levels. For these reasons, SMEs and retail consumers are increasingly turning to the non-traditional lenders for financial services.

## 8.6   ONLINE LENDING

The use of Fintech in lending spreads beyond P2P lending, microlending, and SME lending. Now, banks are quickly adapting the same technology for their traditional loan service, to cut down the cost, reduce the risk, and improve efficiency. One prime example is the German fintech company Kreditech.

Kreditech uses AI to analyze Big Data and calculate an individual's credit score. The data it uses to determine a loan applicant's creditworthiness are essentially the digital footprint of the loan applicant. Such data include location information, social networking information, banking data, hardware data, online shopping behavior, general online behavior, etc. The customer's location information, such as shopping at upscale department stores vs. thrift stores, the types of restaurants frequented, etc., reveals a lot about their shopping habit and economic status. Likewise, is true for hardware data, e.g. iPhone vs. an unbranded phone, the make and model of car they drive .

Another example is CreditEase in China. CreditEase brings a brand new concept to the P2P lending industry. CreditEase matches borrowers and lenders online. The lenders are not banks or financial institutions, but individuals who have money to lend. It is like an auction market for loans. Once the conditions match, the lender grants the loan to the borrower, and the borrower repays the lender in monthly instalments with interest. Most often, the lender's money is disbursed to many borrowers, and the borrower gets a loan from multiple lenders. Such a diversification reduces the risk. If the borrower misses a payment, CreditEase will pay the lender and try to collect from the borrower. Therefore, CreditEase, and not the lender, carries the default risk. CreditEase plays the role of a matchmaker and guarantor of the loan. In fact, CreditEase operates like a bank while getting money from individual investors and lending it to borrowers.

The lender commits funds, which can be automatically allocated among approved borrowers or the borrowers of his choice. The lender, also known as an investor in the platform, can choose to enroll in the automated investing option, which automatically reinvests investors' funds when he receives payments from the borrower. Alternatively, the lender can select lending opportunities to the approved borrowers by the lender himself. Furthermore, the investor's fund is not locked to its maturity. He has the option to sell his loan in the company-operated secondary loan market at any time. This liquidity offers investors the opportunity to enter and exit their investments without waiting until maturity.

Chinese fintech firms are increasingly looking for technology solutions to enhance security and to reduce risk. In March 2017, CreditEase launched an Ethereum- based blockchain service called Blockworm to enhance its security.[17] It is expected that when the Social Credit System (SCS) is deployed, P2P lending can receive another boost in consumers' confidence.

## 8.7 MICROLENDING AND SME LENDING

Fintech creates opportunity for microlending and lending to SMEs. Microlending provides the service of lending small amounts of money, not unlike credit cards. SME lending caters to small businesses. Both types of lending are avoided by traditional financial institutions such as banks, because the risk-to-reward ratio is high. Banks demand stringent qualification and require an extensive and tedious approval process. SMEs, which lack qualified collateral and track records of credit repayment, receive only 20-25% of bank-disbursed loans. Yet they have generated 60% of the GDP and 80% of urban employment, and have contributed to 50% of fiscal and tax revenues in China. SMEs also suffer from asymmetric information, with limited transparency in their financial positions and credit rating assessments. Even if they do secure bank loans, the interest rates are much higher than that of large corporations, based on the risk concerns. Likewise, retail customers also receive lower priority in China's banks. This provides a fertile ground for the growth of the non-bank-operated online lending market. About 160 million people in China took out $180 billion in online loans in 2016. There are many companies operating in the niche markets. For example, Daikuan, an online financing fintech company, which raised $2 billion in 2017, offers online loans to buyers of second-hand cars.

Fintech fill the voids of the bank's lending service. Using fintech, the approval process for such lending is extremely fast, made possible by using personal financial data which are online or in the Big Data. Different from the traditional credit data used by banks, such as credit score, tax documents, bank and/or income statements, records of ownership of assets, etc., the data collected by microlending services are the customers' actual spending data.

Peak Fintech Group is a Canadian fintech company having a major business in China. It caters to the huge market of more than 100 million small businesses in China having a difficult time getting access to credit from banks and traditional lending institutions.

Peak Fintech Group uses Artificial Intelligence analytics to help lenders eliminate the risks associated with lending to small and micro businesses. Since AI requires data, PFG's strategy is to offer its solutions to the lending institutions, which have huge data on their customers. As of 2020, Peak has partnered with 50 lending institutions and 53,000 loan broker reps, whose customers' data become part of PFG's Big Data.

The lending institutions like the service, because PFG's service not only reduces the risk of lending, but also eliminates their labor-intensive work to quality the potential loan customers, cutting the cost. PFG's AI software platform is an ecosystem that brings together lenders, brokers, SMEs, data providers, and automated risk management capabilities. PFG has demonstrated that its AI Analytics-generated lending has a default rate of about 2%, within the same range as commercial and industrial loans. These services allow banks and lenders to safely tap into the huge previously untapped market, but deemed as "too risky." This also allows the small-time borrowers to borrow at a more reasonable interest rate. Meanwhile, there is no need to search for loan customers anymore, as Peak Fintech Group brings ideal clients to them. On the other hand, SMEs get loans they would otherwise not get. In 2018, PFG generated $15 billion in loan requests.

Recently in December 2020, Peak Fintech Group entered into a partnership with e-commerce giant Pinduoduo, the largest interactive e-commerce platform in the world and the second largest online marketplace in China. Such partnership allows Peak Fintech to bring credit solutions to Pinduoduo's 5.6 million online stores and over 600 million active users. It makes the already big AI Big Data even bigger and hence more powerful.

Other microlending and SME lending players in China who are market leaders are Lufax of Ping An Insurance, Yirendai of CreditEase, Rendai, Zhai Cai Bao of Alibaba and Dianrong. The risk for these lenders without the leverage of the e-commerce platform is higher; therefore, the interest rates are also higher. However, their service is open to anyone, not limited to supply chain participants. Lufax had more than 23.3 million users by June 2016, doubled in one year.

The SMEs which take part in the e-commerce supply chain can get loans from the e-commerce company, which lends to SMEs by leveraging SME's merchandise on its platform. There is no risk to them because once the SME products are sold on their platforms they are the ones who receive customer payments. The key participants include Ant Financial and Alibaba's MyBank, WeChat's WeBank, *JD.com's* JD Finance, and GOME Electrical Appliances.

## REFERENCES

1. *http://domustower.com/*.

2. "Domus Tower Blockchain", Rhett Creightoon, *http://www.domustower.com/domus-tower-blockchain-mar-22.pdf*.

3. "Mercuria introduces blockchain to oil trade with ING, SocGen," Dmitry Zhdannikov, Reuters, *https://www.reuters.com/article/us-davos-meeting-mercuria/mercuria-introduces-blockchain-to-oil-trade-with-ing-socgen-idUSKBN1531DJ*.

4. *https://www.acchain.org/en/*.

5. "Overview of blockchain for energy and commodity trading," Ernst & Young LLP, *http://www.ey.com/Publication/vwLUAssets/ey-overview-of-blockchain-for-energy-and-commodity-trading/$FILE/ey-overview-of-blockchain-for-energy-and-commodity-trading.pdf*.

6. "P2P energy transaction and control," *https://www.slideshare.net/John-Lilic/transactive-grid*.

7. "Enerchain: A Decentralized Market on the BlockchainXE "Blockchain" for Energy Wholesalers," Morgen Peck, *https://spectrum.ieee.org/energywise/energy/the-smarter-grid/enerchain-a-decentralized-market-on-the-blockchain-for-energy-wholesalers*.

8. *https://lo3energy.com/*.

9. "Enerchain P2P trading project," *https://enerchain.ponton.de/index.php/21-enerchain-p2p-trading-project*.

10. "Gridchain – blockchain based process integration for the smart grids of the future," *https://enerchain.ponton.de/index.php/16-gridchain-blockchain-based-process-integration-for-the-smart-grids-of-the-future.*

11. "Seven Stars Cloud Announces 27% Purchase of Delaware Board of Trade Holdings, Inc.," *https://www.prnewswire.com/news-releases/seven-stars-cloud-announces-27-purchase-of-delaware-board-of-trade-holdings-inc-dbot-300573871.html.*

12. "Seven Stars Cloud Announces 27% Purchase of Delaware Board of Trade Holdings, Inc. (DBOT)," *The NY Times, http://markets.on.nytimes.com/research/stocks/news/press_release.asp?docTag=201712200914PR_NEWS_USPRX____NY74656&feedID=600&press_symbol=46908.*

13. "Indigenous savings & credit societies in the developing world," F.J.A. Bouman, Rural Financial Markets in the Developing World Bank, Washington, 1983.

14. "Ezubao," *https://en.wikipedia.org/wiki/Ezubao.*

15. China Rapid Finance website, *http://stage.investorroom.com/chinarapidfinance/index.php?s=118.*

16. *http://english.creditease.cn/index.html.*

17. "FinTech CreditEase Launches EthereumXE "Ethereum"-based BlockchainXE "Blockchain" Service," Cindy23, *http://news.8btc.com/fintech-creditease-launches-ethereum-based-blockchain-service.*

# CHAPTER 9

# RENEWED INDUSTRIES

In the digital economy, not only will many new industries be created, but most of the existing industries will be transformed dramatically. In this chapter, we will discuss how the digital technologies will transform some traditional industries.

## 9.1 WEALTH MANAGEMENT

The wealth management industry is huge and is one of the most important financial service industries. According to Ernst & Young,[1] the global net investable assets will be $70 trillion dollars by 2021. This is probably one of the biggest markets in the world. Wealth management companies are reinventing themselves to prepare for the digital economy. Wealth managers now face the challenge of adapting to a market environment, or risk becoming obsolete. New industry structures are emerging and early adapters will enjoy profitable future growth opportunities. Technologies change the cost structures, client requirement, capital flow, regulatory requirement, and financial product offering, such as AI-powered robo-advice, etc.

Big Data and AI have already made inroads into wealth management services. AI-powered products and applications have gradually replaced the traditional ones to provide personalized service to customers. Robots offer investment advisory service in the assessment of individual investors' risk tolerance, profit goals, and other preferences and needs, using machine learning to optimize the portfolio. AI-powered models also offer users advice tailored to the dynamics of the market, with timely recommendations.

The fees for robot investment advisory services are lower than for the traditional investment advisory. The robot is devoid of human emotions, and strict implementation of the strategy removes an important factor of uncertainty in the investment. Robot investment advisory services also can absorb, process and digest huge quantities of data, which humans cannot. More asset management companies now use the robot advisor to provide services to their customers.

Many start-up companies, such as Wealthfront,[2] Betterment,[3] Personal Capital[4], Motif Investing, FutureAdvisor, Hedgeable, and Nutmeg are providing robot investment advisory services. The demand for such a service is huge.

As AI-powered investment advice is gaining popularity, not only investment startups, but traditional brokerage houses are also offering such services. Charles Schwab offers the Schwab Intelligent Portfolio service.[5] Based on the investor's answers to a short set of questions, Schwab Intelligent Portfolio selects from among the 53 low-cost professionally selected exchange-traded funds (ETFs) to create a diversified portfolio designed to meet each investor's specific goal. Merrill Edge of the Bank of America also offers a similar service.

This is also true in Europe. Companies like Wealth Horizon, InvestYourWay, and Swanest in the UK, MoneyFarm in Italy, Vaamo and Owlhub in Germany, and Moneyvane in Swissland, all offer intelligent investment services.

In China, there are three types of intelligent wealth management products: the third-party intelligent investment platform, intelligent products offered by the traditional financial institutions, and Internet wealth management applications. These products include A-share investment advisors, wealth management platforms, etc. Investment vehicles include overseas ETF, A shares, bonds, funds, and so on.

Until now, there has been a lack of investment choices for the Chinese investors. Many of them choose to park their money in real estate. This has driven up the housing price and caused a real estate bubble. Wealth Management (WM) tries to lure people away from real estate investment and seems be successful. The value of wealth management products (WMPs) expanded by 56% to $3.5 trillion in 2015. The online fund management app linked to payment platforms offers ease of access. The investment opportunity is never more than a few clicks away on the smartphone.

The primary participants are Yu'e Bao of Ant Financial, LiCaiTong (Tencent), and Baifu (Baidu). Alibaba's Yu'e Bao is one of the world's top money market funds, with $170 billion in assets in 2017.[6] Licaitong is Tencent's wealth management platform, accessible via WeChat wallet and QQ wallet. It provides Tencent users with quality investment selections in a transparent and user-friendly investment environment. Most of these products offer a yearly return of 4.5 to 5.2% depending on the investment duration and an amount up to $1.5 million. In 2016, the total transaction amount reached $300 billion. China also houses several of the largest mutual funds, such as Yu'e Bao and Tencent's Licaitong.

Wealth management is a rapidly growing market. So far, RoboAdvisor programs are AI powered. Blockchain has not been used. It is conceivable that when the digital currencies are used in trading, or when trading across national boundaries, blockchain-powered products will also be offered.

Online stock and mutual fund trading is another big market. Players include Ant Financial (Alibaba), LiCaiTong (Tencent), Baifa (Baidu), Wacai, Tongbanjie, JD Finance (*JD.com*), and other online brokerage, social network, and information portals, such as Snowball Finance, Xianrenzhang, Yiqiniu, Tiger Broker (backed by China's smartphone maker Xiaomi), and Futu Securities (funded by Tencent). All of them have mobile apps for stock and mutual fund trading. By mid-2016, Yu'e Bao had more than 295 million customers, making it one of the largest global consumer funds.

Most of the Chinese P2P lenders such as RenRenDai and CreditEase are also WM service providers. With their access to massive social and analytical data around customers' creditworthiness and purchasing trends, these fintech firms have opportunities to build advanced finance platforms to support elevated expectations from increasingly demanding investors.

In mid-2016, WM firms introduced a simplified investment advice service using robo-advisors through sophisticated automated online platforms incorporating Big Data and artificial intelligence. The robo-advisor uses modern portfolio theory, Big Data algorithms, XUANJI's asset allocation solution, quantitative modeling, and program trading using machine learning. The result is a substantial lowering of costs to provide universal access to entry-level, affordable, yet customized online financial advisory services.

One of the top robo-advisory providers is CreditEase, which launched its robo-advisory product ToumiRA to provide cost-effective access to international WMPs for Chinese retail investors, using trading algorithms to match investor risk preferences and objectives to build their optimal portfolio. Another robo-advisory platform, Xuanji, launched by PINTEC, provides intelligent investment advice to retail investors with the ability to customize and automatically rebalance a global portfolio.[7] In addition, PINTEC also offers a B2B version for brokers, independent financial advisors, and financial institutions. Both versions can trade USD ETFs and RMB denominated Chinese mutual funds.

Others offering machine-assisted investment advisory include Baidu Gupiao, PingAn One, MiCai and Clipper Advisor. Robo-advisory could well reshape the future of China's WM business. To survive such a competitive market, they will need a breadth and depth of asset offerings, portfolio allocation, and technological superiority in Big Data analytics and machine learning.

Many Chinese fintech companies also form alliances to leverage each other's strength in technology, marketing, or database. For example, China Ledger Alliance, comprising regional exchanges, created an open source blockchain protocol to support IoT development. Financial blockchain Shenzhen Consortium, including members such as Ping An Insurance, a member of the global consortium R3 and Tencent, collaborates on research and group-wide blockchain projects, with a focus on capital markets technology, securities exchange, trading platforms, banking, and life insurance. It aims to create a securities trading platform prototype and develop credit, digital asset registry, and invoice management services.

The Qianhai International Blockchain Ecosphere Alliance aims to establish an efficient ecosystem for developing blockchain technology and its applications. The Alliance includes the world's leading global technology companies such as Microsoft, IBM, and Hong Kong's Applied Science and Technology Research Institute (ASTRI). It hopes to accelerate the commercialization of blockchain R&D and promote its application to support China's social and economic development.

Aggressive Chinese tech firms equipped with skilled IT infrastructure and application development are looking to go global. They are investing in global technology hubs by penetrating new product markets overseas to diversify revenue streams and reduce domestic reliance. Baidu, Alibaba, and Tencent are expanding to serve expats and outbound Chinese travelers abroad, while seeking out new customers in emerging economies from Africa to South and Southeast Asia. They are particularly interested in the future possibilities of new O2O revenue streams. For example, Alibaba currently has more than

86% of revenues from China but aims to generate half of all sales from over-seas. The group is developing an international ecosystem that encompasses targeted marketing, logistics, payment services, and cloud computing.

Their strategy is to achieve globalization via international acquisitions and expansion. For instance, its AliExpress e-commerce platform is already doing brisk business in markets such as Russia and Brazil. Alibaba made its largest international investment to-date in April 2016 with $1 billion for the control of Lazada Group, Southeast Asia's largest clothing and electronics portal. In the summer of 2017, it invested an additional $1 billion and in March 2018, it has doubled down on Lazada with additional $2 billion investment with a total investment of $4 billion.[8] To further increase exposure into Southeast Asia, Ant Financial took a stake in Ascend Money, a Thai provider of online payment.

In 2015, Ant Financial ventured into India with a $680 million purchase for about 40% of Paytm, India's largest mobile commerce platform with 122 million users and 23 million mobile wallet users, and another $100 million for the online marketplace Snapdeal. In 2017, Alibaba invested an additional $177 million in Paytm E-commerce, a spinoff of Paytm.[9] These investments gave Alibaba a payments banking license in India and an immediate foothold in a country with an exponential growth in the online payment industry, with a CAGR of 50% from 2007-2014.

To expand the business, Alipay has announced ambitions for one million offline partner merchants globally within three years, a move that will allow 120 million Chinese tourists traveling abroad every year to pay with Alipay even when they are abroad. The first of these cross-border payment partner-ships was rolled out in 2015, allowing Chinese tourists with an Alipay account to shop and pay at 70,000 overseas merchants with the app. With 450 million active registered users and 200 financial institution partners, Alipay is collabo-rating with leading global payment providers to ensure that international mer-chants can be integrated into handling the Chinese payment platform at home.

Ant Financial and European retail merchant leaders, Germany's Wirecard and Concardis, established a partnership to serve the growing number of Chinese tourists in Europe. Alipay also entered an agreement with Ingenico to embed Alipay into Ingenico's payment portal, the largest in Europe. This allows European merchants to accept customers who use Alipay for their pur-chases. A global agreement with the insurance giant AXA allows Alibaba/Ant Financial to sell AXA travel insurance to outbound Chinese travelers.[10]

Likewise in the U.S., the partnerships with San Francisco-based ride-hailing service Uber Technologies, Airbnb, and Macy's allow Chinese customers to use their Alipay wallet. Baidu has also created its own alliance with overseas merchants, in Thailand, South Korea, Japan, Hong Kong, Macau, and Taiwan.

## 9.2 INSURANCE

Insurance is a big business. The worldwide insurance market in 2015 is around $4.5 trillion.[11] Today, the insurance industry is built on trust. For example, people who buy long-term care insurance must trust the insurance company to pay the cost of long-term care when needed many decades later. An insurance policy is really a contract between the insurance company and the insured.

The global insurers are quick to embrace blockchain technology. The insurance companies can benefit from blockchain technology in many aspects. First, blockchain can simplify the insurance administrative process. However, the usefulness of the blockchain for insurance is due to the nature of the insurance contracts, in which certain specific events trigger the obligations. The insurance policy is essentially a contract to transfer risk from the client to the insurer.

The insurance industry has a set of complex legal and regulatory frameworks, addressing issues of ownership, responsibility, and potentially jurisdiction and dispute resolution. Therefore, with insurance contracts being so complex, there is a need for smart contracts for the insurance industry.

The insurance industry launched the Blockchain Insurance Industry Initiative or the B3i Project[12] in October 2016. B3i is dedicated to developing trading platforms across the insurance value chain using blockchain technologies. It aims at efficiency improvements in underwriting insurance policies. Using blockchain to handle insurance contracts eliminates the need for multiple databases and the errors that arise from maintaining and transferring data among them.

B3i has 38 members comprising insurers, brokers, and reinsurers. Its membership includes big insurance companies, such as Allianz, Swiss Re, Liberty Mutual, Sompo Japan Nipponkoa, Reinsurance Group of America, Hannover, Generali Group, SCOR, and others. The market share of B3i members is around 43% of ceded and 70% of reinsurers' premiums worldwide. The target date to release the platform for commercial use is before 2018.

Besides B3i, there are also other consortia in the same space: RiskBlock,[13] EY /Microsoft /Maersk, and R3.[14] The EY /Microsoft /Maersk project aims for marine insurance but can be applicable to another insurance markets as well in the future. The blockchain platform will reside on Microsoft's Azure. The distributed ledger will be used to capture information about shipments, risk, and liability, and will help firms comply with insurance regulations. It will also ensure transparency across an interconnected network of clients, brokers, insurers, and other third parties.

Symbiont developed an MDL platform to create smart insurance contracts that can execute payments with little or no human involvement. MDL-based smart insurance contracts can automatically authorize and execute the required payment when the condition meets the contractual parameter. MDL is also safer than current database technology because of the encrypted MDL data. The MDL platform also allows an individual to establish a global identity protected by encryption but immediately available to individuals and organizations authorized to access the information.

Another growing market is e-insurance. The insurance premium via the online distribution channel grew at an incredible 235% to $34 billion from 2014 to 2015, as compared to 11% to $331 billion via the traditional channel;[15] there still is a huge room for growth. An increasingly urbanized and well-educated population with rising household incomes and personal financial assets drives life insurance in China. China's auto insurance market is already the second largest in the world, but the penetration rate is still behind that in Western countries. Other insurance products such as home insurance and business insurance are also growing.

Traditional Chinese insurers are scaling up their own digital expertise. More than 100 out of around 130 traditional insurers have introduced online sales platforms, distributing $30 billion more premiums from 2014 to 2015, equivalent to 9% of aggregated premium value.

As traditional insurance companies have strengthened their online presence, it has become increasingly difficult for fintech firms to penetrate this market without collaborating with existing players. Therefore, most fintech firms seek to collaborate with the existing insurers. By doing so, fintech firms benefit from traditional insurers' experience in navigating regulatory hurdles, tapping into risk assessment, pricing analytics, and other technical expertise. Traditional insurers benefit from fintech's new channels. Despite its increasing digital capability, the insurance industry remains receptive to fintech collaboration. Fintech companies offer a huge database of potential customers, enabling traditional insurers to tailor solutions for customers with different risk profiles at competitive premiums.

China's first online-only insurer, Zhong An, was launched in 2013 as a collaboration between Alibaba, Tencent, and China's second-largest insurance firm, Ping An. ZhongAn has a technology development arm to develop technology based on artificial intelligence and Big Data to simplify insurance.

Baidu formed a joint venture with international insurance giant Allianz and Hillhouse Capital and CPPIC, to develop fintech products using Big Data and machine learning for better risk assessment in e-motor insurance. Some fintech players choose the merger and acquisition route. For example, Ant Financial took a 60% stake in Cathay Insurance, the Chinese insurance unit of Taiwanese Cathay Financial Holdings. Alibaba broadened its insurance product offering and made it available on Leyebao, its online insurance sales platform, while creating insurance products to suit the needs of SMEs operating on Taobao.

In China, e-insurance companies sell insurance policies through e-commerce and online wealth management (WM) platforms. The major players are the People's Insurance Company of China (PICC), Ping An, and Zhong An. Many startups are developing blockchain solutions for insurance. The most notable one is Chain B,[16] which is a blockchain startup to target the insurance industry. It aims to develop a decentralized network to provide multiple validation points for claims, without the costs associated with traditional insurers.

The action is not limited to startups; China's big banks are also launching blockchain applications aimed at the insurance sector.[17] For example, the China Construction Bank (CCB) began using a custom blockchain platform, jointly developed with IBM, in Q3, 2017, to sell third-party insurance products to a distributed ledger.

The Shanghai Insurance Exchange conducted a blockchain trial on insurance businesses with nine large insurance companies, including Cathay Life Insurance, Meiji Yasuda Life Insurance, the AIA Group, and others in China in 2017.[18] The platform, in collaboration with IBM, integrates several new technologies including blockchain, Big Data, biological recognition, and artificial intelligence.

## 9.3   SUPPLY CHAIN MANAGEMENT

MDL can offer many breakthrough applications in supply chain management, such as product authentication and innovative supply chain financing. MDL stores a digitized database, which can be shared easily and is trustworthy. In addition, by combining the blockchain and AI technologies, while Distributed Ledger Technology (DLT) securely manages and shares data, AI extracts embedded patterns from the data. It opens up a vast frontier for exploration. A manufacturer can track carbon emissions data at the product or parts level, adding accuracy and intelligence to decarbonization efforts.

In the product authentication application, MDL is the ideal platform to certify the authenticity, fair trade status, and origin of the products, components, or raw materials in a supply chain. Transparency comes with blockchain-based time stamping of a date and location—on ethical diamonds, for instance—that corresponds to a product number. It also reduces the cost, labor, and time in managing the supply chain.

In this arena, UK-based Provenance[19] offers supply chain auditing for a range of consumer goods. Making use of the Ethereum blockchain, a Provenance pilot project ensures that the suppliers in Indonesia have harvested fish sold in Sushi restaurants in Japan in a sustainable way.

For the supply chain financing, companies like Skuchain of Mountain View in California,[20] and Hijro and Fluent in Lexington, Kentucky, are developing financing services for the buyers and sellers.

Since the interests of the parties in a supply chain are interlocked across multiple businesses, supply chain financing can be more creative than regular financing. Supply chain financing provides an invaluable opportunity to strengthen relations with suppliers. The objectives of supply chain financing are not just to earn interest, but also to ensure that the deal goes through.

Supply chain financing by blockchain can optimize the utilization of working capital within the supply chain, creating mutually beneficial arrangements between buyers and suppliers. The smart contract can facilitate lending by financiers against purchase orders, invoices, inventory assets, and payment obligations. The automated release of funds triggered by real-world events offers the assurance for loans. It provides a real-time, reliable view of the transaction state, bringing significant transparency for all participants and helping them build a more trustworthy and stable supply chain ecosystem.

It also enhances the liquidity of collateralized assets in a supply chain by improving upon current trade finance instruments such as Factoring, PO Financing, and Vendor-Managed Inventory Financing.

Services like IMT offered by Skuchain provide inventory financing. The idea is to assign the original purchase contract between the buyer and the seller on the ITM blockchain. The contract provides the collateral to an investor in the IMT fund. IMT uses its funds to purchase goods from the seller. Each purchase order triggers the shipment of the finished goods according to the order. The buyer then pays IMT for the goods.

The platform developed by Fluent is a Bitcoin-like system for supply chain financing.[21] Buyers approve invoices on the Fluent Network once they receive the goods satisfactorily. The Fluent Network's blockchain operates on top of the existing banking infrastructure. The actual funds remain in the banks' custody at all times. On the blockchain, the funds are converted into tokens for the transactions.

Not only tech startups, buy many financial institutions and global enterprises, which are already part of the existing supply chain network, are developing blockchain-based supply chain applications. A single blockchain platform with cryptographically verified invoices, instant settlement, and low operating costs benefits all parties on the system.

Foxconn, the world's largest contract manufacturing company, which makes all the iPhones in the world, has launched a new blockchain-based supply chain finance platform, called Chained Finance based in Shanghai, through its financial service arm – FnConn.[22] It collaborates with Dianrong.com,[23] the first Chinese P2P company to participate in Hyperledger Blockchain Project. The new platform leverages advanced financial technology to meet the financial need of the SMEs involved in the supply chain in China.[24] SMEs make up most of the supply chain, but they have limited financing options. Using the dynamic discounting technique can enable buyers and suppliers to negotiate payment terms and discounts when buyers have capital available that can be redeployed to suppliers in exchange for better trading terms. The smart contract can implement such dynamic discounting schemes easily. Chained Finance enables delivery of the needed capital to these suppliers and provides large multinational manufacturers with enhanced visibility and transparency.

Chained Finance initially targets three major industries: electronics, auto, and garment manufacturing. The blockchain is revolutionizing the finance industry. It can offer solutions to any company operating and financing complicated supply chains. Chained Finance creates a unique ecosystem that will provide supply chains with easier access to funding at competitive rates. In return, supply chain operators will gain greater visibility of their suppliers and the many layers of finance embedded in the process.

By using the Chained Finance platform, every payment, every supply chain transaction, can be more transparent, manageable, and easily authenticated. Chained Finance will help eliminate many of the trust issues faced by counterparties and deliver automated execution. The new platform will be an enabler of supply chains across many major industries and geographies.

Chained Finance has an initial focus on the automotive, electronics, and garment production industries, though it has much wider applications. By using the Chained Finance platform, every payment, every supply chain transaction, can be more transparent, manageable and easily authenticated. Chained Finance will provide timely and efficient support to far more suppliers of all sizes. It will also help ensure the timely delivery of products to the end customers and improve efficiencies across the entire supply chain.

Founded in 2012, Dianrong is now a leader in online marketplace lending in China, dispersing more than $300 million in loan amounts a month to 3.7 million retail lenders. Its products and services include loan originations, investment products, and marketplace lending solutions in a comprehensive, one-stop financial platform supported by industry-leading technology, compliance, and transparency. The company's sophisticated and flexible infrastructure enables it to design and customize lending and borrowing products and services, based on industry-specific data and insights, all supported by online risk-management and operation tools.

In summary, the blockchain will revolutionize the supply chain system to make it more efficient, less costly, and more trustworthy.

## 9.4 HEALTHCARE

One of the most important components of the healthcare industry infrastructure is data management. Both blockchain and AI can greatly improve the healthcare system today. For example, using blockchain-based data enables limiting the access to health records to authorized people only. A community of people, including hospitals, doctors, patients, and insurance companies, could be part of the overall blockchain, reducing fraud in healthcare payments.

A blockchain-based system could ensure that care allowance is spent exclusively on healthcare activities. The system can save time spent on reconciliation after every transaction, helping with straight-through processing.

IBM has teamed up with the Centers for Disease Control and Prevention (CDC) as well as U.S. Food and Drug Administration (FDA) to develop blockchain and DLT applications in the health sector.[25]

The project with FDA is to define a secure, efficient, and scalable exchange of health data using blockchain technology, with an initial focus on oncology-related data. IBM and the FDA are exploring the exchange of owner-mediated data from several sources, such as electronic medical records, clinical trials, genomic data, and health data from mobile devices, wearables, and the Internet of Things (IoT).

In 2016, IBM and the New York Genome Center jointly created a comprehensive and open repository of genetic data to accelerate cancer research and scale access to precision medicine using Watson, IBM's artificial intelligence (AI) system.

The CDC is working on several proofs of concept based on blockchain technology. It plans to build real DLT applications for the public health sector.[26] The CDC, state, and local health departments and other organizations routinely share public health data so they can control the spread of a range of infectious diseases. Currently, the task is managed by the traditional database. Such a database is extremely complicated because of the vast areas, organizations, and nature of data involved. Blockchain technology could automate many of the database management processes, store and share health data faster, ensuring that they are more secure and incorruptible. Patient's data can be guarded with much better privacy and security. Critical data can be trusted. This can be especially important when managing a public health crisis.

The amount of research and clinical data in the healthcare sector is exploding. Blockchain technology is coming at the right time to enable the ecosystem of data in healthcare to have more fluidity.

In the healthcare industry, millions of medical records are scattered around different hospitals, clinics, doctors' offices, or even insurance companies. Such data form a complete history of a patient and can be vital for diagnosis when needed. Today, these medical data are fragmented and difficult to share. Even the patient does not have access to most of these data. Such low efficiency and transparency are a great waste of social resources. Enhancing sharing is critical to the healthcare industry. However, there is also a privacy concern about these data. Safeguarding these data so that only authorized persons can have the access to it is vitally important. Therefore, the healthcare data make an ideal case for the blockchain application.

In October 2017, Hangzhou-Yunphant, a blockchain startup based in Hangzhou, entered a strategic partnership with Inspur to integrate blockchain with healthcare data. Inspur Group[27] is a leading provider of cloud computing and an advanced IT product and solution company, one of the largest IT enterprises in China and the world's third largest server provider. It serves more than 80 countries and regions around the world.

Once implemented, the blockchain will allow multiple organizations to access peer-to-peer networks without worrying about data security and integrity through encrypted data transmission. The platform synchronizes, consolidates, and shares medical data created by various parties in real-time. The Yunphant Network is an enterprise-class consortium blockchain platform, called the Yunphant Chain. It is targets improved efficiency and transparency of the medical industry through blockchain technology. It can be quickly deployed for large-scale user application scenarios. The system supports operations such as authority management, monitoring, maintenance, and online deployment of Chaincode and status query.

AI tools are helping designers improve computational sophistication in health care. For example, Merantix, a German company, applies deep learning to address medical issues. Its AI-powered medical imaging system, trained by Big Data using a machine learning algorithm, can detect lymph nodes in Computer Tomography (CT) images much more precisely and quickly than doctors. AI can also help in predicting congestive heart failure.

## 9.5 FOOD INDUSTRY

Food poisoning is one of the major health issues. Every year, 400,000 people die due to contaminated food worldwide. In the U.S. alone, the CDC estimates that 48 million people get sick, 128,000 are hospitalized, and 3,000 die from food-borne diseases each year.[28] In December 2006, an *Escherichia coli* outbreak affected 71 customers in Taco Bell across five states. Eight people developed kidney failure, and 53 people were hospitalized. From October to

November 2015 an *E. coli* outbreak affected 55 customers of the Chipotle Mexican Grill.[29] In 2009, the Peanut Corporation of America (PCA) experienced a Salmonella outbreak. A total of 714 people got sick and nine died.

Food contamination can happen for many reasons: cross-contamination, the spread of food-borne illness, unsafe practices, etc. From outbreak to identification of the source of contamination can take weeks or longer, causing problems to spread. Blockchain technology can help to trace the contamination much quicker, thereby limiting the scope of the damage, both in terms of the people affected and the business lost. IBM entered a collaboration with major food suppliers, such as Dole, Walmart, Golden State Foods, Kroger, and many others to address food safety issues worldwide, using blockchain technology.[30]

Blockchain technology can improve food traceability by providing trusted information on the origin and state of the food. All participants in the food supply chain, from growers to distributors, all way to consumers, can gain access to the known and trusted data of the origin and state of food for their transactions. Such chained information greatly shortens the tracing time.

The food supply members of the consortium identify and prioritize deficiencies in the current food tracing system, while IBM provides technical solutions. Once developed, IBM's fully integrated, enterprise-grade production blockchain platform, which runs on IBM Cloud, can be adopted in areas beyond food supply chain applications.[31] The platform includes new features developed in collaboration with the Hyperledger community, including the Hyperledger Fabric and Hyperledger Composer hosted by the Linux Foundation.

Recently, IBM and Walmart conducted platform trials in both China and the U.S. The trial was a success – the platform can track a product throughout the supply chain's every stage in seconds instead of days or weeks needed in the traditional system. Blockchain technology enables a new era of end-to-end transparency in the global food system.

## 9.6  DEFENSE INDUSTRY

Like any other industry, defense companies already use a variety of technologies to address operation and product development to improve visibility and efficiency. The U.S. Department of Defense launched Project Maven, working with Google to deploy AI in defense. Project Maven helps human analysts sort troves of video footage to find targets. It can sift through the massive troves of data and video captured by surveillance and then alert human analysts when it detects patterns or when there is abnormal or suspicious activity. The project's initial objective is to automate the processing, exploitation, and dissemination of massive amounts of full-motion video collected by intelligence, surveillance, and reconnaissance assets around the globe. Special algorithms could search for, identify, and categorize objects of interest and flag them. It is one of the many contracts Google has to provide the Pentagon with cyber-security services.[32]

Big Data analytics will profoundly affect intelligence analysis, as massive amounts of data are sifted in real time, thereby providing commanders with a more thorough intelligence analysis at a much faster rate. Commanders can even delegate certain routines and decisions to AI platforms, reducing the time associated with the decision and improving the effectiveness of the subsequent action. Since timing is the essence of warfare, fast decision and action will generally prevail.

Blockchain offers additional value in maintaining classified information along with their supply chains and critical defense-related infrastructures, such as to track and audit transactions across multiple supply chain and operational partners.[33]

Defense industry infrastructure is dispersed across different locations. Some of these locations serve both defense and non-defense markets. Blockchain technology can be used to ensure security against any unauthorized access to these important networks and hardware equipment by consensus-based access.

For example, blockchain can perform the certification of people, partners, and parts; e.g., a key component used in the F-35 jet requires certification of the part's origin. The blockchain-based system can manage the supply chain of hundreds of thousands of components that go into a highly sophisticated defense product by recording each transaction step of each component, from raw material to finished part. It can also serve as security clearance, allowing certain employees, customers, and partners the privilege to use certain facilities and tools or to access certain data. It eliminates the possibility of a back door or a bug being implanted in a critical electronic component that becomes a key component in the operation of the final product.

Blockchain technology can find applications both in the defense industry and in military operations. The blockchain is an ideal platform to deliver hack-proof messages. The blockchain platform-based system can send and receive smart documents and contracts securely.[34,35] Crypto-Chat, a subsidiary of Indiana Technology and Manufacturing Companies (ITAMCO), developed a secure messaging and transaction platform for the U.S. military.[36]

On the national security side, the National Security Agency (NSA) engages Amazon Web Services in a $10 billion cloud computing contract known as WildandStormy. The CIA also awarded a contract of an amount equivalent to five companies – AWS, Microsoft, Google, Oracle, and IBM – for its intelligence needs.

The WildandStormy project is the NSA's attempt to modernize its primary classified data repository, the Intelligence Community GovCloud, which is an internally operated data lake. The NSA also intends to use a commercial cloud provider to meet the growing demands in data volume, processing, and analytics requirements, called the Hybrid Compute Initiative, to move its intelligence data from its own servers to servers operated by a commercial cloud provider.[37]

Likewise, the Homeland Security Department has been working on a project to move its biometrics database and apps to a new, cloud-based system called the Homeland Advanced Recognition Technology (HART) system. The new system will be able to match biometric indicators like face, iris, and fingerprints to other forms of identity, like Social Security numbers and immigration registration numbers.

## 9.7 CYBERSECURITY

By nature, the blockchain database or MDL is secure because it is encrypted and distributed. One might ask: How can it be used to improve the security of Internet and telecommunication (such as 5G) in general?

The project called InterPlanetary File System (IPFS), developed by IPFS Corp. in 2015, aims at exactly this purpose. The system seeks to replace the existing server–client architecture with the distributed storage of online data. The blockchain manages the storage of Internet data by spreading them to connected participating nodes so as to make that data not only censor-proof but also resilient against attack. Nodes get paid with a cryptocurrency called Filecoin, as incentive for their contribution to the storage and bandwidth.

The system works like a P2P network, with each new requestor of a file becoming an additional host. That data would be represented on a blockchain as a cryptographic hash and linked to a built-in IPNS (InterPlanetary Name System), akin to the Domain Name System. Unlike the conventional DNS, which translates between the numerical IP addresses and more readily memorized domain names, a name in IPNS is the hash of a public key. The hash is created from a dataset signed by the corresponding private key. The identity of the owner of the dataset, such as an email or a financial record, is thus hidden under the hash. This is unlike DNS, in which the Domain name, IP, can be traced to its owner. This can prevent DDoS attacks and identity tracking.

Another project to use blockchain to enhance Internet security is called Orchid. Orchid is actually a cryptocurrency-powered VPN. It allows conventional VPN providers to sell their excess bandwidth to users by becoming a part of a decentralized P2P privacy network. The platform allows people to hop between different VPN providers who contribute bandwidth to the Orchid's VPN platform. This ensures that not even the individual providers have the full picture of users' web activity.

VPNs route traffic through a separate, encrypted server, so web activity appears to travel to and from an IP address which differs from that of the user. From the point of view of an Internet Service Provider (ISP), identifiable traffic is initiated but appears to travel only to the VPN server. At the other end of the journey, the destination website sees visiting traffic as originating from the same encrypted server, rather than the user's actual IP address.

VPNs are not 100% fail-proof. There are several potential weaknesses, also known as leaks. Leaks can be the fault of the VPN provider, or the fault of apps, plug-ins, or operating systems routing traffic through default servers. Using social media apps makes it much more difficult to maintain privacy, even with a VPN.

Domain Name Systems (DNS), which convert web domain names into numeric IP addresses, can also be a leak. ISPs assign a DNS server to their users to identify and log the web domains their customers are accessing. When you use a VPN, the privacy solution routes your traffic through a different DNS server, making it harder for the ISP to log you or your destination websites to see who or where you are.

But when DNS requests are sent outside the VPN server, your ISP sees the sites you visit. DNS leaks can occur if an operating system continues to access the default DNS server rather than the one assigned by the VPN.

Likewise, blockchain can also offer security solutions to the 5G communication network. Blockchain can provide privacy by distributed trust models, thus making 5G capable of protecting itself from the security breach. Since the bandwidth of 5G is huge, the encryption and distribution of blockchain to 5G does not pose too much burden to its performance.

5G is a cloud-based communication technology, which utilizes the Software Defined Network (SDN), such as NFV (Network Function Virtualization). Its core network actually resides in the Cloud. Many of its functions reside in the Edge Clouds. This makes the integration of blockchain with 5G not only more compatible but also highly desirable. Blockchain opens the opportunity for storing and managing data on 5G networks via a distributed ledger. Blockchain is the key to ensure security and network performance.

Decentralized Blockchain makes use of asymmetric cryptography and hash algorithms to help in protecting user identity. Blockchain can register the devices with their blockchain address, further preventing identity loss.

However, to integrate blockchain into 5G protocol, many structural and technical frameworks need to be developed, including the regulatory frameworks to implement agreements like smart contracts. The scalability of Blockchain also needs to be improved to deal with a high number of devices.

## 9.8 AUTONOMOUS VEHICLES

Autonomous vehicles (AVs) represent a major area of AI and machine learning innovations. Since AV development is intimately linked to the Electrical Vehicle, it is difficult to separate the investment in these two areas. There are several levels of autonomous driving: from level 1 to level 5. Level 1 is the simplest driver-assisted system, while level 5 is fully autonomous driving without the need of a human driver. As one can imagine, level 5 Autonomous vehicles must be equipped with human-level intelligence, at least from the driving point of view.

The AV features automated vehicle guidance, braking, lane-changing, collision avoidance, auto-parking, adoption of traffic rules, and many others. AV uses an array of cameras and sensors to determine its circumstances, which change quickly. It also uses AI to analyze information in real time to make decisions according to its new circumstances.

One of the sensors used in AV is the LIght Detection And Ranging system (LIDAR). The LIDAR system combines light and radar sensors. They are mounted on the top of vehicles with a 360-degree view to measure the speed and distance of surrounding objects. LIDAR and all other on-board sensing systems provide information that keeps fast-moving AV in motion without driver, helping it avoid other vehicles and objects.

AI algorithms enable AVs to learn from experience and adjust their guidance systems based on changes in weather and driving or road conditions. Therefore, the AV is a much more advanced AI-equipped computer on wheels than a vehicle.

Since these cameras and sensors compile a huge amount of information and need to process it instantly, AVs require a powerful computer, advanced algorithms, and deep learning systems. The capabilities of these systems differentiate AVs into different levels.

Ride-sharing companies are very interested in AVs. All of the major ride-sharing companies, such as Uber and Lyft in the U.S., Daimler's Mytaxi and Hailo in the UK, and Didi in China, are exploring driverless cars, called RoboTaxi. Uber recently signed an agreement to purchase 24,000 RoboTaxis from Volvo.

In the U.S., Waymo and Cruise are the leading RoboTaxi developers. They have raised $8 billion in investment and completed over 6.8 million miles of testing combined. Waymo started its autonomous ride-hailing service in Phoenix in October, 2020 and Cruise recently signed a deal to deploy 4,000 RoboTaxis in Dubai by 2030.

According to some investigation, an AV is safer than cars with human drivers.[38] However, accidents do happen. AV suffered a setback in March 2018 when an Uber RoboTaxi hit and killed a pedestrian in Arizona. It raised a profound and philosophical question: Who is responsible for the accident? – The AV's owner, manufacturer, or the system developer? Or even the careless pedestrian? After all, the pedestrian could have disobeyed the traffic signal and rushed in front of the car before it could react. In any case, the accident became a news headline and brought AV testing to a temporary halt. Even though the state actively tested Uber's RoboTaxi, given that the issue is not entirely technical, but to some extent philosophical, it is difficult to arrive at a conclusion.

# REFERENCES

1. *https://www.ey.com/en_us/wealth-asset-management/how-the-global-wealth-management-industry-is-evolving*

2. *https://www.wealthfront.com/*

3. *https://www.betterment.com/*

4. *https://www.personalcapital.com/*

5. *https://intelligent.schwab.com/*

6. "AlibabaXE "Alibaba" 's Yuebao becomes world's largest money market fund", Yang Jing, *https://news.cgtn.com/news/3d41544f79637a4d/share_p.html*

7. "Chinese robo-advisor Xuanji launched by PINTEC group in Beijing", Steven Hatzakis, *https://www.financemagnates.com/fintech/investing/chinese-robo-advisor-xuanji-launched-by-pintec-group-in-beijing/*

8. "Alibaba doubles down on Lazada with fresh US$2 B investment and CEO", Jon Russel, *https://techcrunch.com/2018/03/18/alibaba-doubles-down-on-lazada/*

9. "Alibaba to invest US$177 m in India's Paytm", Simon Mundy, *https://www.ft.com/content/5cbb69bf-a2ae-3288-8500-27656a12067b*

10. "AXA, AlibabaXE "Alibaba" and Ant Financial Services announce global strategic partnership", *https://group.axa.com/en/newsroom/press-releases/axa-alibaba-ant-financial-services-announce-global-strategic-partnership*

11. "Global insurance market trend", EY report, *http://www.ey.com/Publication/vwLUAssets/ey-global-insurance-trends-analysis-2016/$File/ey-global-insurance-trends-analysis-2016.pdf*

12. *https://b3i.tech/home.html*

13. *https://www.theinstitutes.org/guide/riskblock*

14. "R3XE "R3" 's partnership with ChainThat is one giant leap for insurance", *https://www.the-digital-insurer.com/blog/insurtech-r3-chainthat-partnership-giant-leap-insurance/*

15. "China's insurance market", whitepaper, *http://www.aon.com/inpoint/bin/pdfs/white-papers/ChinaWhitepaper2016.pdf*

16. "Digital insurance in action", The digital insurer, *https://www.the-digital-insurer.com/dia/chain-b-blockchain-enabled-insurance/*

17. "Big Four' Chinese Bank to Launch BlockchainXE "Blockchain" Bancassurance Product", *https://www.coindesk.com/big-four-chinese-bank-launch-blockchain-bancassurance-product/*

18. "10 insurance firms test blockchain for insurance in China", Wolfie Zhao, *https://www.coindesk.com/insurance-firms-blockchain-test-insurance-china/*

19. *https://www.provenance.org/*

20. *http://www.skuchain.com/*

21. "How Fluent Wants to Streamline Financial Supply Chains With a BlockchainXE "Blockchain" ", Aaron Van Wirdum, *https://bitcoinmagazine.com/articles/how-fluent-wants-to-streamline-financial-supply-chains-with-a-blockchain-1465318410/*

22. "Foxconn reveals plan for blockchain supply chain domination", Michael del Castillo, *https://www.coindesk.com/foxconn-wants-take-global-supply-chain-blockchain/*

23. *http://en.dianrong.com/*

24. "Chained Finance: First BlockchainXE "Blockchain" Platform for Supply Chain Finance", *https://www.prnewswire.com/news-releases/chained-finance-first-blockchain-platform-for-supply-chain-finance-300418265.html*

25. "IBM XE "IBM" partners with CDC to bring blockchains to public health" by Giuliu Prisco, *http://distributed.com*

26. "Why CDC wants in on BlockchainXE "Blockchain" " by Mike Orcutt, MIT Technology Review.

27. *http://en.inspur.com/inspur/2225886/index.html*

28. CDC, *https://www.cdc.gov/foodborneburden/index.html*

29. "Worst Food borne Illness Outbreaks in Recent U.S. History", *https://www.healthline.com/health/worst-foodborne-illness-outbreaks*

30. "IBM XE "IBM" announces major blockchain collaboration with food suppliers", *http://www-03.ibm.com/press/us/en/pressrelease/53013.wss*

31. "IBM XE "IBM" deploys blockchain technology to provide enterprise solutions to food safety", Brigid McDermott

32. *https://www.defenseone.com/technology/2018/06/general-project-maven-just-beginning-militarys-use-ai/149363/*

33. "BlockchainXE "Blockchain" in aerospace and defense", Accenture consulting, *https://www.accenture.com/t20170928T023222Z__w__/us-en/_acnmedia/PDF-61/Accenture-Blockchain-For-Aerospace-Defense-PoV-v2.pdf#zoom=50*

34. "U.S. Defense finding use cases for BlockchainXE "Blockchain" technology?", J R Cornel, *https://steemit.com/blockchain/@jrcornel/u-s-defense-finding-use-cases-for-blockchain-technology*

35. "ITAMCO to Develop BlockchainXE "Blockchain" -Based Secure Messaging App for U.S. Military", *https://www.prnewswire.com/news-releases/itamco-to-develop-blockchain-based-secure-messaging-app-for-us-military-300464063.html*

36. *http://www.crypto-chat.com/*

37. *https://www.nextgov.com/it-modernization/2021/09/state-federal-cloud/185242/*

38. *https://magazine.jhsph.edu/2016/fall/forum/open-source-lifesaving-autonomous-vehicles/*

# *INDUSTRIE 4.0*

The term "Industrie 4.0" was first introduced in 2011 at the Hannover Fair in Germany. It designates the goal of industry to use newly developed digital technologies to automate manufacturing. Progress in automation has been an on-going process in the manufacturing industry for many years. The maturity of digital technologies takes automation to a higher level.

There are three aspects in manufacturing automation: equipment automation, factory automation, and data automation. Industry 4.0 will not only integrate these technologies within the factory but also integrate the upstream and downstream supply chains, all way from raw material suppliers to the end customers. The product design can also be well integrated into manufacturing. Flexible manufacturing allows products to be highly customized. The Industry 4.0 factory is also known as the intelligent factory and/or the "Lights-out" factory. The intelligent factory can be fully flexible and much more efficient in using resources.

Not since 1913, when Henry Ford demonstrated the world's first assembly line which vastly improved the production efficiency and turned out identical products in huge volume, has the factory found a way to custom-make products without losing efficiency. This has been achieved using digital technologies.

There is tremendous potential for the applications of Blockchain in Industry 4.0. It essentially solves the problem of data security, transparency, and immutability to develop effective solutions for industrial and business operations and processes. In other words, it guarantees the data integrity and creates a tamper-proof history of the products through their lifecycle with many stakeholders. Each object, physical property, or raw material will have its own secured identity.

## 10.1 THE FOURTH INDUSTRIAL REVOLUTION

2010 is marked as the starting point of the 4th industrial revolution, which applies digital technologies in all aspects of the economic activities. The scope of the 4th industrial revolution extends way beyond the traditional manufacturing industry. It is also known as the digital revolution.

When it is applied to the manufacturing industry, it is known as Industry 4.0. In the factory of Industry 4.0, manufacturing is entirely automated using robots. These robots have extraordinary sensors that can see and hear. They are also intelligent. They can recognize images and perform certain cognitive services. At the same time, the Big Data collected from the factory provide information on the production status in the factory, its supply chain, and all aspects of the factory's operation, such as production loading, labor productivity, equipment status and its utilization rate, bottleneck, WIP distribution, throughput, factory actual output vs. planned output, overall cost and cost per unit, efficiency, inventory turn, quality, and many others. Using such information in real time, the factory Big Data-trained AI will manage the factory. In some extreme cases, there is no need to have people on the factory floor; therefore, lights can be turned off. Such a factory acquires the name of "Lights-Out" factory. The Lights-Out factory can run 24 hours a day, non-stop and without a worker.

Data collected from the factory and supply chain will allow the manufacturing execution system to decide on production and materials flow to make the most efficient use of resources such as equipment and materials. Much of the managerial work can be automated. When the factory is linked to its upstream and downstream supply chains, or even the market, certain tasks are to be guided by the supply chain requirements. For example, it allows participants of the delivery process, such as shipping and courier companies, to globally track their freight in real time.

End customers can even specify how they want their products made. The factory is said to be "personalized" and the products are "customized." In a personalized manufacturing environment, factories can cater quickly and creatively to customer demands. They are flexible and specialized to produce personalized products without hiring and training more skilled labor.

The 4th industrial revolution will have equal impact on the world, if not more, when compared to the first three industrial revolutions. These advances are merging the physical, digital, and biological worlds in ways that create both huge promise and potential peril. The speed, breadth, and depth of this revolution are forcing us to rethink how countries develop, how organizations create value, and even what it means to be human.

## 10.2 EQUIPMENT AUTOMATION

Equipment is the basic workhorse in the factory. As the complexity of products and manufacturing processes increases, equipment also becomes more sophisticated. Today, most of the equipment is driven by onboard computers, which are capable of handling the complicated instructions set to operate the equipment. The equipment itself also generates a lot of process data and machine parameter data. Equipment automation provides a means of accurate and timely data collection, process controls, and optimization efforts.

Equipment automation not only simplifies equipment operation, it also provides valuable information for maintenance. It benefits operators, production engineers, equipment maintenance engineers, and quality engineers. It also helps managers to allocate resources. It improves equipment efficiency, and reduces the scrap caused by equipment error, increasing the yield by controlling and adjusting the process automatically. There is a wide range in the level of equipment automation. High-technology equipment, such as that used in the semiconductor industry, can have a very high degree of automation. Equipment for simple product manufacturing may not need such a high level of automation.

Equipment automation serves two purposes during the process: to operate the equipment automatically using the preprogrammed instruction set, and to collect all relevant process data and machine operating data. The preprogrammed instruction set, called the recipe, controls process parameters such as temperature, power, current, pressure, process time, etc. During the process, the sensors in the equipment monitor all these process parameters. If they are out of range, the process deviates, possibly due to a malfunction in the equipment. It will notify the engineer to shut down the process or will shut down the process automatically. Such a capability stops the equipment from continuing to process further lots under the failed conditions, which not only reduces the scrap and improves quality, but also improves equipment utilization.

When the equipment is shut down due to error, it performs a self-diagnosis. The diagnostic report is sent to the maintenance engineers for them to know exactly what is wrong with the equipment and to perform proper repair without having to spend time on fault identification. This greatly improves the maintenance efficiency.

Equipment automation also automatically identifies the lot number that is to be processed, and applies the proper recipe. When the lot is processed, it informs the Automated Materials Handling System (AMHS) to send the lot to the next process station.

## 10.3 FACTORY AUTOMATION

Factory automation refers to the automation of the entire factory. A factory has much equipment, and is running production lines for many products using different processes. Factory automation automates all the production processes.

There are two key systems in factory automation: the Manufacturing Execution System (MES), and the Automated Materials Handling System (AMHS). MES is the heart of factory automation. It controls all aspects of the operation.

The MES database holds all the data about the lots in production, such as their process routes, current process location, starting date, scheduled finish date, process parameter data, metrology data, etc. The process route contains all the necessary information to manufacture the lot from beginning to end, step by step – which recipe is to be used, which equipment is assigned to process a given step, all the process parameter data for each step, and metrology data collected from the lot. All these data are linked to a unique lot ID. Even when the product leaves the factory, all its manufacturing data can be traced, if necessary.

MES also has a dispatch function. It can assign a priority status to the lot to be processed in the given equipment. By doing so, it directs the traffic of WIP (Work in Progress) in the factory, so that the work load of the equipment is maintained evenly to avoid congestion in the factory. Congestion can happen due to bottlenecks in capacity. Bottlenecks can develop because some equipment is down unexpectedly or there is a constraint in the capacity design. MES also assigns priority for equipment maintenance, performs a line balance function to make sure that the WIP is uniformly distributed across the factory, acts as the depository of the authorized process recipes, and many other functions.

The second most important system for factory automation is the WIP transport system. Since a factory is large and WIP and other raw materials need to move around, a materials transport system is essential. In general, there are two types of AMHS; one is an Automatically Guided Vehicle (AGV). The AGV is a self-driven vehicle that can carry WIP and other materials around. It is similar to an autonomous vehicle but designed for factory use only. It has robot arms to load and unload WIP. The other kind is AMHS. It is a raised rail system suspended from the ceiling. Operators can lift or lower WIP from equipment to the suspended rail, and transport the WIP to a destination in the factory in a carrier similar to the monorail transport system. Both types of transport systems are equipped with RFID readers so that they can recognize the WIP they carry and take it to the destination defined by MES.

## 10.4 DATA AUTOMATION

The third component of automation in the manufacturing site is data automation. Both factory automation and equipment automation need to work with data. Data are collected from equipment, WIP, and factory automation systems, including lot data, WIP data, equipment data, process data, quality data, metrology data, and many others. Data automation is like the Big Data in the factory. It is the precursor of AI in the factory. The movement of lots, equipment, and transport system is all controlled by the data. The outcome of the data dictates where to move the WIP to for next processing step, whether the equipment is in good working condition, the priority status of the WIP in the bottleneck equipment, which piece of equipment needs to be maintained first, which lot is to be accelerated for production, and many others.

Data automation helps work processes, analyzes work patterns, and improves cycle time, productivity, quality, etc. Factory data also feed supply chain management systems and ERP. For example, if stock of a raw material or spare part for equipment is below a certain level, it automatically places a purchase order through the supply chain management system. Or, the production data feed the ERP to calculate the actual production cost of a particular product in the factory. Or, if a product already sold and working in the field shows a defect, data automation will be able to trace the original process step that caused the defect.

In Industrie 4.0, data can be aggregated and expanded to allow total process simulation of an actual production process. This makes it possible to "see" the manufacturing of a product before committing the actual resources to run the production line. It is called the Digital Twin. The Digital Twin is the virtual design of the physical object. It allows designers to see how the final design will be and how it will change when the design changes or the object's environment changes. Best of all, the digital twin can be implemented at any scale: as small as a component or as large as an entire factory. Large-scale objects such as cars, airplanes, buildings, and ships can all be designed using their digital twins. For example, car designers can learn from the digital twin of a vehicle that they design on how the vehicle would behave when driving in adverse conditions. Not only objects, but also processes can use the digital twin technology. For example, in the 3D printing process, a powerful laser is used to melt layers of metallic powders stacked on top of each other to form a 3D object. The laser energy needs to be extremely accurate to control the thin slice of the molten metal layer. The digital twin allows experimenting with the control of such laser energy to observe the heat map and optimize the process. This is not possible without using deep learning to enhance digital twin technologies.

Semiconductor companies have been using the digital twin concept for a long time. Today, such a concept is expanding to encompass the various sub-systems that make up products. Systems companies are turning to model-based systems engineering, before designing begins, to bring together different disciplines in a comprehensive digital twin at a systems-architecture level.

The digital twin concept extends to cover both design and manufacturing. This enables design and manufacturing teams to better collaborate to speed up the design process. This is familiar in the semiconductor industry as Design for Manufacturability (DFM). Streamlining the transition from design to manufacturing requires sharing a complete understanding of the product and the manufacturing technology and enabling early exchange of data between design and manufacturing. For example, in the semiconductor industry, technology used in the production line defines the design rules. Design must comply to these design rules to achieve manufacturability. Using a digitally integrated platform helps teams develop a complete and accurate interface between design and manufacture. A strong connection between system design and production further complements the system-of-systems approach needed to create the manufactured products.

To take the digital twin concept one step further, the Virtual Twin Experience is an executable virtual model of a physical system.[1] The virtual model updates the digital twin model by taking the experiences from the real world. This feedback loop closes the gap between the virtual and real worlds.[2] The real-usage data of a product or a system is re-collected and fed back to the virtual model for improvement or redesign. The virtual model contains all the history of the product from design to final use. Thus, the virtual model has a lifecycle of its own. The technology involved in the Virtual Twin Experience is called the Virtual Twin Technology.

The quality control monitoring will also be in real time, and will no longer rely on the metrology data taken from the semi-finished product. AI will predict quality issues before they occur, and quickly trace to the origin through the use of digital twins, machine learning models, advanced analytics, and the ability to embed intelligence quality controls.

When a large manufacturing company operates multiple factories at different locations around the world, the data are usually consolidated in the cloud. A fix in a production step in one factory can be quickly applied to different locations. A capacity shortage in one factory can be easily made up by a factory in another location.

## 10.5 FROM PRODUCT DESIGN TO MARKET

Industry 4.0 adds flexibility to the manufacturing system. Flexibility means that a factory can be configured to produce different products or customized products easily, produce new product types, and has the ability to change the order of operations executed on a part. This can be done by process routing, machine reconfiguration, or additive manufacturing. This is the biggest innovation of manufacturing since Henry Ford invented the assembly line to produce automobiles in December 1913. Assembly-line production brought many revolutionary improvements in the manufacturing industry, such as reduced manufacturing cost, lower cost per unit produced, greater labor productivity, greater machine efficiency, improved quality, and many others. However, it does have a major drawback, that is, it has lost the flexibility. All products manufactured are identical copies under the same tooling. To make a new product, the factory needs to be retooled, which is not economical if the production volume is small.

Industry 4.0 promises to bring back the lost flexibility. It allows product variation and process variation without retooling. The Flexible Manufacturing System (FMS) deploys intelligent robots, automated equipment, and Computer Numerical Controlled machines (CNC). Robots are very flexible tools, sometimes on par with human labor.

Additive manufacturing adds additional flexibility. It can be used to create complex geometries that would be difficult or impossible to achieve with traditional manufacturing methods. Additive manufacturing uses design created by computer-aided-design (CAD) software or scanned object in 3D to deposit material, layer upon layer, to form a part. Sometimes, it is called 3D printing. Since each part is created by a computer file, there is no retooling needed to make different parts. This adds more flexibility to the manufacturing. With such flexibility, it is possible to custom-make products in the factory to meet the market demand or for a particular product design.

## REFERENCES

1. *https://virtual-twin-experience-whitepaper.3ds.com.*

2. *https://discover.3ds.com/sites/default/files/2021-01/Cloud-digital-twin-ebook-en.pdf.*

# CHAPTER 11

# SMART CITY

## 11.1 WHAT IS A SMART CITY?

A smart city is designed and built by applying digital technologies to the city's infrastructure. It is implemented through a public–private partnership that combines government and business data to improve governance. For example, cities could integrate information from ride-sharing services and from traffic and highway congestion, with public transportation services, such as buses and subway, to improve transportation. That would help metropolitan areas deal with traffic jams and assist in highway and mass-transit planning. The Fire Department can use data analytics to optimize the use of resources while responding to medical emergencies AI can deal with large volumes of data and provide the most efficient ways of responding to public requests.

The European Investment Bank defines smart city projects in six major categories: governance, economy, mobility, environment, people, and living.[1] Each area, in turn, is divided into several subcategories. They are:

- Participation, transparency, public and social services in the governance category;
- Innovation and entrepreneurship in the economy category;
- Traffic, public transport, ICT infrastructure, and logistics in the mobility category;
- Network and environmental monitoring, energy efficiency in the environmental category; digital education and creativity in the people category;
- Tourism and culture, health and safety, and technology accessibility in the living category.

Such a list is not exclusive. Different definitions could apply to the different regions of the world, may depending on their current issues of urbanization that need to be addressed.

Worldwide, there are an estimated 600 cities with the smart city program in 2020.[2] These projects aim at improving service delivery, environmental planning, resource management, energy utilization, and crime prevention using AI. In the U.S., cities like Seattle, Boston, San Francisco, Washington D.C., and New York City are the top adopters of smart city projects. Seattle is using AI to manage energy and resource usage. Boston has deployed cameras to monitor and manage traffic. Most other cities have smart city projects that are tailored in some way to solve their most urgent issues. Examples are smart meters for utilities, intelligent traffic signals, e-governance applications, Wi-Fi kiosks, radio frequency identification sensors on pavements, and intelligent garbage recycling. These smart city projects with AI and data collection devices are gradually transforming basic operations and decision making in urban areas.

A smart city project is built on top of Information and Communication Technologies (ICT) and cloud computing with AI, to develop, deploy, and promote sustainable development practices. The Big Data collected from around the city is fed into the AI system to form decisions on the city's management.

Smart city projects have been developed at the right time, to meet the increasing population and urbanization worldwide. A few decades ago, a city with a population of 10 million was considered a megacity. Today, Tokyo, Delhi, Shanghai, and Sao Paulo all have a population that exceeds 20 million. There are over 30 cities in the world with a population exceeding 10 million.

As the megacities in proximity merge, the metropolitan area can have more than 100 million people. The population of the Beijing–Tianjin–Hebei metropolitan area is 112 million; the Yangtze Delta centered on Shanghai, and the Pearl Delta centered in Shengzhen both have populations exceeding 100 million as well, spurring the demand for resources and services, which are skyrocketing. Traffic, pollution, healthcare, utility, and garbage collection and treatment become unmanageable. Traveling from one part of the city to another can take hours. Cities already consume 70% of the world's energy and the majority of other resources. The demand for municipal water, power, garbage disposal, and flow of traffic will only increase. If not carefully managed, it can lead to a chaotic situation, as is already happening in the slum areas in many big cities around the world.

Smart City technology enables cutting-edge intelligence and flexibility that are necessary to help cities use resources more efficiently – to improve everything from the quality of the air and water to transportation, energy, and communication systems. As the infrastructure becomes more intelligent and connected, citizens will benefit from the improved management of resources and other positive social and economic impacts. Many see the smart city project as the only hope of rescue.

In the smart city project, cloud-based IoT applications receive, analyze, and manage data in real-time to help municipalities, enterprises, and citizens make better decisions that improve the quality of life. In the smart city, the information interpreted and stored is critical to its growth and security.

The physical components of IT systems are crucial for smart city development. Both wired and wireless infrastructures are required to support interconnected living. A wired city environment provides general access to continually updated data of digital and physical infrastructures, such as the quality of water, traffic congestion, or even the hospital intensive care unit loading. Pairing devices and data with a city's physical infrastructures and services can cut costs and enable real-time feedback. A smart city provides access to public services through any connected device. Citizens can engage with smart city services using smartphones and mobile devices, and connected cars and homes.

Communities can improve energy distribution, streamline trash collection, decrease traffic congestion, and even improve air quality with help from the IoT. Smart cities employ a combination of data collection, processing, and disseminating technologies in conjunction with networking and computing technologies and data security and privacy measures, encouraging the application of innovation to promote the overall quality of life for citizens. The technology covers dimensions that include utilities, healthcare, security, transportation, entertainment, and government services.

The smart city project can make more efficient use of infrastructure, such as roads, streets, power plants, water supply, and hospitals to support economic, social, and cultural development, thereby improving the quality of life for its residents.

It also engages effectively with local governance officials, improving the collective intelligence of the city's institutions with citizen participation. It allows learning, adaptation, innovation, and responsiveness more effectively and promptly to changing circumstances.

## 11.2  SMART CITY PROJECTS IN THE WORLD

There are many smart city projects around the world,[3] each implemented with a different approach. Barcelona in Spain hosts the annual Smart City Expo, the largest such event in the world. With a tourism-based economy, Barcelona has a very robust smart city program covering everything from ubiquitous public Wi-Fi to becoming energy self-sufficient. It has made the city more tourist friendly, simultaneously becoming an innovation hub.

Copenhagen is another example. It innovates green building requirements, expansion of green spaces, public transit, and a growing use of renewable energy to supply residents with sustainable heating and cooling from sources such as the neighboring waterway and the landfill. Copenhagen has invested in smart technologies for their transportation system. For example, traffic lights are centrally monitored and synchronized, and give right-of-way to public transportation.

In Asia, Singapore has a bold Smart Singapore strategy, which aims to convert the city-state to the first smart nation through a range of initiatives that leverage intelligence, integration, and innovation to become a major player on the world stage.[4] The city has excellent public transit and a handful of powerful incentives to discourage personal vehicle use. It also has a very active smart governance program, including a strong commitment to online service delivery. Singapore is committed to greening its infrastructure.

China has many smart city projects.[5] Most of its mega cities have embarked on a smart city program. Unmanned supermarkets, unmanned restaurants, and mobile payments are a part of daily life in Hangzhou. Alibaba's AI (artificial intelligence) City Brain system has been adopted for Hangzhou's city management. Real-time traffic conditions are monitored and the vehicles on the road are counted. The system can adjust traffic lights according to the traffic conditions.

There are many smart city projects in North America as well, in cities such as Vancouver, Montreal, Dallas, Chicago, Austin, Seattle, San Francisco, Washington D.C., and New York, just to mention a few.[6] In the United States, by 2016, there were 54 cities that had embarked on smart city projects.[7]

Not to be left behind, Brazil, as the largest country In Latin America, began its smart city efforts early on.[8] Both the federal and the local governments provide initiatives for smart city projects. Connected Smart Cities or CSC is a platform that brings entities, governments, and companies together with a vision of innovation and improvement in cities. CSC considers 11 development indicators in its smart city program, including mobility and accessibility, environment, urbanism, energy, technology and innovation, health, education, economy, governance, security, and entrepreneurship. CSC analyzed 700 Brazilian cities based on these 11 indicators and ranked them according to their growth potential: Curitiba, Vitoria, Belo Horizonte, São Paulo, and Rio de Janeiro occupy the top 5 slots.

Curitiba is the smartest and the most connected city in Brazil. Its population increased from 300,000 in the 1950s to 1.9 million in 2020. The city's development has always followed the path of sustainability. Curitiba has one of the most sustainable transport systems in the world. The city received the Sustainable Transport Award in Washington. It boasts 55 square meters of green public space per capita. Following the policy of reduce, reuse, and recycle, the city recycles 70% of its waste. With the arrival of smart city technologies, Curitiba is able to expand its sustainable city growth to greater scope.

São Paulo, the largest city in Brazil and one of the most populated cities in the world, is using digital technologies to streamline bureaucracy together with other Brazilian smart cities. *Descomplica* is the latest initiative, through which the city offers to simplify government services, such as parking cards for the disabled and elderly, issuance of municipal taxes and other documents, etc. The Mayor of São Paulo has outlined his vision for a smart city which includes digitizing public services, providing and enhancing public security through the use of technology, and reducing bureaucracy. The Public services will be completely digitized. These initiatives are led by the newly-appointed secretary of innovation and technology. Another project is the introduction of digital processes geared at those who want to start a business. When it is completed, the process to register a business in the city will speed up, from the current 128 days to just one week.

São Paulo has installed 10,000 surveillance cameras to improve public security. The cameras are linked to Detecta, a monitoring system provided by Microsoft and used by São Paulo's military police. The city has also implemented drone programs to detect areas that might be infested with the mosquito Aedes aegypti, which transmits the zika virus.[9]

## 11.3 SMART CITY PROJECT – TRANSPORTATION

One of the major headaches today in big cities is transport. No matter how much infrastructure is built to accommodate the ever-growing number of vehicles, it seems never enough. Streets are always congested, polluted, and noisy. The smart city project may provide a breakthrough solution to the problem. It deploys technologies such as 5G, AI, IoT, AR, Wi-Fi, and edge computing to solve the current problems faced in the transport system.

The project involves smart parking, intelligent route planning, autonomous vehicles, and integrated traffic control systems. The project will create a so-called smart digital ecosystem for all transport systems. It aims at effective operation by creating a digital environment. It will result in huge savings for the city because resources are better utilized. People will also spend less time in commuting, enabling them to be more productive. The air will be cleaner, thereby favoring better health of its people.

For example, the last-mile solution provides autonomous vehicle transport from home to metro station and from metro station to office. The hassle of parking is completely eliminated. The requirement for city parking is reduced. Each passenger occupies the vehicle for 10 to 20 minutes only. Vehicles are shared by many people, thus greatly reducing the number of automobiles in circulation.

Data are collected constantly from mobile phones, parking sensors, congestion charging zones, and smart card ticketing, and sent to the cloud/ edge computing centers using AI to optimize traffic in real time. 5G wireless, edge computing, radar, LIDAR, GPS, and Intelligent Transportation Systems (ITS) are all integrated in a single unified system.

Cities leading the smart city initiative are already demonstrating excellent results. Citizens in Hamburg, Germany, can use an app on their phones that track their current location and constantly match this to available buses and trains. The app also pays for tickets in real time. Helsinki integrates bike and car-sharing services with the public transport, a service accessed via the smartphone. Smart traffic lights lead to a reduction in travel time by a substantial percentage.

The city generates a huge amount of data every day. These data offer transport companies, governments, automotive manufacturers, and mobile broadband providers the insights they need to evolve their services. Such data need to be digested, analyzed, and processed to operate. This is achieved by AI.

## 11.4 SMART CITY PROJECT – UTILITY MANAGEMENT

The smart city project also plays an important role in managing the city's utilities: the advanced metering system for managing electricity, gas, Internet cable, water, street lights, and garbage collection. Until now, utility companies have independently handled their services, along with the related billing, consumption, and management. Smart utilities are connected, which improves efficiency and usability. Creating a shared network infrastructure enables different city departments responsible for different services – such as lighting, traffic, or transportation – to leverage resources to increase efficiency, reduce cost, and provide better services.

For example, the health department works with the sewage department to coordinate the monitoring of potential disease-bearing bacteria or viruses in sewage. The hospital works with the fire department to coordinate industrial-scale incidents. The smart grid framework allows the distribution of electrical power to achieve optimum performance. It connects power generation, consumption, distribution, and transmission as one entity, thus allowing quicker restoration of electricity after the outage. It reduces operational and management costs, regulates peak demand, integrates large-scale renewable energy systems, and improves security. It can integrate renewable energy, decrease carbon emissions, help to balance needs, increase operational flexibility, enhance transmission and distribution systems, and reduce the risk of grid failure.

In addition to the connectivity to infrastructures, social media also connects the city's government to its citizens in all kinds of areas related to the city governance. Such a feedback loop helps communication between individuals, businesses, and research facilities while handling the issues as they arise, thus improving quality of life and fostering innovation.

Detection of new and developing problems in the utility system in real-time can improve maintenance and prolong equipment life. Decision-support systems powered by AI allow for autonomous knowledge and understanding of when there is a need for service and respond accordingly.

Utilizing the real-time data provided by smart technology can enhance operational efficiency, inform better business decisions, and enable inaccessible meters and sensors to be remotely monitored. Improved smart grids will allow for more responsive adjustments to system overload, including alternative sources of energy such as solar and wind power.

## 11.5 SMART CITY PROJECT – CRIME PREVENTION

The crime prevention program in the smart city uses AI to predict crime occurrence, thus providing policing in the most effective way. This is also known as predictive policing, done by collecting surveillance and crime-related data to use AI to identify the patterns of crime, catalog them, and flag patterns that develop.. It is like a detective on steroids. The police can respond more effectively. One of the well-known companies to offer the predictive policing technology is Palantir Technologies.[10] In 2018, it provided the New Orleans Police Department with a predictive policing system. It also exports the technology to the Danish and Israeli governments.

Even before AI for crime prevention is available, the police are already patrolling the parts of the city with a higher crime rate. Video surveillance cameras throughout the city can monitor streets to spot suspicious activities. Facial recognition technology coupled with surveillance cameras installed at key points of streets and stores can spot people with previous criminal records and track them. Tracking vehicle license plates is another way to locate people under surveillance. Fake license plate or the license plate of a stolen car can be spotted easily and red-flagged. Not to mention that location tracking of cell phones and message monitoring of the target are routine procedures.

With AI, not only is such monitoring automated, all the random pieces of the puzzle are strung together by Big Data. Previously random information, seemingly irrelevant and unrelated, now suddenly makes sense. Cities such New York, Chicago, Los Angeles, New Orleans, and others have experimented with predictive policing programs.

Of course, such monitoring raises the issue of privacy invasion. Today, surveillance cameras have been installed at most of the major cross roads in the city, and at the entrances to most of the stores. There is nothing to prevent such camera images from being shared with the crime-fighting units of the police.

As the technology becomes more advanced, such tracking and monitoring become easier. It will be increasingly difficult to strike a balance between privacy and security. The tendency is tilted in favor of law enforcement and security. The questions are: How much surveillance is too much? What is the right balance between security and liberty? Who can decide? How are data used? George Orwell's famous fiction novel "1984" published in 1949 is the reality today.[11]

## 11.6 SMART CITY PROJECT – HEALTHCARE AND DISEASE PREVENTION

Healthcare requires resources, and smart city projects coordinate resources. In a smart city, the citizens engage with smart healthcare services. The system interacts and engages with all healthcare providers. In a broader sense, the healthcare system includes both health-related services and non-health service programs.

Health-related services include doctor's visit, hospitalization, medical emergency response, medicine supply, remote patient monitoring, etc. Non-health services are public safety, environmental health, social services, emergency services, disease prevention, etc. The interoperability and integration of these systems and services into smart city programs enables real-time response to all services in healthcare.

Like other smart city programs, the smart city healthcare program also utilizes digital technologies, such as Big Data, broadband Internet, and AI to deliver services to the residents of the city. The smart city program for healthcare collects, analyzes, and disseminates the relevant health-related data, including disease tracking and environmental conditions. Disease surveillance in the early stage involves the monitoring of public health, hospital patient trend, seasonal disease pattern, vital statistics of the population, food supply system, public water supply system, and sewage system. Environmental conditions such as air quality and ultraviolet radiation may also affect the population's health.

Monitoring and surveillance form an important part of the health agenda. The smart city project can offer significant value to health surveillance. It is the ongoing systematic collection, assembly, analysis, and interpretation of population health data, and the communication of the information derived from these data to stimulate response to emerging health problems. The project aids in the planning, implementation, and evaluation of health services and programs. Such a task is ideal for the digital infrastructure. A small population, such as sick, disabled, or older adults, requires remote patient monitoring.

With detailed monitoring and surveillance, the smart city project can greatly improve disease prevention. Currently, most healthcare data collected are from people who seek healthcare. These data include healthcare utilization registries, health services statistics, or hospital/ clinic/ CDC administrative records. Additional data need to be collected from the population, air quality, water quality, and sewage quality. All these data can provide crucial information about the potential disease. This is especially true after the COVID pandemic.

Medical emergency response is focused on determining management in emergency situations, management of ambulance, and emergency management applications, such as rescue in a fire, building collapse, or flooding. Smart cities allow for distributed monitoring and remote-control facilities, which might be the basis for effective emergency responses. The availability of incident control and crisis management intelligence by collecting, integrating, and processing all the possible data might be one of the most interesting and useful smart city services. Senior citizens require social participation, maintenance of health conditions, and safety to promote their quality of life as they age. They, together with a small population, such as the sick or disabled, require remote patient monitoring.

Unlike the smart city program for transportation, which collects data largely from infrastructures, the implementation of the smart city program for healthcare is complex, because it requires the cooperation of different stakeholders (e.g., public and private sectors, citizens, or domain experts), and complex distributed applications supporting a vast amount of data.

# REFERENCES

1. *http://www.eiburs-ascimer.transyt-projects.com.*

2. *https://www.techrepublic.com/article/smart-cities-6-essential-technologies/.*

3. *https://nexxworks.com/blog/the-most-innovative-smart-city-projects-in-the-world.*

4. *https://www.weforum.org/agenda/2019/11/singapore-smart-city/.*

5. *https://www.uscc.gov/sites/default/files/China_Smart_Cities_Development.pdf.*

6. *https://www.digi.com/blog/post/smart-cities-in-the-us-examples.*

7. *https://www.usmayors.org/wp-content/uploads/2017/02/2016SmartCities Survey.pdf.*

8. *https://smartcity.press/brazil-smart-cities/.*

9. *https://www.zdnet.com/article/sao-paulo-mayor-outlines-smart-city-plan/.*

10. *https://finance.yahoo.com/news/25-most-dangerous-prisons-world-140306577.html.*

11. *https://en.wikipedia.org/wiki/Nineteen_Eighty-Four.*

# CHAPTER 12

# GOVERNANCE, LEGAL APPLICATIONS, AND REGULATION

## 12.1 GOVERNANCE AND VOTING

A public blockchain allows people who do not know each other to agree to a set of rules for governance purposes. For example, blockchain can verify that no one has tampered with a file that stores digital signatures and provides identity verification. This could allow citizens to carry out self-service for many bureaucratic transactions that require the attention of civil servants and lawyers today.

Different public blockchains have different rules and incentives, but are fundamentally aimed at bring people together to perform certain functions. This is the definition of governance. Best of all, with blockchain, it can be done without relying on a centralized organization to reach consensus. Therefore, blockchains are ideally suitable for governance.

By making the results fully transparent and publicly accessible, MDL technology could bring full transparency to elections or any other kind of polling. Ethereum-based smart contracts help to automate the process. As such, there are efforts to develop blockchain technology for governance purposes. It can potentially redesign our interactions in business, politics, and society.

Blockchain platforms can manage social interactions and governing rules. They can be useful and important tools for the responsible party in governance, but they cannot replace the traditional central authorities that define the rules. Thus, the blockchain apps for governance are mostly permissioned blockchains. The ownership must rest with a responsible governing entity rather than an anonymous public.

For example, Boardroom[1] is an app that enables organizational decision-making on the blockchain. With Boardroom, a Governance DApp, individuals and companies can manage their smart contract systems on the Permissioned Ethereum blockchain. It can conduct proxy voting on the board proposal, for shareholders. It is an administrative tool for organizations. These are very narrowly defined organizations, simply concerned with bookkeeping of address balances, but they meet all the requirements of decentralized decision-making.

Like any organization, the Decentralized Autonomous Organization (DAO) is comprised of participating members following a set of rules. However, it is virtual in the blockchain. The rules are organized by those who constitute the 'governance.' Once the rules are defined, the DAO operates automatically, without authority. The DAO is most suitable for the applications with which the consensus protocol will generate desirable decision-making.

Since decision-making is generated by the consensus protocol, DAO is a democratic process. It improves transparency and integrity. The voting process is particularly suitable to employing blockchain technology, to make it tamper-proof.

Today, the voting systems are either a paper-based system or a digital voting system. The security risk of digital voting is even higher than that of the paper voting system because it is more prone to fraud.

The digital voting system identifies a voter through their ID card. The platform must confirm a voter's identity before they can cast their vote at the polling station. When a voter submits their vote, it goes to a vote storage server. The vote storage server encrypts the vote, and strips the voter's ID data from the vote before sending it to a vote-counting server. The vote-counting server decrypts and counts the votes and then outputs the results. In the current digital voting platform, there is a risk of an attack before the votes are transferred to the counting server.

The DAO-based voting system is more secure and robust. In the DAO-based voting system, the voters are participating members, the rules are set by the government, and the result of voting is by consensus protocol. Once the rules are set, not even the government can change them.

The blockchain does not need to replace the current voting system but rather to improve it. The DAO voting system first registers the voter into the so-called registration blockchain. The registration creates a transaction unique to the voter. The government miner validates the user. Upon validation, the voter will receive a ballot card with their information on it. This is the same process as the voter registration in the U.S. today, except that the registration is a record in a blockchain.

The voting itself actually takes place in a separate blockchain – the voting blockchain. Each vote is a transaction. The platform validates a voter by three-factor authentication; their identification number, the password supplied on registration, and their ballot card that contains a QR code. The voter can only vote in their constituency where they is registered.

The separation of registration and voting blockchains ensure voter anonymity. Certified observers and election officials will monitor and audit the voting process. Instead of reading the ballots and counting them, they will host the nodes in the voting blockchain and verify that the unencrypted results match the encrypted votes. Each transaction is encrypted with public and private keys. The polling station nodes contain the public keys of their voters to allow them to encrypt any vote cast at that polling station.

Each constituency counts the votes and builds blocks. They act as miners during the counting process. They build the blocks by including the votes for the same candidate in a block. A block can contain 5,000 or 10,000 votes. This happens in the local constituencies all over the country. The local polling stations then broadcast their voting blocks to all nodes of the voting blockchain network of the same constituency to build the blockchain. Once the vote has been confirmed or built into a block, the polling station will then generate a transaction to remove the vote to its pooled memory. Such a voting system is tamper-proof.

Besides the voting system, many other blockchain technology applications can benefit the government's bureaucratic process. Governments are known for their inefficiency because of their size, inertia, bureaucracy, and lack of incentives. The services are normally slow, negatively impacting citizens. Linking the data between the departments with blockchain ensures the real-time release of critical data. For example, real-time consumer information can help to formulate economic and monetary policy. Real-time nationwide clinical data can help to contain the spread of a contagious disease.

Blockchain technology could improve transparency and check corruption in governments worldwide. For example, the U.S. Navy's Innovation department recently announced its interest in using blockchain technology for their manufacturing system. They plan to add blockchain technology to their 3D printing in order to help securely transfer data through the manufacturing process.[2] The Naval Innovation Advisory Council will test the blockchain technology's integration into their system. The initial test is to prove the concepts, share data, and secure digital designs throughout the Navy's network of information.

They also plan to create a data-sharing layer among the 3D printing sites using Blockchain technology. Other government departments, such as the Department of Homeland Security, and the Science and Technology Directorate, awarded a total sum of $9.7 million to several small businesses for technology research on Blockchain usage, such as contract bidding.[3]

## 12.2 REGULATORY APPLICATIONS AND ISSUES

Government regulation is possibly one of the most important factors as to whether or how AI and blockchain will eventually develop into a full-fledged fintech industry. There are two aspects to the issue: one is the development of RegTech (Regulatory Technology), as a branch of fintech.[4] The other is government regulation in data collection. Both apply to the regulation-related challenges of fintech, including fraud detection and prevention.

Overall, the scope of regulatory issues relates to both: what data are allowed to be collected, and once collected, how they can be used and how they are protected. Furthermore, in the more globalized world, the question arises on whether a country's regulation can be applied to its multinationals operating in other countries.

There are challenges to understand, implement, embed, and enforce the new legislation and regulation in the AI, fintech, and Blockchain systems. RegTech explores how firms can benefit, leverage, better understand, and manage the risks to comply with the new legislation and regulation. Since AI, fintech, and Blockchain technologies are still evolving quickly, the related legislation and regulations are still fluid.

The development of Regulatory Technology requires expert knowledge of both technology and regulation. RegTech provides executives with the tool to introduce new capabilities to leverage systems based on the new legislation and regulation. It also allows them to analyze regulatory data and report in a cost-effective, flexible, and timely manner, and to be able to respond and react as new regulations emerge. RegTech can assist the industry in complying with regulation, which regulators can use. Most important of all, since the legislation and regulations are constantly evolving, RegTech allows companies to update the legislation and regulation when changes occur.

The scope of RegTech is big: it needs to cover everything from the monitor and control of core ledgers to apps at the user end. RegTech solutions are mostly Cloud-based. RegTech apps provide tools for analysis, compliance, management, reporting, activity monitoring, training, etc.

RegTech can help firms to automate the mundane compliance tasks and reduce operational risks associated with non-compliance. It can also make risk choices and suggest how to mitigate and manage those risks. RegTech is more than a tool to meet the regulatory requirements. It also queries legislation and regulations in order to identify compliance imperatives.

Companies such as Hadoop,[5] Tableau, and Pentaho[6] develop tools to organize data and create reports to meet regulatory requirements. In addition, these tools apply analytics to Big Data. For example, Tableau is a visualization tool that makes it easy to look at data in new ways to help identify trends and to analyze from a regulatory perspective.

Traditional financial institutions are also investing in regulatory fintech: HSBC created a $200 million fund to heighten levels of regulation in the fintech sector, aiming at improving new compliance demands.

Examples of RegTech companies include FundRecs,[7] which developed reconciliation software for the Funds Industry; Silverfinch,[8] which creates connectivity between asset managers and insurers through a fund data utility in a secure and controlled environment; TransUnion,[9] which prevents online fraud by scanning transactions in real time; and FunDapps,[10] which offers tools for compliance monitoring and reporting.

One of the challenges of RegTech development is that the legislation and regulation differ from country to country. While Europe has a European Banking Authority which sets the standard, the U.S. has a different standard. As long as there is no standardized regulatory baseline or data interchange format across the regions, it is difficult to develop a universal RegTech app.

## 12.3 OVERCOMING PRIVACY ISSUES IN DATA COLLECTION

One of the most debated issues about Big Data is privacy vs. the data collection neto build up Big Data. On the one hand, data is crucial to train AI. On the other hand, bluntly collecting data not only intrudes on privacy, but be damaging if the data are wrongly used. Many Western countries regulate data collection out of privacy concerns. For example, the European Union passed a General Data Protection Regulation in 2018 on data collection and analysis. Its rules restrict companies from collecting data on streets. Such data include those emitted from unencrypted home Wi-Fi networks along a street. Data have been collected both with and without the knowledge of the data owner. Indeed, since 2007, Google has been gathering personal web activity from home Wi-Fi networks through the Street View cars as they cruise streets.[11] The General Data Protection Regulation (GDPR) in Europe is enacted exactly to prevent this from happening in Europe. In addition, it places severe restrictions on the use of these data in AI and machine learning.[12]

The GDPR-like development is prevalent worldwide. In the U.S., there is no single legislation for data protection. Instead, there are numerous laws, at both the federal and state levels. These laws prohibit businesses from collecting data from consumers. Some states are more restrictive than the others. For example, California has a CCPA (California Consumer Privacy Act), effective from January 1, 2020.[13]

China, once thought of as the land of free data collection, is also acting on the more restrictive GDPR. On October 21, 2020, China released the first draft of the Personal Information Protection Law (PIPL) – similar to the GDPR in Europe. It will have significant influence on business operation. It not only restricts data collection, but also data exportation.[14]

On the other hand, the U.S. does not have a uniform standard in data access, sharing, and protection. Data collection and privacy are viewed as two opposite sides of the coin – a law favoring one will sacrifice the other. However, this is not necessarily true. For one thing, anonymous data does not intrude on privacy. If the identity of the data owner can be stripped from the data itself, there is no privacy issue for the data owner. This is exactly where Blockchain or MDL fits in.

Remember that we have discussed that the MDL database separates into three parts: Identity MDL, Transaction MDL, and Content MDL. The Content MDL is devoid of identity. The content is linked to the identity only for those who have been authorized, such as a government agency like DMV, or insurance companies for their policy holders. Such a link can only be used for a pre-specified purpose. The user of the data will have to apply for a new license for any additional use of the linked data.

For example, a patient's medical database, located in the Content MDL, is linked to his identity data, located in the Identity MDL. Only his medical doctors or hospital have the access to this pair (patient's identity with patient's medical record). When he visits a doctor, which is considered as a transaction, the MDL is updated. His doctor and hospital get updated MDL, but not his insurance company, which has only a subset of this patient's medical database in the content MDL. Even though the patient adds a transaction of doctor's visit, this added transaction does not automatically enter in the content MDL accessible by the insurance company.

At the same time, since the patient's medical database is in the Content MDL, which contains his X-ray images, diagnosis, or blood test reports, but not his identity, there is no risk of this information being shared with the medical AI development companies from this database, The Content MDL can be used to train AI. What is needed is a data regulation that forces data collectors to comply with the separation of identity from the content. It is also easy to audit, since the separation is done by rules in the algorithms.

In this way, one can achieve both innovation and consumer protection. Right now, there are no regulations governing data access, sharing, and protection. Such a regulation is so important that if it is not established, it can hinder the development of AI.

The National Cancer Institute has a similar data-sharing protocol where certified researchers can query health data pre-stripped of identity. That enables researchers to use the data for their research without compromising the privacy of patients. Such a protocol, though it uses the same principle as MDL, is however not as secure, because MDL, by nature, is further protected by encryption and distribution.

## 12.4 LAND TITLE REGISTRATION AND REAL ESTATE

A number of countries are undertaking blockchain-based land registry projects. The Honduras announced such an initiative in 2015. In 2016, the Republic of Georgia contracted the Bitfury Group to develop a blockchain system for property titles. More recently, Sweden also announced that it was experimenting with a blockchain application for property titles.

Japan probably put in the biggest effort in such blockchain applications. The lack of sufficient and updated data has been a major problem for the Japanese authorities because many ownership cases cannot be properly solved due to insufficient data. The Japanese government wants to upgrade their real-estate registration systems using blockchain technology to improve the efficiency in collecting, managing, and updating real-estate data, and to make the data tamper-proof. A blockchain-based registry would allow authorities to better maintain real-estate property transactions and boost recovery efforts of properties, in the event of a natural disaster like the infamous tsunami of 2011. The Japanese land ministry will launch a trial version of the new system as early as the summer of 2018. The government will select a few cities for testing. The Japanese government is planning to roll out the system nation-wide within 5 years after proving its feasibility.

Likewise, the Ukrainian government also plans to implement Blockchain solutions to solve problems of a depressed land market due to the lack of suit-able financial instruments for leases and land transfers. The lease price is low because of a deeply entrenched black market. The application of a Blockchain system will be able to protect the auctions from black market controls, thereby stabilizing the land price slide and increasing the income for farmers. Their pilot project is to transfer the State Land Cadastre to blockchain technology.

These are examples of the blockchain applications in the governmental administration of the land ownership. At the same time, blockchain technol-ogy also finds its use in private real estate business. Real estate transactions have always been cumbersome and complicated. Property titles are a case in point. They tend to be susceptible to fraud, as well as costly and labor-in-tensive to administer. Blockchain technology can have a great impact on the financial verification of the sales process itself. As publicly-accessible ledgers, blockchains can make all kinds of record-keeping more efficient.

The most costly and complicated process is the use of escrow and title companies for third-party verification, which is, of course, necessary to pre-vent the risk of fraud. With blockchain, there will no need for an escrow company.

By using a blockchain-distributed database to prove authenticity, home-owners could legitimately transfer ownership immediately without the need to pay for third-party verification.

Blockchain technology can be useful in the rental business as well. The blockchain would effectively make forged ownership documents and false listings outdated, making selling or advertising properties that you do not own almost impossible.

Blockchain technology also improves the mortgage business, which is always slow and plagued with red tape and administrative issues. Using the blockchain, the buyer, seller, as well as the real estate asset can all have digital IDs. The mortgage process and transfer of ownership would be seamless and much faster. Verification of the buyer's credit history and income would be instant, avoiding time-consuming trips to banks, lawyers, and estate agents. Homeowners would be able to prove ownership of their property with a record of their purchase transaction. Houses could acquire digital identities as well, including the chain of ownership, a list of repairs and renovations, and the history of real estate tax payment. When this is implemented, the real estate transaction can happen not in one or two months, but in one week. This will have a profound impact on the real estate market.

## 12.5 LAW AND JUSTICE

Laws are actually contracts between citizens and the government. A Blockchain smart contract can implement many civil laws. For example, DMV can revoke a driver's license using a smart contract for three consecutive traffic offenses automatically. The fines of traffic tickets can be automatically deducted from the offender's bank account. A restaurant's license can be voided if it does not pass the food safety inspection. The smart contracts will have a profound impact on industries. Smart contracts eliminate the intermediary, such as a legal firm, as payment will happen based on meeting certain milestones. By its very nature, the smart contract is easily enforceable electronically, creating a powerful escrow by taking it out of the control of a single party.

Blockchain smart contracts will not replace lawyers anytime soon, but they can greatly help lawyers to do their jobs more efficiently. In 2017, ten law firms and four legal institutions including Cooley, Debevoise & Plimpton, Hogan Lovells, and others jointly formed the Ethereum Enterprise Alliance (EEA).[15] Their objective is to create the framework of legally binding smart contracts.

EEA is not the only entity interested in the application of blockchain in the legal field. A large law firm, Frost Brown Todd (FBT) has also taken the initiative to deploy smart contracts in the legal field.[16] FBT developed a prototype smart contract to be used in software escrow agreements.

The smart contract, once written, will execute on its own. As the lawyers are not skillful in programming the smart contract and the programmers are not skillful in legal terms and conditions, the gap may cause undesirable consequences. However, the trend will prevail that smart contracts will bring developers and attorneys together to collaborate and provide progressive solutions for the legal industry.

In addition to the blockchain, cloud service also enters judicial applications. Ali Cloud is one of China's top providers of cloud computing services, domain services, emails, network security, and Big Data analysis. With its data and emails preserved for judicial departments as courtroom evidence, this may be the first instance of blockchain being utilized by a state judiciary.

AI is being deployed in criminal justice. The city of Chicago has developed an AI-driven "Strategic Subject List" that analyzes people who have been arrested for their risk of becoming future perpetrators. It ranks 400,000 people on a scale of 0 to 500, using items such as age, criminal activity, victimization, drug arrest records, and gang affiliation. In looking at the data, analysts found that youth is a strong predictor of violence, being a shooting victim is associated with becoming a future perpetrator, gang affiliation has little predictive value, and drug arrests are not significantly associated with future criminal activity.

An AI-based justice program can actually reduce human bias in law enforcement and lead to a fairer sentencing system. Machine learning, automated reasoning, and other forms of AI also enhance the predictive risk analysis. Such analysis can determine whether a criminal is likely to commit repeated offense, or whether they pose further danger to the society once released. Thus, the wide adaption of such AI programs can cut crime without increasing the jailing rates, or reduces jail populations without the increase in crime rates.[17] On the negative side, critics worry that such AI programs may predict a crime that someone is yet to commit. Such tools may be wrongly used to target people of disadvantaged groups unfairly.

Despite these concerns, some countries are moving ahead with rapid deployment in this area. In China, companies already have access to voices, faces, and large volumes of other biometric data to help them the develop technologies to enable the use of AI to improve national security and law enforcement – to keep track of criminals, potential law-breakers, and terrorists.

## 12.6 PROTECTION OF INTELLECTUAL PROPERTY

Computers can easily reproduce digital contents, such as movies, music, and books, and widely distribute them, causing rampant piracy of illegal copies of the intellectual properties. The unauthorized copies of digital intellectual properties deprive their creators of financial gains. Smart contracts can protect copyright and automate the sale of creative works online, eliminating the risk of file copying and redistribution. Blockchain protects IP in two ways: registering the content to prove the ownership and collecting the payments when the content is being used.

Blockchain tracks the rights and transactions attached to any type of digital content – from music and books, to videos. Blockchain technology registers the IP rights, catalogs and stores the original works, and makes the content widely available. By registering the IP rights to a blockchain, authors possess tamper-proof evidence of ownership. This is because a blockchain transaction is immutable. Once a work has been registered to a blockchain, that information cannot ever be lost or changed.

The Ethereum platform uses blockchain to issue smart contracts to verify contractual agreements. There are now startups using the Ethereum platform to focus on IP solutions and other alternative blockchain applications. Mycelia uses the blockchain to create a peer-to-peer music distribution system.[18] Founded by the UK singer-songwriter Imogen Heap, Mycelia enables musicians to sell songs directly to audiences, as well as license samples to producers and share royalties to songwriters and musicians through automated smart contracts. By doing so, it empowers a fair, sustainable, and vibrant music industry ecosystem involving all online music interaction services.

There are many other startups who do such work. Ascribe, a digital IP platform, offers solutions to solve the issues surrounding IP[19] and digital content on the Internet. InterPlanetary File System (IPFS), another startup company, developed a peer-to-peer protocol to do the same.[20]

The blockchain and timestamping services can be used to create an auditable trail of content ownership, from creation through to the transfer of rights, and beyond. Platforms such as Blockai[21] and Ascribe are allowing authors to make a record of copyright ownership, which can then be used to see where and how the work is being used on the Internet and to seek licenses from third parties.

Registering a work in a blockchain gives the author a digital certificate of authenticity, which can help third parties identify the author of a work. The blockchain, being a permanent immutable record, is the perfect solution for providing proof of creation. There is now a universal database for the record of ownership of IP content, and making the payment for its use indisputable.

Once a work is registered and verified in the blockchain platform, authors can make the IP content unusable for those who do not pay for the right to use, or be notified to see who is using their work. Blockchain registration reduces the cost of transactions and creates a direct link between authors and users.

No less important is the fact that blockchain can help in collecting the payments from IP users. Smart contracts assist in the sale and licensing of intellectual property through micropayments. With each use, a user using the content makes a small payment to the author. As a result, the author can be remunerated each time their IP is being used without having to pay brokerage fees. Such a method is simpler and more transparent than many other existing means of payment for authors.

Ujo Music,[22] an Ethereum-based and ConsenSys-backed music software services company, has used its blockchain application with singer-songwriter Imogen Heap to release her songs on the blockchain. Users are able to purchase licenses to download, stream, remix, and sync the song via smart contracts, with each payment automatically split on the blockchain and sent to Imogen Heap directly.

## REFERENCES

1. *http://boardroom.to/*

2. "The US Navy wants to connect its 3D printers with a blockchain", Stan Higgins, *https://www.coindesk.com/the-us-navy-wants-to-connect-its-3-d-printers-with-a-blockchain/*

3. "BlockchainXE "Blockchain" applications for Homeland Security analytics", *https://www.sbir.gov/sbirsearch/detail/867813*

4. "Is RegTech the new FintechXE "Fintech"?", *https://www2.deloitte.com/ie/en/pages/financial-services/articles/RegTech-is-the-new-FinTech.html*

5. *http://hadoop.apache.org/*

6. *http://www.pentaho.com/*

7. *https://www.fundrecs.com/*

8. *https://www.silverfinch.com/*

9. *https://www.transunion.com/idvision*

10. *https://www.funDapps.co/*

11. *https://www.theguardian.com/technology/2010/may/15/google-admits-storing-private-data*

12. *https://docs.microsoft.com/en-us/compliance/regulatory/gdpr*

13. *https://iclg.com/practice-areas/data-protection-laws-and-regulations/usa*

14. *https://www.taylorwessing.com/en/insights-and-events/insights/2020/12/chinas-gdpr-what-you-need-to-know-about-the-pipl*

15. "Legally Binding Smart Contracts? 10 Law Firms Join Enterprise EthereumXE "Ethereum" Alliance", Michael Del Castillo, *https://www.coindesk.com/legally-binding-smart-contracts-9-law-firms-join-enterprise-ethereum-alliance/*

16. "How the Legal Industry is Adopting EthereumXE "Ethereum"-based Smart Contracts", *https://cointelegraph.com/news/how-the-legal-industry-is-adopting-ethereum-based-smart-contracts*

17. *https://www.brookings.edu/research/how-artificial-intelligence-is-transforming-the-world/#footnote-24*

18. *http://myceliaformusic.org/*

19. "How Ascribe uses BitcoinXE "Bitcoin" tech to help underserved artists", Stan Higgins, *https://www.coindesk.com/ascribe-bitcoin-tech-underserved-artists/*

20. "An introduction to IPFS", *https://medium.com/@ConsenSys/an-introduction-to-ipfs-9bba4860abd0*

21. "Blockai taps the BitcoinXE "Bitcoin" blockchain to protect creative content", Martin Hsu, *https://www.ccn.com/blockai-taps-bitcoin-blockchain-protect-creative-content/*

22. *https://blog.ujomusic.com/*

# CHAPTER 13

# CONCLUSION

Just as the previous three industrial revolutions, the coming digital revolution will also bring major changes in the world economy and social structure. In fact, every sign indicates that this digital revolution will have a much stronger impact.

Like every paradigm shift, the impact will be positive in some aspects and negative in others. We only hope that the positive impacts will overshadow the negative ones.

## 13.1 NEAR-FUTURE POSITIVE IMPACT

On the positive side, we are going to see increased productivity worldwide. In manufacturing, smart factories will use resources more efficiently and will significantly reduce the cost of manufacturing. This will make products more affordable to many. Energy usage will be more efficient, and energy production will leave less waste, which will benefit the environment. Product customization can meet customer demand better. Product quality will also improve.

In the healthcare industry, development of new drugs will be much faster and more cost-effective. Customized drugs will be more effective for patients, with lower side effects. Remote surgery will become commonplace. Telemedicine will allow healthcare professionals to evaluate, diagnose, and treat patients at a distance using telecommunications technology. It will enable greater efficiency in the use of human resources in healthcare, and save patients the trip to visit a doctor. In the healthcare industry, AI will greatly accelerate the research for new drugs, thereby exerting a positive influence on healthcare. AI-assisted medical diagnosis will also able to detect diseases at an early stage, improving the cure rate. Remote surgery will become common practice. AI-assisted medical services will facilitate the life of many and relieve the burden of having to attend patients for minor problems.

Applying digital technologies for the agriculture industry can increase food production while consuming fewer natural resources, thereby increasing productivity. Drones equipped with sensors can detect the area of plantation infected by diseases. AI can annotate the diseases and prescribe precise pesticides for dissemination. Automated agriculture can estimate crop yield and monitor livestock health. It can promote the so-called precision agriculture.

In financial services, the digital economy will provide banking services to the millions of unbanked people in the world for the first time in history. Therefore, it will be a great equalizer. People can transact online and make payments across borders without huge transaction fees. This will greatly accelerate the world economy and push globalization further. Digital currencies, whether decentralized or issued by the central banks, will accelerate the exchange of money, thus increasing the money velocity and the efficiency of the economy overall. The cross-border movement of capital will also be much easier.

Blockchain technology will make the transactions much more secure. These transactions not only include monetary transactions, but also the exchange of messages and information, including the voice messages in phone conversations and the messages in social media. Digital currency using blockchain technology makes payments possible without a third party, across the world and as easy as face-to-face. Smart contracts allow transactions to be conducted without the need for trust verification.

The shared services economy enabled by the digital revolution will benefit the population in general. For example, ride sharing greatly reduces the number of cars needed; therefore, fewer cars need to be produced. After all, more than 90% of the time, our cars are parked at garages at home or in the office. When the RoboTaxi becomes a reality, there will be no need to own a car. RoboTaxi will assist in pick-up and drop, making travel easier. For most people, it will be cheaper, eliminating the costs of depreciation, fuel, maintenance, and parking that come with owning a vehicle. All the resources saved with less auto production will be a boon for the environment.

In governance, the AI-assisted crime prevention program, including face recognition and video surveillance, will be able to spot crimes much easier and apprehend the criminals faster. Crime rates will reduce. The voting system using blockchain will also be fraud-free.

Identity, Transaction, and Content-separated MDL will integrate all types of personal databases without the concern of privacy. For the banks or rental agencies to check the financial background of their customers, it will be as easy as typing a few words into their system. Mortgage and other loans can be approved or disapproved in minutes rather than days. Smart contracts embedded in the blockchain will inspire confidence and avoid potential legal fights.

## 13.2 FUTURE JOB MARKET

There are also downsides to this digital revolution. Firstly, many people dread that AI will replace many of the working labor, not only blue-collar labor but also white-collar labor. This is inevitable, because AI and robots will be cheaper and much more efficient than human labor. They do not need vacations, do not ask for a raise, and can work 24 hours a day.

However, the rate of jobs that will be lost to AI will be slow, because technology adoption lags behind technology development due to delays and costs in implementation, acceptance, and regulatory hurdles. For example, driverless trucks will not replace normal trucks overnight. We have roughly a generation's worth of time to work on the issues.

In general, the new jobs created in the digital economy are specialized and require high levels of education. The jobs being eliminated are low-level labor/clerk and repetitive work, mostly unskilled. Without elevating the job skills of the population in general, there will be gaps between the skill requirements and the job seekers.

While many people will be unable to find jobs, many jobs will also remain vacant without suitable candidates. To solve this problem, the society and the government have to collaborate to provide re-skilling and training programs to prepare the population for the change before it is too late. The shortage of key AI and data scientists will slow down AI deployment.[1] Unprepared, the economy risks facing social and political destabilization – caused by the disruption in the job market.

At all levels of schooling, education must follow a curriculum geared for a future world where AI will be ubiquitous. Educators must be conscious of the kinds of skills that will be needed in the digital economy. Today, data scientists, computer scientists, engineers, coders, and platform developers are all in short supply. The administrators in the education department must mobilize resources to make up for such shortage.

Fortunately, in the U.S., both state and federal governments have recognized such a need and have been investing in AI human capital. For example, in 2017, the National Science Foundation funded over 6,500 graduate students in computer-related fields and has launched several new initiatives designed to encourage data and computer science. The goal is to train more AI and data analytics personnel so that the U.S. can be competitive in the digital economy era, and continue to lead the technology innovation.

As a private enterprise, IBM's Teacher Advisor program helps teachers bring the latest knowledge into the classroom. It enables instructors to develop new lesson plans, and helps students get the most out of the classroom.

On the personal level, a young work force will have to understand the future job perspective and be prepared for the career that might have a high demand in the future. At the same time, the impact of such job displacement will vary greatly from country to country, industry to industry. It will also vary at different levels of education, socio-economic status, age, and gender.

## 13.3 WEALTH REDISTRIBUTION

Besides job displacement, we can also expect wealth re-distribution, which happened in every industrial revolution. In the digital economy, data are the equivalent of crude oil. The dominance of data resources through digital platforms creates power, influence, and profitability. Whoever controls data will control wealth. The entry barrier to controlling such resources is huge.

With the ever more integrating world economy, such a control can be extended across the globe. Those individuals will be richer than many countries and more powerful than many heads of state. Today, the richest 1% of the population owns half of all household wealth worldwide. The top 62 individuals control more assets than the poorest half the world's population. Entering the digital economy, the gap can grow wider, if the governments do not take any action.

The unchecked growth of fintech companies can also bring other undesirable consequences. China has a case in point: In 2020, China has cracked down on Ant Financial IPO, which might reap $34.5 billion dollars from the market and place Ant Financial valuation over $313 billion dollars, more than twice that of Goldman Sachs – the largest investment bank in the world. Its IPO was hailed as the largest IPO in history. A few days before the IPO, the

Chinese government brought it to a halt.[2] This move perplexed the world. Why would the Chinese government destroy the IPO of its most successful fintech company? It does not make sense.

Ant Financial operates many financial services. The most well-known is Alipay, the world's largest mobile and online payments platform. Alipay owns 53% of the Chinese mobile payment market; $41 trillion dollars annually in 2020.[3] This means that Alipay handled almost $22 trillion dollars of mobile payment in 2020, roughly the size of the U.S. economy.

One might ask how the mobile payment market in China could exceed its GDP by so much, roughly $15 trillion dollars. It is easy to explain: Let us say that a factory sold $1 million dollars' worth of products to a distributor. The distributor in turn sold the same products to retail stores for $1 million, and the retail stores sold the same products to end customers for $1 million. The aggregated transactions from factory to the end users are worth $3 million dollars, but only $1 million is counted as GDP. Transactions that do not add value to the economic activity do not contribute to GDP. In this case, only the factory's activity contributed to the GDP. If the distributor and retail stores each added 10% or $100,000 as the cost of their service, then the contribution to the GDP will be $1.2 million dollars.

Ant Financial has many other financial services: one of the world's largest money market and wealth management funds, a credit rating system, a credit payment service, online bank, microlending, and a platform to allow financial institutions to sell their financial products as well as Medicare-like health insurance products. It has even been working with the People's Bank of China to develop and test DCEP, the Chinese official digital currency.

Such a concentration of financial power positions Ant Financial as one of the world largest financial service companies. Yet, it is classified as a technology company, not subject to the regulation of banks.

What worries the Chinese government the most is its microlending product. Microlending is the service of lending small amounts of money to customers. The amount of each microloan is small, $10,000 dollars or less, much like a credit card. However, since China has a large population, the aggregated amount of the loan is huge. It uses AI to qualify the borrower and approves a loan within a few minutes online. Therefore, it is very popular among the young people to get some quick money. The loans are funded by the asset-based securities (ABS). In 2017 alone, its microlending amounted to $40 billion dollars – a 4-fold increase from 2016. By the time of its scheduled

IPO in 2020, the microloan amount reached $330 billion dollars. What is more scary is that Ant's microlending is highly leveraged, up to 100 times its funding in ABS and without collateral.[4] This is not possible under bank regulations. Ant Financial was betting that not all of the borrowers would be defaulters at the same time. This may be true when the economy is doing OK, but not when the economy enters a downturn.

Ant Financial takes advantages of the loophole that it is a hi-tech company and is not regulated by the bank rules. Although the total microlending amount is not as large as the sub-prime mortgage in the U.S. during 2005 and 2006, which reached $600 billion dollars a year, the effect can still be devastating, especially in view of the leverage. Moreover, the $600 billion subprime mortgage was owned by many banks, while the $300 billion microlending loan is owned by Ant Financial alone. The downfall of Ant Financial will not only destroy its microlending business and all the banks and institutions underwriting ABS, but also all of its other financial services, including Alipay.

Chinese authorities may have realized that an unregulated fintech sector growing exponentially could provoke a domestic financial crisis and could eventually damage the real economy. Since then, the Chinese government has been tightening the regulation in the fintech area to prevent the over concentration of power in the hands of a few. This lesson shows that unchecked run-away expansion of fintech can distort and pose danger to the economy. It is not an exaggeration, to say that the timely action to control Ant Financial has possibly averted a financial disaster in the making.

This example shows how important it is to update the regulations in the fintech industry to prevent run-away disasters before it is too late.

The digital revolution also enlarges the gap between the have and the have-not countries. Just like in the first industrial revolution, UK, empowered by its newfound industrial prowess, colonized half of the world. Likewise, the U.S., leading the second and third industrial revolutions, became the world's leading superpower for almost a century. The 4th industrial revolution is no different.

Countries without digital technologies will depend on the countries with the technologies to build the digital economy infrastructure. As a result, the former will lose some autonomy, especially in economy. In addition, smart factories in the advanced countries have a production cost so low that they no longer need to outsource to the countries with cheap labor. This is the amplified phenomenon of robots and AI replacing blue-collar workers. The countries dependent on the cheap labor export today will be devastated.

The increasing inequality among countries creates instability around the world. It could lead to famine, social unrest, terrorist activities, mass migration and destruction of natural resources, worldwide pandemics, war, and many other unthinkable disasters. It creates the conditions for violent extremism and other security threats.

## 13.4 TECHNOLOGY-EMPOWERED EXTREMISM

Technology can be used both productively and destructively. The most notable example is nuclear technology. It is used to generate clean energy; while on the other hand, it makes nuclear bombs with terrible destructive power. Today, Internet hacking is probably the most prevalent Internet-based crime. Tomorrow, AI-, IoT-, and Big Data-empowered crime will be much worse. The digital technologies are creating new forms of extremism. These technologies can be lethal and harder to govern and negotiate.

People worry that one day, AI will be beyond human control and can act on its own, against human beings. However, the likelihood of this happening is lower than that of AI-related crime and terrorism. After all, AI is trained by humans feeding data to it. There is nothing to prevent bad elements from training AI to destroy, steal, control, or achieve any other objective. AI can be trained to attack the electrical grid, nuclear power plant or water dam, sabotage an airplane, destabilize financial markets, or even trigger a nuclear bomb. AI war is likely when a country is using AI to defend against AI intrusions. As such, cyberspace is now a field of warfare engagement, just as land, sea and air. Drones, autonomous tanks, and missiles equipped with AI can all be formidable weapons. Miniature drones the size of a fly can monitor enemy activities and trigger an attack at the right moment. Assassination can be carried out without a human assassin. Weaponized digital technologies pose tremendous challenges to defense.

A malicious attack can be triggered by an event, using IoT, under the command of smart contract or AI. Digital currency can be hacked across a national boundary. Airplanes can be hijacked without a hijacker on the plane. Cloud computing centers can be shut down, causing thousands of businesses to go down. These enemies are invisible and attack unexpectedly, when the targets are most vulnerable. It is therefore important for the national governments to formulate strategies to prevent such future occurrences. Such an effort should be coordinated across nations using platforms like, for example, the United Nations, in order to be effective.

## 13.5 LONGER-TERM IMPACT

Prediction into the distant future is more difficult. However, we can be certain that the progress of technology is ever faster. We can expect that AI singularity – when AI exceeds human intelligence – will happen.

AI singularity will be the greatest event in the human history. Until now, human beings, being more intelligent than all other living species, dominate the earth and create civilization. After AI singularity, this will no longer be true. Human beings will no longer hold the important position as the most intelligent species on earth. Our dominant position will be challenged. Even though AI is a human creation, it does not diminish the fact that AI will be able to do what humans cannot do. It will outsmart human beings.

There is no law in the universe that says that evolution has to be biological. One might argue that AI resides in computer hardware and cannot reproduce. However, the human–machine fusion, also known as cyborg, provides a clear path to overcome such shortcomings. Cyborgs may be the next step of evolution.

Cyborgs will be equipped with both biological and intellectual power, beyond human imagination. They will be able to perform tasks that humans cannot, such as travel beyond the solar system, colonization of remote planets, and spreading the earth's civilization throughout the galaxy. In this way, they will carry genes evolved on earth to the far corners of the universe, to realize the dream that humans have always had.

History provides a parallel situation. Neanderthals existed on earth as early as some 800,000 years ago, and became extinct around 40,000 years ago. The world was then taken over by human beings. We may be following the footsteps of Neanderthals. Although Neanderthals are extinct, humans continue to carry their genes. In one sense, Neanderthals fused into human beings. It is estimated that they contribute 1 to 4% of genomes for most people on earth.[5]

AI singularity may be a remote possibility for our generation. However, if it happens in the next hundred years, it is a blink of the eye on the evolutionary timeline. In comparison, the fusion of Neanderthal and human happened over hundreds of thousands of years.

What will happen after AI singularity is anybody's guess. Stephen Hawking, the renowned British scientist, once said that AI could spell the end of the human race and it could be the worst event in the history of our

civilization. Elon Musk, the CEO of Tesla and the richest man on earth, has also warned of the AI apocalypse. We do not know whether they are right or wrong. No one knows. However, being a top scientist and a top businessman, both successful in their own right, their words and vision must be given credit. The evolution toward cyborg is indeed a disaster for the human race, from our point of view as a species. However, it allows the human genomes to be carried on for much longer, and to spread further into the universe. It may not be a bad thing, as explained in Richard Dawkins' book, The Selfish Gene.[6]

## REFERENCES

1. *https://venturebeat.com/2021/04/19/survey-finds-talent-gap-is-slowing-enterprise-ai-adoption/*

2. *https://en.wikipedia.org/wiki/Ant_Group*

3. *https://www.brookings.edu/wp-content/uploads/2020/04/FP_20200427_china_digital_payments_klein.pdf*

4. *https://news.cgtn.com/news/2020-11-05/Ant-Group-s-failed-IPO-and-overleveraging-in-the-financial-market-VahQDnbIYg/index.html*

5. *https://en.wikipedia.org/wiki/Neanderthal*

6. *https://www.amazon.com/s?k=the+selfish+gene&i=stripbooks-intl-ship&crid=OLWWHU42APHG&sprefix=the+selfish+gene%2Cstripbooks-intl-ship%2C202&ref=nb_sb_noss_1*

# INDEX

## A

Access, 78
ACChain, 148
AI as a Service, 12
Alibaba, 76, 77, 80–82, 84–86, 97, 109,
   119–122, 126, 127, 129, 131, 132, 157,
   158, 163–165, 168
Alternative Trading System (ATS), 151, 152
Amazon, 80, 87, 109, 129, 131, 132, 146
AML, 79–80, 112, 113, 134, 138, 139
Anti-Money Laundering. *See* AML
APIs, 45, 105, 109
Application programming interfaces.
   See APIs
Artificial General Intelligence (AGI), 51
Artificial Narrow Intelligence (ANI), 51
Artificial Super Intelligence (ASI), 51
Autonomous Decentralized Peer-to-Peer
   Telemetry (ADEPT), 39
Autonomous Vehicles (AVs), 178

## B

Baseband Unit (BBU), 30, 31
Big Data, 4–6, 9, 10, 37, 38, 47, 51–68,
   81, 88, 95, 96, 98, 106, 109, 111,
   117–119, 123, 129–131, 155–157, 161,
   163, 164, 168, 173, 184, 187, 199, 205,
   206, 210

Bitcoin, 75, 78–80, 105, 107, 113, 114, 116,
   117, 170
Blockchain, 5, 12, 39, 40, 47–49, 67, 74,
   77, 78, 103, 105–108, 114, 125, 126, 129,
   133–134, 136, 146, 147, 151, 153, 163,
   164, 166, 170, 172, 174, 175, 178, 183,
   201, 204, 206, 208, 209, 211, 212, 216
Blockchain as a Service, 12

## C

Central Bank Digital Currency (CBDC), 140
Centralized Unit (CU), 30, 31, 33
Chatbot, 10, 59
Cloud Network Functions (CNFs), 34
Composable infrastructure, 19
Cryptography, 108, 137
Cybersecurity, 176

## D

dBFT, 137
Decentralization, 108
Decentralized autonomous organizations
   (DAO), 202
Design for Manufacturability (DFM), 188
Digital currency, 104, 135, 139–141, 151
Digital economy, 1–7, 37–49
Distributed Unit (DU), 30, 31, 33
Domain Name Systems, 177

**E**

Edge computing, 19–21
Ethereum, 39, 105, 129, 135, 150, 156, 169, 201, 202, 209, 211, 212

**F**

Fintech, 40, 45, 46, 82, 84, 85, 87–89, 95–98, 103–131, 151, 154, 156, 163, 164, 167, 168, 204, 205

**G**

General Data Protection Regulation, 206
Google, 43, 45, 104, 129, 131, 132

**H**

High-bandwidth memory (HBM), 42
High-Performance Computers (HPC), 9, 11, 17, 21, 23, 24
Hybrid cloud, 18
Hyperledger, 115, 130, 170, 174

**I**

IBM, 39–41, 43, 104, 121, 126, 164, 168, 172, 174
Industrie 4.0, 1, 6, 104, 183
Infrastructure as a Service, 11
Initial Coin Offering (ICO), 135, 153
Intel, 41, 43, 104
Intelligence Processor Cores (IPCs), 43
Internet of Things (IoT), 8–10, 15–17, 20, 29, 35, 37–40, 71, 73, 148, 164, 172, 193, 196
IOTA Foundation, 71, 72

**K**

Keyless Signature Infrastructure (KSI), 48
Know Your Customer (KYC), 79–80, 97, 108, 133, 134, 138, 139

**L**

Light Detection And Ranging system (LIDAR), 179
Linux Foundation, 174

**M**

Manufacturing Execution System (MES), 186
MDL, 47, 92, 93, 137–139, 167, 169, 176, 201, 205–207, 217
Mobile Network Operator (MNO), 34
Mobile Virtual Network Operator (MVNO), 34
Moore's Law, 3, 40, 41, 43
Mutual Distributed Ledger. *See* MDL

**N**

NAND, 41
Nanowire technology, 41
New Radio, 30

**P**

Permissioned blockchain, 107, 146, 201
Physical network functions (PNFs), 33
Platform as a Service, 11
PoW, 39, 138, 139, 147
Private keys, 203
Proof-of-Concept, 137

**Q**

Quantum Key Distribution (QKD), 25

**R**

R3, 114, 125, 145, 164, 167
Remote Radio Head (RRH), 31
Remote Radio Unit (RRU), 30, 31
Rotating Savings and Credit Association (ROSCA), 152, 153

## S

Service-Based Architecture (SBA), 30, 35
Software as a Service (SaaS), 11
Software defined network (SDN), 32–34

## T

TARGET2-Securities (T2S), 91–93
Tensor Processing Units (TPU), 42

## V

Validation, 139
Virtualized network functions (VNFs), 33
Virtual Private Network (VPN), 30, 32, 35, 177

## W

Wallet, 75, 84, 86, 126, 127, 163, 165, 166
Wealth Management, 162

www.ingramcontent.com/pod-product-compliance
Lightning Source LLC
Chambersburg PA
CBHW061409210326
41598CB00035B/6148